The Book of
GENESIS

The Book of
GENESIS

A Layman's Practical Expository

MICHAEL J AKERS

Copyright © 2020 by Michael J Akers.

Library of Congress Control Number: 2020911714

HARDBACK: 978-1-952155-53-6
PAPERBACK: 978-1-952155-52-9
EBOOK: 978-1-952155-54-3

All rights reserved. No part of this publication may be reproduced, distributed, or transmitted in any form or by any electronic or mechanical means, without the prior written permission of the publisher, except in the case of brief quotations embodied in critical reviews and certain other noncommercial uses permitted by copyright law.

Ordering Information:

For orders and inquiries, please contact:
1-888-404-1388
www.goldtouchpress.com
book.orders@goldtouchpress.com

Printed in the United States of America

CONTENTS

Chapter 1:	The Creation	1
Chapter 2:	The Creation of Man and Woman	9
Chapter 3:	The Fall of Man	14
Chapter 4:	Cain and Abel	20
Chapter 5:	Descendants of Adam	24
Chapter 6:	The Corruption of Mankind	27
Chapter 7:	The Flood	32
Chapter 8:	The Flood Subsides	35
Chapter 9:	Covenant of the Rainbow	38
Chapter 10:	Descendants of Noah	42
Chapter 11:	Universal Language, Babel, Confusion	46
Chapter 12:	Abram Journeys to Egypt	49
Chapter 13:	Abram and Lot	54
Chapter 14:	War of Kings and God's Promise to Abram	57
Chapter 15:	Abram Promised A Son	60
Chapter 16:	Sarai and Hagar	64
Chapter 17:	Abraham and the Covenant of Circumcision	67
Chapter 18:	Birth of Isaac Promised	71
Chapter 19:	The Doom of Sodom	75
Chapter 20:	Abraham Treachery	79
Chapter 21:	Isaac Is Born	83
Chapter 22:	The Offering of Isaac	87
Chapter 23:	Death and Burial of Sarah	90
Chapter 24:	A Bride for Isaac	93
Chapter 25:	Abraham's Death	99
Chapter 26:	Isaac Settles in Gerar	104
Chapter 27:	Jacob's Deception	109

Chapter 28: Jacob Is Sent Away 115
Chapter 29: Jacob Meets Rachel 118
Chapter 30: The Sons of Jacob 122
Chapter 31: Jacob Leaves Secretly for Canaan 128
Chapter 32: Jacob's Fear of Esau 136
Chapter 33: Jacob Meets Esau 142
Chapter 34: The Treachery of Jacob's Sons 145
Chapter 35: Jacob Moves to Bethel 149
Chapter 36: Esau Moves 154
Chapter 37: Joseph's Dream 159
Chapter 38: Judah and Tamar 164
Chapter 39: Joseph's Success in Egypt 168
Chapter 40: Joseph Interprets a Dream 173
Chapter 41: Pharaoh's Dream 176
Chapter 42: Joseph's Brothers Sent to Egypt 182
Chapter 43: The Return to Egypt 188
Chapter 44: The Brothers Are Brought Back 192
Chapter 45: Joseph Deals Kindly with His Brothers 196
Chapter 46: Jacob Moves to Egypt 200
Chapter 47: Jacob's Family Settle in Goshen 204
Chapter 48: Israel's Last Days 208
Chapter 49: Israel's Prophecy Concerning His Sons 211
Chapter 50: The Death of Israel 218

CHAPTER 1

The Creation

¹ In the beginning God created the heavens and the earth. ² The earth was formless and void, and darkness was over the surface of the deep, and the Spirit of God was moving over the surface of the waters. ³ Then God said, "Let there be light"; and there was light. ⁴ God saw that the light was good; and God separated the light from the darkness. ⁵ God called the light day, and the darkness He called night. And there was evening and there was morning, one day.

Three huge questions in verse 1.
    What is the beginning?
    Who is God?
    How did He create the heavens and the earth?

The Beginning

What is the beginning? The word "beginning" mean re'shiyth (pronounced "re-sheth") that means "first fruits". There is no time when the beginning occurred. It is unknown. Yet God, the Son, and the Holy Spirit were together in the beginning.

Who Is God?[1]

Who is God? - The Fact

The fact of God's existence is so conspicuous, both through creation and through man's conscience, that the Bible calls the atheist a "fool" (Psalm 14:1). Accordingly, the Bible never attempts to prove the existence of God; rather, it assumes His existence from the very beginning (Genesis 1:1). What the Bible does is reveal the nature, character, and work of God.

Who is God? - The Definition

Thinking correctly about God is of utmost importance because a false idea about God is idolatry. In Psalm 50:21, God reproves the wicked man with this accusation: "You thought I was altogether like you." To start with, a good summary definition of God is "the Supreme Being; the Creator and Ruler of all that is; the Self-existent One who is perfect in power, goodness, and wisdom."

Who is God? - His Nature

We know certain things to be true of God for one reason: in His mercy He has condescended to reveal some of His qualities to us. God is spirit, by nature intangible (John 4:24). God is One, but He exists as three Persons—God the Father, God the Son, and God the Holy Spirit (Matthew 3:16-17). God is infinite (1 Timothy 1:17), incomparable (2 Samuel 7:22), and unchanging (Malachi 3:6). God exists everywhere (Psalm 139:7-12), knows everything (Psalm 147:5; Isaiah 40:28), and has all power and authority (Ephesians 1; Revelation 19:6).

Who is God? - His Character

Here are some of God's characteristics as revealed in the Bible: God is just (Acts 17:31), loving (Ephesians 2:4-5), truthful (John 14:6), and holy (1 John 1:5). God shows compassion (2 Corinthians 1:3), mercy (Romans 9:15), and grace (Romans 5:17). God judges sin (Psalm 5:5) but also offers forgiveness (Psalm 130:4).

---

[1] https://www.gotquestions.org/who-is-God.html

Who is God? - His Work

We cannot understand God apart from His works, because what God does flows from who He is. Here is an abbreviated list of God's works, past, present, and future: God created the world (Genesis 1:1; Isaiah 42:5); He actively sustains the world (Colossians 1:17); He is executing His eternal plan (Ephesians 1:11) which involves the redemption of man from the curse of sin and death (Galatians 3:13-14); He draws people to Christ (John 6:44); He disciplines His children (Hebrews 12:6); and He will judge the world (Revelation 20:11-15).

Who is God? - A Relationship with Him

In the Person of the Son, God became incarnate (John 1:14). The Son of God became the Son of Man and is therefore the "bridge" between God and man (John 14:6; 1 Timothy 2:5). It is only through the Son that we can have forgiveness of sins (Ephesians 1:7), reconciliation with God (John 15:15; Romans 5:10), and eternal salvation (2 Timothy 2:10). In Jesus Christ "all the fullness of the Deity lives in bodily form" (Colossians 2:9). So, to really know who God is, all we have to do is look at Jesus.

God is "elohiym" that means "God-creator". This word is used 2,606[2] in the Old Testament. God is the creator of all things on earth. How did God create the heavens and the earth? To create means that everything was made-out of nothing.

Have you ever been asked by your children or any small child, "Where did God come from?" You don't know how to answer other than "I don't know". Yet, you don't want to admit to your child that you don't know something. So how do you answer the question? The best answer I've heard is simply this-----God is neither like humans nor like any created thing. Yet we humans have been created in God's image (Genesis 1:27, both male and female). The Bible simply assumes that God has always existed. God is the uncreated Creator who created the universe and everything in it. If you do not agree with this simple-truth that assumes God's existence, then prove the Bible wrong. Not to believe the Bible is not proving it wrong. In fact,

---

[2] Used many times in various books, too many to count.

by believing that there is no God because you do not have proof where He came from, you are described as a fool (Psalm 14:1).

How did He create the heavens and the earth?

The word "created" in the Hebrew is the combination of two Hebrew words, "bara" and "asa". Bara is creation out of nothing. Asa is to prepare what is created for use. God created everything from nothing (Hebrews 11:3) and then prepared creation for us. Thomas Aquinas once said that "any error about creation also leads to an error".

The earth was formless and void, darkness over the surface of the deep and the Spirit of God was moving over the surface of the waters. Formless and void means nothing, no life yet, no boundaries, just nothing. Darkness was over the surface of the deep, just water and air. We have no idea how long this occurred. The Spirit of God moved over the surface of the waters, perhaps preparing them for God's ultimate creation of land, sun and moon, vegetation, and various forms of life, ultimately human beings.

The Days of Creation: One Week

"In the beginning, **God created the Heaven & the Earth** ..." – Genesis 1:1-2

Genesis 1:3-5	Genesis 1:6-8	Genesis 1:9-13	Genesis 1:14-19	Genesis 1:20-23	Genesis 1:24-31	Genesis 2:1-3
"let there be **light**"	"a firmament in the midst of the waters"	"waters gathered & **dry land** appears"	"lights ... for signs, seasons, days & years"	**Winged Creatures** & **Water Creatures**	"God created man in his own image" **Beasts of the Earth** & **Man**	"God **blessed** the seventh day and **sanctified** it: because that in it He had rested from all His work"
Day & Night	Heaven	Grass, Herbs & Fruit Tree	Sun, Moon & Stars			
Day 1	Day 2	Day 3	Day 4	Day 5	Day 6	Day 7

https://www.sutori.com/story/
the-old-testament--Apr17sTq2XVcMaxUaJH6GtBJ

The First Day

The first day of God's creation occurred in Genesis 1:3-5. God said, "Let there be light". Whatever God said, it was done. God saw that the light was good and He separated the light from the darkness. The light (not yet the sun) cleared up the darkness and murkiness of the of the water and air at least part of the day. God called the light day and the darkness night. The first day was completed, half dark and half-light.

The Second Day

⁶ Then God said, "Let there be an expanse in the midst of the waters, and let it separate the waters from the waters." ⁷ God made the expanse, and separated the waters which were below the expanse from the waters which were above the expanse; and it was so. ⁸ God called the expanse heaven. And there was evening and there was morning, a second day.

The second day was described in Genesis 1:6-8. God said "Let there be an expanse in the midst of the waters and let the expanse separate the waters from the waters". The expanse or firmament is a hemisphere above the waters. It separate waters before the expanse from waters above the expanse. God called the expanse heaven. Expanse is something that we humans cannot see.

The Third Day

⁹ Then God said, "Let the waters below the heavens be gathered into one place, and let the dry land appear"; and it was so. ¹⁰ God called the dry land earth, and the gathering of the waters He called seas; and God saw that it was good. ¹¹ Then God said, "Let the earth sprout vegetation, plants yielding seed, and fruit trees on the earth bearing fruit after their kind with seed in them"; and it was so.¹² The earth brought forth vegetation, plants yielding seed after their kind, and trees bearing fruit with seed in them, after their kind; and God saw that it was good. ¹³ There was evening and there was morning, a third day.

The third day is described in Genesis 1:9-13. God said "Let the waters below the heavens be gathered in one place and let the dry land appear"; and it was so. The dry land was called earth and the waters become the seas. God saw that this was very good. Whatever God says will happen, it happens. Why don't we believe this about everything written in the Bible? Then God said, "Let the earth sprout vegetation, plants yielding seed, and fruit trees on the earth bearing fruit after their kind with seed in them and it was so. All this was so good, God said so. Any plant that God created is good for animals and man.

The Fourth Day

[14] *Then God said, "Let there be lights in the expanse of the heavens to separate the day from the night, and let them be for signs and for seasons and for days and years;* [15] *and let them be for lights in the expanse of the heavens to give light on the earth"; and it was so.* [16] *God made the two great lights, the greater light to govern the day, and the lesser light to govern the night; He made the stars also.* [17] *God placed them in the expanse of the heavens to give light on the earth,* [18] *and to govern the day and the night, and to separate the light from the darkness; and God saw that it was good.* [19] *There was evening and there was morning, a fourth day.*

The fourth day of God's creation was filled with lights in the expanse of the heavens to separate the day from the night. These lights were for signs and for seasons and for days and years. They separated days from night for as long as the earth has existed. God made two great lights, the greater light to govern the day and the lesser light to govern the night. He also made stars. Do you ever look up at all the starts on a quiet night realize God made them? Do you also realized that many stars you see no longer exist but takes so long for the light of the star to travel to the earth. God placed them in the expanse of the heaven to give light on the earth, to govern days and nights, and to separate the light from the darkness. God saw that it was good. The fourth day has been completed.

The Fifth Day

[20] *Then God said, "Let the waters teem with swarms of living creatures, and let birds fly above the earth in the open expanse of the heavens."* [21] *God created the great sea monsters and every living creature that moves, with which the waters swarmed after their kind, and every winged bird after its kind; and God saw that it was good.* [22] *God blessed them, saying, "Be fruitful and multiply, and fill the waters in the seas, and let birds multiply on the earth."* [23] *There was evening and there was morning, a fifth day.*

On the fifth day God said, "Let the waters teem with swarms of living creature, let the birds fly above the earth in the open expanses of the heavens". God created fish of the sea and birds in the air. Fish of the sea would include reptiles and whales and other great sea monsters as evidence in Genesis 21. Every winged bird would include eagles and all else that could fly. God blessed them all and said, "Be fruitful and multiply and fill the waters of the sea and birds everywhere".

The Sixth Day

²⁴ Then God said, "Let the earth bring forth living creatures after their kind: cattle and creeping things and beasts of the earth after their kind"; and it was so.²⁵ God made the beasts of the earth after their kind, and the cattle after their kind, and everything that creeps on the ground after its kind; and God saw that it was good. ²⁶ Then God said, "Let Us make man in Our image, according to Our likeness; and let them rule over the fish of the sea and over the birds of the sky and over the cattle and over all the earth, and over every creeping thing that creeps on the earth." ²⁷ God created man in His own image, in the image of God He created him; male and female He created them. ²⁸ God blessed them; and God said to them, "Be fruitful and multiply, and fill the earth, and subdue it; and rule over the fish of the sea and over the birds of the sky and over every living thing that moves on the earth." ²⁹ Then God said, "Behold, I have given you every plant yielding seed that is on the surface of all the earth, and every tree which has fruit yielding seed; it shall be food for you; ³⁰ and to every beast of the earth and to every bird of the sky and to everything that moves on the earth which has life, I have given every green plant for food"; and it was so. ³¹ God saw all that He had made, and behold, it was very good. And there was evening and there was morning, the sixth day.

On the sixth day God created cattle, creeping things, beasts of the earth, all of which created after themselves. This means all the wild animals of the earth, both big and small. Then in verse 26 God said, "Let Us make man in Our image, according to our image, Our likeness and let man rule over the fish of the sea, birds in the sky and cattle over all the earth". Our image and Our likeness. Man was created in the image of God the Father, God and Son, and God the Holy Spirit. Man was created in the image and the likeness of God's righteousness. Man's righteousness was destroyed with Eve and Adam's original sin and was not truly renewed until Jesus came to earth and died for our sins. Righteousness returns to man when we accept

Christ as our Savior and Lord. Then Scriptures such as II Corinthians 5:17 and Ephesians 4:24 defines our lives in Christ. Verse 27 repeats that God created man in His own image, male and female He created them. Eve was created in Chapter 2. God blesses them and said to them, "Be fruitful and multiply and fill the earth and subdue it. Man shall rule over fish and birds and over every living thing that move on the earth. All mankind, regardless of race, are part of one species and one family. In verses 29-31 God saw that everything He created had a place in His world. Thus, at the end of the 6th day, God saw that all He had made was very good.

CHAPTER TWO

The Creation of Man and Woman

The Seventh Day

¹ Thus the heavens and the earth were completed, and all their hosts. ² By the seventh day God completed His work which He had done, and He rested on the seventh day from all His work which He had done. ³ Then God blessed the seventh day and sanctified it, because in it He rested from all His work which God had created and made.

The heavens and earth were completed, and all their hosts. Who are the hosts? Hosts are the complete creation, including the sun, moon, stars, different vegetation, fish, birds, all animals and man himself. On the seventh day God rested. This becomes one of the Ten Commandments, Exodus 20:8-11. God blessed the seventh day and sanctified it because He rested from all His work that He created. We are to spend one day a week without any work. Yet today how many people truly follow this commandment?

⁴ This is the account of the heavens and the earth when they were created, in the day that the Lord God made earth and heaven. ⁵ Now no shrub of the field was yet in the earth, and no plant of the field had yet sprouted, for the Lord God had not sent rain upon the earth, and there was no man to cultivate the ground. ⁶ But a mist used to rise from the earth and water the whole surface of the ground.⁷ Then the Lord God formed man of dust from the ground, and breathed into his nostrils the breath of life; and man became a living being. ⁸ The Lord God planted a garden toward the east, in Eden; and there He placed the man whom He had formed. ⁹ Out of the ground the Lord God caused to grow every tree that is pleasing to the sight and good for food; the tree of life also in the midst of the garden, and the tree of the knowledge of good and evil.

In verse 4 of Genesis 2, there is a second account of the creation when God made heaven and earth. However, both describe the same creation event[3]. Genesis describe six days of creation (and a 7th day of rest, included Genesis 2:1-3) while Genesis 2 covers only the 6th day. Genesis 2 gives a more detailed description of the creation of man. Only two major differences between the two accounts exists. Genesis 1:11 records God creating vegetation on the third day while Genesis 2:5 states that prior to the creation of man "no shrub of the field had yet appeared on the earth and no plant of the field had yet sprung up, for the LORD God had not sent rain on the earth and there was no man to work the ground." Genesis 1:11 uses a term that refers to vegetation in general. Genesis 2:5 uses a more specific term that refers to vegetation that requires agriculture, i.e., a person to tend it, a gardener. Genesis 1:11 speaks of God creating vegetation, and Genesis 2:5 speaks of God not causing "farmable" vegetation to grow until after He created man.

The second claimed contradiction regards animal life. Genesis 1:24-25 records God creating animal life on the sixth day, before He created man. Genesis 2:19, in some translations, seems to record God creating the animals after He had created man. However, a good and plausible translation of Genesis 2:19-20 reads, "Now the LORD God had formed out of the ground all the beasts of the field and all the birds of the air. He brought them to the man to see what he would name them, and whatever the man called each living creature, that was its name. The man gave names to all the livestock, the birds of the air and all the beasts of the field." The text does not say that God created man, then created the animals, and then brought the animals to the man. Rather, the text says, "Now the LORD God had [already] created all the animals." There is no contradiction. On the sixth day, God created the animals, then created man, and then brought the animals to the man, allowing the man to name the animals.

---

[3] https://www.gotquestions.org/two-Creation-accounts.html

10 Now a river flowed out of Eden to water the garden; and from there it divided and became four rivers. 11 The name of the first is Pishon; it flows around the whole land of Havilah, where there is gold. 12 The gold of that land is good; the bdellium and the onyx stone are there. 13 The name of the second river is Gihon; it flows around the whole land of Cush. 14 The name of the third river is Tigris; it flows east of Assyria. And the fourth river is the Euphrates.

The Garden of Eden was located somewhere in southern Iraq near the northwest edge of the Persian Sea. Of course, no one knows the exact location because in Genesis 3:24 God put permanent barriers to the location so no one today knows exactly where it was. While the rivers Tigris and Euphrates still exist, we don't know where the rivers Pishon and Gihom existed. A couple of maps are given to show where the Garden of Eden might have existed.

Possible Location of Garden of Eden

15 Then the Lord God took the man and put him into the garden of Eden to cultivate it and keep it. 16 The Lord God commanded the man, saying, "From any tree of the garden you may eat freely; 17 but from the tree of the knowledge of good and evil you shall not eat, for in the day that you eat from it you will surely die."

God took the man and put him into the garden of Eden to cultivate it and keep it. The Lord God commanded the man saying, "From any tree of the garden you may eat freely, but from the tree of knowledge of good and evil you shall not eat for in the day that you eat from it you will surely die". The first man had a God-given purpose. God did not create man to live a life of luxury. Work of part of man's original design although his work became far worse after original sin (Genesis 3:17-19). Evil was not in the fruit of the tree of knowledge of good and evil, but evil was in man's choice to eat it. God had to give man a choice. God wanted them to choose Him rather than evil, but they chose to disobey. The tree of the knowledge of good and evil represented a man's choice to do what was moral or immoral. The man eventually chose to do what God considered was immoral. And all humankind has paid for this ever since.

[18] Then the Lord God said, "It is not good for the man to be alone; I will make him a helper suitable for him." [19] Out of the ground the Lord God formed every beast of the field and every bird of the sky, and brought them to the man to see what he would call them; and whatever the man called a living creature, that was its name. [20] The man gave names to all the cattle, and to the birds of the sky, and to every beast of the field, but for Adam there was not found a helper suitable for him. [21] So the Lord God caused a deep sleep to fall upon the man, and he slept; then He took one of his ribs and closed up the flesh at that place. [22] The Lord God fashioned into a woman the rib which He had taken from the man, and brought her to the man. [23] The man said,

*"This is now bone of my bones,
And flesh of my flesh;
She shall be called Woman,
Because she was taken out of Man."*

[24] For this reason a man shall leave his father and his mother, and be joined to his wife; and they shall become one flesh. [25] And the man and his wife were both naked and were not ashamed.

God decided that man needed what God called a helper suitable for him. First, God asked the man to name each animal, God created its name. Man gave names to all cattle, all birds, and every beast of the field. Fish are not mentioned. The man's name was Adam, the first man, and this is the first-time man was called Adam. Yet no animal was fitting for Adam. God put Adam in a deep sleep and while he slept, God took one of his ribs and closed-up the flesh at that place. God fashioned into a woman the rib that He has taken from the man. Adam gave a love poetry (that was resumed in the Song of Solomon) because God took from him one rib to prepare a woman and brought the woman to man. She was called "Woman" because she was taken out of a man. The man and the woman because one flesh (verse 24), not ashamed of each other even though they were naked. Verse 2:24-25 still used by pastors to describe the beautiful union between a man and a woman, both who chose to leave their father and mother and be one flesh. Disobedience in Genesis 3 ruined this ideal relationship between a man and a woman although even today some couples abide by the original purpose of God.

CHAPTER THREE

The Fall of Man

¹ Now the serpent was more crafty than any beast of the field which the Lord God had made. And he said to the woman, "Indeed, has God said, 'You shall not eat from any tree of the garden'?" ² The woman said to the serpent, "From the fruit of the trees of the garden we may eat; ³ but from the fruit of the tree which is in the middle of the garden, God has said, 'You shall not eat from it or touch it, or you will die.'" ⁴ The serpent said to the woman, "You surely will not die! ⁵ For God knows that in the day you eat from it your eyes will be opened, and you will be like God, knowing good and evil." ⁶ When the woman saw that the tree was good for food, and that it was a delight to the eyes, and that the tree was desirable to make one wise, she took from its fruit and ate; and she gave also to her husband with her, and he ate. ⁷ Then the eyes of both of them were opened, and they knew that they were naked; and they sewed fig leaves together and made themselves loin coverings.

Who was the serpent who was more-crafty than any other beast the Lord God had made? The serpent was a snake, but was used by Satan to speak in a language that Eve could hear. He said to the woman that God told her not to eat from any tree of the garden. This is the first level of deception that Satan, through the serpent, told Eve. No, she replied, we can eat from any tree of the garden but not from the fruit of the tree in the middle tree or we will die if we eat or touch that fruit. The Satan in the serpent said to the woman, you surely will not die. The second level of deception by the serpent was in verse 4, You surely will not die! Note that the serpent is calling God a liar. Satan is a liar and a murderer according to Jesus in John 8:44. God knows that in the day you eat from the tree of knowledge of good and evil, your eyes will be opened and you will be like God, knowing good and evil. The serpent wanted Eve to believe that God's true motive for not eating the fruit from the tree of good and evil was God's selfishness. Is not this motive for disobeying God been true ever since? Eve want to see just as God's sees. In verse 6 when the woman saw that the true was good for food and it looked fabulous to the eyes and the food would all them to be wise like God, Eve took the fruit and ate it, and then she took some of the fruit to her husband and he ate. Thus, Eve and Adam committed the first sin in human history. Their eyes were open to good and evil, but they did not have the maturity of God; instead they saw perversion. The evil they saw opened them to shame, fear, worry, and pain. Satan robbed them away from the love of God and, indeed, a lack of trust in Him. This has been the conditions of humans ever since.

⁸ They heard the sound of the Lord God walking in the garden in the cool of the day, and the man and his wife hid themselves from the presence of the Lord God among the trees of the garden. ⁹ Then the Lord God called to the man, and said to him, "Where are you?" ¹⁰ He said, "I heard the sound of You in the garden, and I was afraid because I was naked; so I hid myself." ¹¹ And He said, "Who told you that you were naked? Have you eaten from the tree of which I commanded you not to eat?" ¹² The man said, "The woman whom You gave to be with me, she gave me from the tree, and I ate." ¹³ Then the Lord God said to the woman, "What is this you have done?" And the woman said, "The serpent deceived me, and I ate."

What must it be like to hear the sound of the Lord walking in the garden? Only Adam and Eve would know as well as the Lord Jesus. The man and wife hid themselves from the Lord God. Why? Because they were naked. God asked where they were. Did God not know where they were? God knew, but He still asked the question. There are hundreds of questions God and Jesus asked. How many questions did God asked in Job 38-41…. at least 77 questions. How many questions did Jesus asked? According the book by Martin B. Coperhaver (Abingdon Press, 2014), Jesus asked 307 questions, but only answered three of them. Yet God knew the answers because He is omniscient. God knew the answers that the man and woman being naked and that they ate from the tree of knowledge of good and evil. The man blamed the woman and the woman blamed the serpent. They both disobeyed the Lord God. They both admitted it although they blamed someone else. They know they sinned and they are moved to repentance. They now experience the results of sin---shame, embarrassment, guilt, and perhaps sorry that they were caught. Yet we can never escape the watching eyes of the Lord God (Proverbs 15:3).

[14] The Lord God said to the serpent, "Because you have done this, cursed are you more than all cattle, and more than every beast of the field; on your belly you will go, and dust you will eat all the days of your life; [15] And I will put enmity between you and the woman, and between your seed and her seed; he shall bruise you on the head, And you shall bruise him on the heel." [16] To the woman He said, "I will greatly multiply your pain in childbirth, in pain you will bring forth children; yet your desire will be for your husband, and he will rule over you."

God became the man and woman's defender once they admitted their sin although there are always consequences to sin. We now see that the serpent is not a snake although will become one because of God's curse. Paul referred to the serpent as Satan masquerading as an "angel of light" (II Corinthians 11:14). The serpent becomes a snake and crawls on its belly forever. Why was the serpent so anti-God? Perhaps because he wanted to be like God (Isaiah 14:14) but never was. So our history deals with his evil until he is smothered forever in the lake of fire (Revelation 20:10).

Genesis 3:15 is a remarkable verse, a great promise of all of Scripture that God placed in the third chapter of the Bible. God writes that "I will put enmity between you and the woman, and between your seed and her seed; he shall bruise you on the head, And you shall bruise him on the heel." God puts an enmity between the serpent and the woman and between your seed and her seed. Enmity means hatred in the Hebrew. The woman would certain hate the serpent (Tempter) who betrayed her and led her astray. The tempter would hate her because she is now the object of God's love. The seed of the woman is defined as "he" and he is Jesus Christ. The seed of the serpent (tempter) is the death of Jesus through all the hatred of Him. The other bruising of the head of the serpent was the resurrection of Jesus. There will always be a hatred between Christ-followers and those against Him.

God then said to the woman, I will greatly multiply your pain in childbirth, in pain you will bring forth children, yet your desire will be for your husband and he will rule over you. Eve, the woman, had never borne children before so she would be the first woman to experience pain in childbirth. Additionally, she would desire her husband and he will rule over her. She would not rule over him although she would like to. Both seek to rule the other, but now God said that he would rule over her. Sin tainted the relationship between husband and wife and now only a right relationship between husband and wife, as discussed in Ephesian 5:22-30, will husband and wife truly live like Christ and the church.

¹⁷ Then to Adam He said, "Because you have listened to the voice of your wife, and have eaten from the tree about which I commanded you, saying, 'You shall not eat from it'; Cursed is the ground because of you; In toil you will eat of it all the days of your life. ¹⁸ "Both thorns and thistles it shall grow for you; And you will eat the plants of the field; ¹⁹ By the sweat of your face You will eat bread, Till you return to the ground, Because from it you were taken; For you are dust, And to dust you shall return."

One of my favorite books on the topic of suffering is James Dobson's <u>When God Doesn't Make Sense</u> (Tyndale House, 1993). One of his main conclusions is the fact that we all live in a fallen world, a world that was cursed because of man's original sin. That curse is found in these two verses of Genesis. When "curse" is used in the Bible, it means that God has judged someone or something and has condemned it. In this passage, God put a curse on the ground. The original Hebrew word used "adamah" means "land". Scholars have questioned whether this curse refers to a specific geographic area or all land on the earth. Note that the curse involves (1) having to work very hard to eat, (2) the ground will contain thorns and thistles (weeds), and (3) "you will eat the plants of the field".

The original Garden of Eden contained food that God already had planted and provided so now Adam would have to work painfully hard (some translations use the word "sorrow") to replace the food that God removed. It will not be easy to grow food on land now containing thorns and thistles. The real curse is the last part that some scholars believe is the confirmation that Adam and Eve were kicked out of the Garden of Eden because no longer would there be food already provided.

Therefore, the "world" that God had provided, represented by the Garden of Eden, was no more because of the original sin of Adam and Eve (disobedience of God's commands and believing in the serpent more than believing in God). This describes a fallen world, a world not originally designed by God. His kingdom and His will are being done in heaven, not on earth although, via the Lord's prayer, we pray that someday His kingdom and will may be done on earth. Original sin has been passed down to every generation since Adam and Eve and that's why sin and evil and suffering are so common and rampant in our world today. There is natural evil (natural disasters), moral evil (Romans 3:23, James 1:13-15—note the LSD of sin), and demonic evil, all the result of original sin and God's curse upon mankind. That's why it is so important—so essential—that all mankind believe in God's redemption that removes this curse for eternity—and that is to believe in His Son, Jesus Christ. Otherwise, God's original curse remains on mankind forever. Read Romans 5 and come to your own conclusions about mankind's need for Christ.

All mankind death was pronounced by God in verse 19. The man would eat bread by the sweat of his face meaning that he would work very hard to eat until he returned to the ground. God created him from dust and because of original sin he will return to dust as will every human who will ever live. God, who formed man and woman out of dust of the ground, will cause man to die and return to dust. Death entered the life of the man on the day he ate the fruit of the tree of good and evil. Every one of us who live are aware that one day will die because of original sin of man and woman.

[20] Now the man called his wife's name Eve because she was the mother of all the living. [21] The Lord God made garments of skin for Adam and his wife, and clothed them. [22] Then the Lord God said, "Behold, the man has become like one of Us, knowing good and evil; and now, he might stretch out his hand, and take also from the tree of life, and eat, and live forever"— [23] therefore the Lord God sent him out from the garden of Eden, to cultivate the ground from which he was taken. [24] So He drove the man out; and at the east of the garden of Eden He stationed the cherubim and the flaming sword which turned every direction to guard the way to the tree of life.

In verse 20 this was the first time the woman was called Eve by her husband. Eve means "living" in Hebrew. Adam was looking forward to the generation of humans to come. God will also provide for Adam and Eve as He does today. He provided them clothing since all they were wearing were fig leaves. The clothing they wore was from an animal. God killed the animal to provide for humans. Later he had a lamb die to save Isaac and eventually Jesus became the lamb that died for human sin. Who was God talking to in verse 22? The man has become like one of Us, knowing good and evil. He must be speaking to Jesus Christ and the Holy Spirit. He might stretch out his hand and take also from the tree of life and ate and live forever. God cannot let this happen. Therefore, the Lord God sent Adam and Eve out of the garden of Eden, to cultivate the ground from which he was taken. Note that God did not finish His sentence about removing the man from the garden of Eden before He drove the couple out of Eden. God banished Adam and Eve from living with Him to a life characterized by hard work, lots of problems, illness, and eventual death. In verse 24 God drove the man out and at the east end of the garden of Eden He stationed the cherubim (angels) and the flaming sword which turned in every direction to guard the way to the tree of life. Cherubim are mentioned over 90 times in the Old Testament. Ezekiel chapters 1 and 10 describe them as powerful winged creatures and typically guard what belongs to God. These cherubim guard the way to the tree of life. God also assigns a flaming sword that turns in every direction so that no one can get near the tree of life. Now the only way to come to God is spiritual, not physical. Cherubim and the flaming sword remove any physical way to God other than through our spirits (Ephesians 2:18, John 4:23-24).

CHAPTER FOUR

Cain and Abel

¹ Now the man had relations with his wife Eve, and she conceived and gave birth to Cain, and she said, "I have gotten a manchild with the help of the Lord." ² Again, she gave birth to his brother Abel. And Abel was a keeper of flocks, but Cain was a tiller of the ground. ³ So it came about in the course of time that Cain brought an offering to the Lord of the fruit of the ground. ⁴ Abel, on his part also brought of the firstlings of his flock and of their fat portions. And the Lord had regard for Abel and for his offering; ⁵ but for Cain and for his offering He had no regard. So Cain became very angry and his countenance fell. ⁶ Then the Lord said to Cain, "Why are you angry? And why has your countenance fallen? ⁷ If you do well, will not your countenance be lifted up? And if you do not do well, sin is crouching at the door; and its desire is for you, but you must master it." ⁸ Cain told Abel his brother. And it came about when they were in the field, that Cain rose up against Abel his brother and killed him.

The Bible does not say where Adam and Eve were after being exiled from the Garden of Eden. He has relations with Eve and she bore him a manchild (man in the original Hebrew) with the help of the Lord. Note that she is very thankful that the Lord helped her have her first child. She likely had pain during child bearing but we don't know. She conceived again and gave birth to Abel. We don't know how much older Cain was than Abel. We also don't know how many other children Adam and Eve had, but there had to be more for Cain to marry and have his own children. Scripture often does not provide other details, only what is most important. The brothers' occupations are known, Abel keeps sheep while Cain farms.

In verse 3 Cain brought an offering to the Lord of the fruit of the ground. We know Cain and Abel had a relationship with the Lord. Abel, on his part, brought the firstlings of his flock and their fat portions. We do not know why the Lord had regard for Abel's offering and no regard for Cain's offering. We read in I John 3:12 that we should not be like Cain, who belonged to the evil one and murdered his brother. And why did he murder him? Because his own actions were evil and his brother's were righteous. We read in verse 5 that Cain became very angry and his countenance (his face) fell. In verse 6 the Lord said to Cain, "Why are you angry and why has your countenance fallen? If you do well, will not *your countenance* be lifted up? And if you do not do well, sin is crouching at the door; and its desire is for you, but you must master it." God asks Cain to adjust his understanding to what is good to God. There is no reason for Cain to be angry about God rejection. God will accept Cain's adjustment. But, if Cain chooses his own way, sin is crouching at the door. He must overcome sin's desire for him and not give in. Yet in verse eight Cain saw Abel his brother while they were in the field, Cain's anger rose up against Abel his brother and killed him. Cain allow sin to win. The two went into the field and Cain killed Abel. Cain refused to believe God's way. He was so angry over God rejected his offering and he was jealous with his brother. Why did Cain murder his brother? The Bible does not say other than I John 3:12. Interesting stories about Cain and Abel appear in Wikipedia[4].

9 Then the Lord said to Cain, "Where is Abel your brother?" And he said, "I do not know. Am I my brother's keeper?" 10 He said, "What have you done? The voice of your brother's blood is crying to Me from the ground. 11 Now you are cursed from the ground, which has opened its mouth to receive your brother's blood from your hand. 12 When you cultivate the ground, it will no longer yield its strength to you; you will be a vagrant and a wanderer on the earth." 13 Cain said to the Lord, "My punishment is too great to bear! 14 Behold, You have driven me this day from the face of the ground; and from Your face I will be hidden, and I will be a vagrant and a wanderer on the earth, and whoever finds me will kill me." 15 So the Lord said to him, "Therefore whoever kills Cain, vengeance will be taken on him sevenfold." And the Lord appointed a

---

4   https://en.wikipedia.org/wiki/Cain_and_Abel

sign for Cain, so that no one finding him would slay him. *¹⁶ Then Cain went out from the presence of the Lord, and settled in the land of Nod, east of Eden.*

God again asks a question, "Where is Abel your brother?" Cain's answer has been a standard answer for siblings ever since, "Am I my brother's keeper?". This shows both dishonesty and disrespect for God. God quickly replied that Cain did something for Abel's blood is crying to God from the ground. Despite God showing justice and not killing Cain, God show mercy along with justice. Now Cain is cursed from the ground which has opened its mouth to receive your brother's blood from your hand. God cursed Cain, say that when he cultivates the ground it will no longer yield its strength to Cain. Cain lost his livelihood and would his life end, but this is not the final aspect of his curse. He will become a vagrant and wanderer on the earth. Cain protested that his punishment was too great to bear. Behold, God has driven him this day from the face of the ground and from Your face I will be hidden and I will be a vagrant and a wanderer on earth and whoever find him will kill him. Note that there is no sense of repentance, remorse, or apology from Cain. He's only angry for his punishment. No, the Lord said, whoever kills Cain, vengeance will be taken upon him sevenfold. Then God appointed a sign for Cain so that no one finding him would kill him. Thus, there are other people in existence by now. We don't know what the sign was, but God is preventing the never-ending cycle of revenge. Then Cain went out from the presence of the Lord and settled in the land of Nod, east of Eden. Cain left God's presence. Sin separates us from God and, often from other people. Cain settled in Nod which means "wandering" in the Hebrew. No other mention of Nod in the Bible.

¹⁷ Cain had relations with his wife and she conceived, and gave birth to Enoch; and he built a city, and called the name of the city Enoch, after the name of his son. ¹⁸ Now to Enoch was born Irad, and Irad became the father of Mehujael, and Mehujael became the father of Methushael, and Methushael became the father of Lamech. ¹⁹ Lamech took to himself two wives: the name of the one was Adah, and the name of the other, Zillah. ²⁰ Adah gave birth to Jabal; he was the father of those who dwell in tents and have livestock. ²¹ His brother's name was Jubal; he was the father of all those who play the lyre and pipe. ²² As for Zillah, she also gave birth to Tubal-cain, the forger of all implements of bronze and iron; and the sister of Tubal-cain was Naamah. ²³ Lamech said *to his wives, "Adah and Zillah, listen to my voice, you wives of Lamech, give heed to my speech, for I have killed a man for wounding me; and a boy for striking me; ^{24} If Cain is avenged sevenfold, Then Lamech seventy-sevenfold."*

Cain had relations with his wife, she conceived and gave birth to a son, Enoch. Where did his wife come from? Adam and Eve had many more children than Cain and Abel. Remember people back then lived hundreds of years and there were no potential diseases affecting the unborn (genetic diseases) from marrying siblings as there are now. Cain built a city and called it Enoch after his son. Verse 18 onward is the first of many genealogies in the Bible. They are present to help us remember that people lived and died and we should remember this. Genealogies give one person born in a new generation, not to give lots of information about others within the family. This is the genealogies of Cain that includes Lamech who in verse 23-24 killed others. It is known that all of Cain's family were anti-God. For example, Lamech had two wives, against what God called a family of one husband, one wife. This atheistic family someday gives rise to the population that God needed to destroy during the days of Noah. Cain and Lamech and others were deeply perverse.

^{25} Adam had relations with his wife again; and she gave birth to a son, and named him Seth, for, she said, "God has appointed me another offspring in place of Abel, for Cain killed him." ^{26} To Seth, to him also a son was born; and he called his name Enosh. Then men began to call upon the name of the Lord.

Seth was born many years later, we don't how many. We are told in Chapter 5 that Adam was 130 when Seth was born and Eve was the same age. Eve said that Seth represents another offspring in place of Abel. To Seth, a son was born, Enosh. Then men began to call upon the name of the Lord. Seth's family were very faithful to God, unlike Cain's family. The men began to call upon the name of the Lord, perhaps being public in their faith.

CHAPTER FIVE

Descendants of Adam

¹This is the book of the generations of Adam. In the day when God created man, He made him in the likeness of God. ²He created them male and female, and He blessed them and named them Man in the day when they were created. ³When Adam had lived one hundred and thirty years, he became the father of a son in his own likeness, according to his image, and named him Seth. ⁴Then the days of Adam after he became the father of Seth were eight hundred years, and he had other sons and daughters. ⁵So all the days that Adam lived were nine hundred and thirty years, and he died. ⁶Seth lived one hundred and five years, and became the father of Enosh. ⁷Then Seth lived eight hundred and seven years after he became the father of Enosh, and he had other sons and daughters. ⁸So all the days of Seth were nine hundred and twelve years, and he died. ⁹Enosh lived ninety years, and became the father of Kenan. ¹⁰Then Enosh lived eight hundred and fifteen years after he became the father of Kenan, and he had other sons and daughters. ¹¹ So all the days of Enosh were nine hundred and five years, and he died.

The descendants of Adam in Genesis 5 compare to what we can read of the legacy of Jesus Christ both in Matthew 1 (Adam) and Luke 3 (Mary). The genealogy of Adam through Noah a are given listed in Genesis 5. The period between the creation of Adam and the advent of the flood is 1656 years. Adam had Seth when Adam was 130 years old. Seth was created in Adam's image. Adam lived another 800 years and he was the first to died naturally, not murdered like Abel. Seth lived 105 years before becoming the father of Enosh. Seth lived another 807 years and he had many other sons and daughters. Back then people could live over 900 years and apparently could have children for hundreds of years so the population expanded rapidly.

[12] Kenan lived seventy years, and became the father of Mahalalel. [13] Then Kenan lived eight hundred and forty years after he became the father of Mahalalel, and he had other sons and daughters. [14] So all the days of Kenan were nine hundred and ten years, and he died. [15] Mahalalel lived sixty-five years, and became the father of Jared. [16] Then Mahalalel lived eight hundred and thirty years after he became the father of Jared, and he had other sons and daughters. [17] So all the days of Mahalalel were eight hundred and ninety-five years, and he died. [18] Jared lived one hundred and sixty-two years, and became the father of Enoch. [19] Then Jared lived eight hundred years after he became the father of Enoch, and he had other sons and daughters. [20] So all the days of Jared were nine hundred and sixty-two years, and he died. [21] Enoch lived sixty-five years, and became the father of Methuselah. [22] Then Enoch walked with God three hundred years after he became the father of Methuselah, and he had other sons and daughters. [23] So all the days of Enoch were three hundred and sixty-five years. [24] Enoch walked with God; and he was not, for God took him. [25] Methuselah lived one hundred and eighty-seven years, and became the father of Lamech. [26] Then Methuselah lived seven hundred and eighty-two years after he became the father of Lamech, and he had other sons and daughters. [27] So all the days of Methuselah were nine hundred and sixty-nine years, and he died. [28] Lamech lived one hundred and eighty-two years, and became the father of a son. [29] Now he called his name Noah, saying, "This one will give us rest from our work and from the toil of our hands arising from the ground which the LORD has cursed." [30] Then Lamech lived five hundred and ninety-five years after he became the father of Noah, and he had other sons and daughters. [31] So all the days of Lamech were seven hundred and seventy-seven years, and he died. [32] Noah was five hundred years old, and Noah became the father of Shem, Ham, and Japheth.

Ten main names from Adam to Noah. Of course, many other people born during this time as the Scripture repeats many times (Genesis 5:4,7,10,13,16,19,22,26,30). Yet, these 10 mean are the first 10 men in the ancestry of Jesus Christ (Luke 3:26-38). The Hebrew and English names, the age of the first child and how long each person lived are given in the following table:

Hebrew	English	Age of First Son	How Long He Lived
Adam	Man	130	930
Seth	Appointed	105	912
Enosh	Mortal	90	905
Kenan	Sorrow	70	910
Mahalalel	The Blessed God	65	869
Jared	Shall come down	162	962
Enoch	Teaching	65	365
Methuselah	His death shall bring	187	969
Lamech	The Despairing	182	777
Noah	Rest	500	950
Start of flood	---	100	1656 year from Adam's birth

Each man listed was a righteous man. This cannot be the case of men born in the line of Cain. Each man lived a very long life for various reasons--- many other children, advanced intelligence, gathered knowledge to live so long and increase their knowledge. Yet, one man, Enoch 4:17, 21-23), did not live as long as the others because he walked with God. We read about Enoch in Jude 1:14-15: Enoch, the seventh from Adam, prophesied about them: "See, the Lord is coming with thousands upon thousands of his holy ones to judge everyone, and to convict all of them of all the ungodly acts they have committed in their ungodliness, and of all the defiant words ungodly sinners have spoken against him." Enoch spoke, as we read in Jude, preached against false teachers. One day Enoch walked with God one day and walked right into heaven. He did not die on earth. Hebrews 11:5 writes "By faith Enoch was taken up so that he would not see death; and he was not found because God took him up; for he obtained the witness that before his being taken up he was pleasing to God."

Noah was the tenth man born of Lamech and lived 500 years before he then had Shem, Ham, and Japheth. We don't know how many years apart these three sons were. Shem was part of the in-line ancestry of Jesus Christ. All three sons had wives before the flood came. Only Noah, wife, the three sons and their wives survived the great flood.

CHAPTER SIX

The Corruption of Mankind

¹Now it came about, when men began to multiply on the face of the land, and daughters were born to them, ²that the sons of God saw that the daughters of men were beautiful; and they took wives for themselves, whomever they chose. ³Then the LORD said, "My Spirit shall not strive with man forever, because he also is flesh; nevertheless, his days shall be one hundred and twenty years." ⁴The Nephilim were on the earth in those days, and also afterward, when the sons of God came in to the daughters of men, and they bore children to them. Those were the mighty men who were of old, men of renown.

There may be more disagreement among these few verses (Genesis 6:1-4) than anywhere else in the Bible. Who are the sons of God and who are the Nephilim? I've read several commentaries on these verses and still not sure who they are. Were the sons of God spirit-beings or fallen angels? This seems to be the prevalent view although some scholars still don't agree. The sons of God saw the daughters of men being so beautiful and took them as wives. Yet the Lord said that His Spirit will not strive with man forever and reduced their maximum age from the high hundreds to only one hundred and twenty. Did the sons of God and the beautiful women product the Nephilim (giants). The Bible writes (verse 4) that the Nephilim were on earth in those days and also afterward so they could have originated from sons of God and daughters of men. The Nephilim were giants with physical superiority. Only one other place where Nephilim were mentioned (Numbers 13:33). This race of half human creatures was wiped out by the flood, along with mankind in general.

⁵Then the LORD saw that the wickedness of man was great on the earth, and that every intent of the thoughts of his heart was only evil continually. ⁶The LORD was sorry that He had made man on the earth, and He was grieved in His heart. ⁷The LORD said, "I will blot out man whom I have created from the face of the land, from man to animals to creeping things and to birds of the sky; for I am sorry that I have made them." ⁸But Noah found favor in the eyes of the LORD.

Genesis 6:5 is where the Lord saw that the wickedness of men was great on the earth and all they thought about were evil continually. He was sorry that He had made man on the earth and was grieved in His heart. The Lord then said "I will blot out man whom I have created from the face of the land. It is so incredible that so soon after God created man in His own image, man had become totally evil. In Genesis 1, you read that God created everything, including human beings, and saw that it was good. Five chapters later, you read "God saw how great man's wickedness on the earth had become". How could this happen?

Note the absolute words that Scripture uses to describe man's evil. God saw that "every" inclination of the thoughts of the heart of man was evil. He also saw that man's heart contained "only" evil and evil was present "all the time".

You'd think after the great flood when God erased all evil from the earth that mankind would not return to being so evil. Yet you read the following verses written centuries later that tragically emphasis the same thing, that evil of the heart prevails:

- This is an evil among all things that are done under the sun...... also the heart of the sons of men is full of evil, and madness is in their heart while they live (Ecclesiastes 9:3)
- The heart is deceitful above all things, and desperately wicked: who can know it? (Jeremiah 17:9)
- For out of the heart proceed evil thoughts, murders, adulteries, fornications, thefts, false witness, blasphemies (Matthew 15:19)

I vaguely recall watching a movie about Noah (long before Russell Crowe 2014 movie) building the ark while people laughed and made fun of him. The image that horrified me was men wearing necklaces with human skulls, many skulls. Like watching a bunch of killers laughing while they perform the most-evil acts possible. If this was the kind of image that God saw, no wonder he wanted to destroy what He had created.

Do you recall the aftermath of Hurricane Katrina in New Orleans and all the television images and reports of people, without law enforcement, resorting to all kinds of rampant evil---looting, squalor, all kinds of rampant violence. When society is left without boundaries, law enforcement, any kind of control of people's natural inclinations, what are the results? Evil. Wasn't the main message of William Golding's <u>The Lord of the Flies</u> (Faber and Faber, 1954) that there is evil within everyone and it's a fine line between someone allowing that evil to run rampant or not?

What's keeps evil from running rampant in a person's life? The simple answer---the presence of God in a person's life where you allow good to triumph over evil. God gave you the choice to choose good or evil and it's a matter of conscience which choice you make. God is sorry He created man and all animal living things. Yet one man---Noah—found favor with God. Why? Because despite the wickedness that upon the earth, there is one man who stands out—a man whose life was characterized by the hand of God's grace upon him. Noah found favor with the Lord. God was about to send judgment upon the world for its wickedness, but He extends His saving grace to Noah and his family.

⁹These are the records of the generations of Noah. Noah was a righteous man, blameless in his time; Noah walked with God. ¹⁰Noah became the father of three sons: Shem, Ham, and Japheth.

Noah represents the tenth generation from Adam. The genealogical account of Noah reads, "When Lamech had lived 182 years, he had a son. He named him Noah and said, 'He will comfort us in the labor and painful toil of our hands caused by the ground the LORD has cursed'" (Genesis 5:28-29). Genesis 6:9 marks the beginning of the flood narrative, and it is here that we learn the most about Noah's life. We learn that Noah was a righteous man, blameless in his generation, and that he walked with God. Noah was not a perfect man, as we will read in Genesis 9:20-27, but still revered by others. Noah is an example of a life of faith. Noah was the result of generational obedience and faithfulness toward God. If we were to model our lives after Noah, there is no better rule to follow that to be "righteous, blameless in our generation, and to walk with God"

¹¹Now the earth was corrupt in the sight of God, and the earth was filled with violence. ¹²God looked on the earth, and behold, it was corrupt; for all flesh had corrupted their way upon the earth.

God saw the earth was correct in His sight and the earth filled with violence. Violence can mean cruelty, wrongdoing, murder, injustice. Much of our world today can be described as hedonistic, people filled with drugs, alcohol, parties, pleasure seeking, decadent people. The Lord looked on the earth and behold it was corrupt, for all flesh had corrupted their way upon the earth. Therefore, God decided to get rid of them all except for Noah, his wife, his 3 sons and their wives. He describes what He will do in Genesis 6:13-22.

¹³Then God said to Noah, "The end of all flesh has come before Me; for the earth is filled with violence because of them; and behold, I am about to destroy them with the earth. ¹⁴"Make for yourself an ark of gopher wood; you shall make the ark with rooms, and shall cover it inside and out with pitch. ¹⁵"This is how you shall make it: the length of the ark three hundred cubits, its breadth fifty cubits, and its height thirty cubits. ¹⁶"You shall make a window for the ark, and finish it to a cubit from the top; and set the door of the ark in the side of it; you shall make it with lower, second, and third decks. ¹⁷"Behold, I, even I am bringing the flood of water upon the earth, to destroy all flesh in which is the breath of life, from under heaven; everything that is on the earth shall perish. ¹⁸"But I will establish My covenant with you; and you shall enter the ark—you and your sons and your wife, and your sons' wives with you. ¹⁹"And of every living thing of all flesh, you shall bring two of every kind into the ark, to keep them alive with you; they shall be male and female. ²⁰"Of the birds after their kind, and of the animals after their kind, of every creeping thing of the ground after its kind, two of every kind will come to you to keep them alive. ²¹"As for you, take for yourself some of all food which is edible, and gather it to yourself; and it shall be for food for you and for them." ²²Thus Noah did; according to all that God had commanded him, so he did.

God said to Noah, "The end of all flesh has come before Me, for the earth is filled with violence because of them (people still living everywhere) and, behold, I am about the destroy them with the earth." For Noah to hear that all of humankind except for his immediate family would have been devastating to him. In verse 14 God gives specific instruction how Noah should build the ark. The original Hebrew work is "chest", same word used to describe the vessel Moses was placed in as a baby, also same work used to carry the Ten Commandments after the Israelis left Egypt. This is not a boat, does not have sails or rudder. It is used to float, not travel. The wood is gopher wood although we don't know what kind of wood it really was. Some people believe it was cypress wood. The structure had rooms within and spaces between the wood covered with pitch, perhaps like asphalt. Noah had help from his sons and God perhaps had angels help.

A cubit is 18 inches (46 centimeters). The ark that God describes Noah to build would be 450 feet long (one and one-half football fields), 75 feet wide, and 45 feet high. In verse 16 God tells Noah to construct a rood with about 1 cubit all the way around the top. The ark would have three decks and a single door on one side, big enough to accommodate the entrance and exit of all animals. In verse 17 God reveals to Noah how He will destroy all life. He will bring a flood of water to kill everyone that needs air. All humans and all animals except those who will be in the ark. He will establish His covenant with Noah and his family. Noah also will bring two of each animal, male and female, to restart the animal life. Noah will bring for his family some of all food that is edible and it will sustain humans and animals during the long time in the ark. In verse 22 Noah demonstrates his faith and submission to what God asked him to do. Noah is an example of obeying God completely. Throughout all that God told Noah, there are so many details missing, but the writer only gives us the main points. Noah surely would have many more questions and concerns than what is given, but He obeyed the Lord. Noah was a righteous, blameless man who walked faithfully with God as we were told in Genesis 6:9 and in Genesis 7:1

CHAPTER SEVEN

The Flood

¹Then the LORD said to Noah, "Enter the ark, you and all your household, for you alone I have seen to be righteous before Me in this time. ²"You shall take with you of every clean animal by sevens, a male and his female; and of the animals that are not clean two, a male and his female; ³also of the birds of the sky, by sevens, male and female, to keep offspring alive on the face of all the earth. ⁴"For after seven more days, I will send rain on the earth forty days and forty nights; and I will blot out from the face of the land every living thing that I have made." ⁵Noah did according to all that the LORD had commanded him.

The Lord told Noah to enter the ark, you and all your household. Noah's family is the only one of millions or more people on the earth that would be saved. Only Noah was righteous before God. What happened to all the other people? God viewed them as unrighteous. This would have included Noah's parents and Methuselah, the oldest man who ever lived. Noah should take with you of every clean animal by sevens, a male and a female, and of animals that are not clean two, and male and his female; also birds of the sky, by sevens, male and female, to keep the offspring alive on the face of the earth. Why seven pairs of clean animals? When the flood is over, only clean animal are acceptable as sacrifice. Noah will need more than one pair of those for a while and not sacrifice all of them. What animals are not clean? At this time, we do not know as the difference between clean and unclean animals since they are not characterized until Leviticus 11. However, God and Noah knew the difference. In verse 4 Noah had one week to get everything inside the ark. Animal were not urged, they knew through God that they were to board. They had one week to have everyone on board. For after that one week God will send rain on the earth forty days and forty nights and He will blot out from the face of the land every living thing that He had made. Noah did as God commended him.

⁶Now Noah was six hundred years old when the flood of water came upon the earth. ⁷Then Noah and his sons and his wife and his sons' wives with him entered the ark because of the water of the flood. ⁸Of clean animals and animals that are not clean and birds and everything that creeps on the ground, ⁹there went into the ark to Noah by twos, male and female, as God had commanded Noah. ¹⁰It came about after the seven days, that the water of the flood came upon the earth. ¹¹In the six hundredth year of Noah's life, in the second month, on the seventeenth day of the month, on the same day all the fountains of the great deep burst open, and the floodgates of the sky were opened. ¹²The rain fell upon the earth for forty days and forty nights.

Noah was six hundred years old when the flood of water came upon the earth. His three sons were perhaps around one hundred years old. The eight-people entered the ark because of the water of the flood. The animals were sent to the ark by God. Noah did not have to lure them. After seven days, the water of the flood came upon the earth. In verse 11 all the fountains of the great deep burst open and the floodgates of the sky were opened. The rain fell, as God predicted, for forty days and forty night. From the beginning of time, the earth started to revert to the whole earth covered by water.

¹³On the very same day Noah and Shem and Ham and Japheth, the sons of Noah, and Noah's wife and the three wives of his sons with them, entered the ark, ¹⁴they and every beast after its kind, and all the cattle after their kind, and every creeping thing that creeps on the earth after its kind, and every bird after its kind, all sorts of birds. ¹⁵So they went into the ark to Noah, by twos of all flesh in which was the breath of life. ¹⁶Those that entered, male and female of all flesh, entered as God had commanded him; and the LORD closed it behind him.

Verses 13-16 basically repeat what we have believed, that Noah and his family entered the ark, and all the animals, male and female, entered also so that the life God created could be continued. Those that entered, male and female of all flesh, entered as God had commanded and then

Lord closed the door behind him. We are reminded that God's will and His knowledge are specific. When He says that something will occur, it happens exactly as He said. Everything God says is the exact truth. There are people who believe that the ark and the flood were a huge lie, but they do not believe in the miracles of God.

[17]Then the flood came upon the earth for forty days, and the water increased and lifted up the ark, so that it rose above the earth. [18]The water prevailed and increased greatly upon the earth, and the ark floated on the surface of the water. [19]The water prevailed more and more upon the earth, so that all the high mountains everywhere under the heavens were covered. [20]The water prevailed fifteen cubits higher, and the mountains were covered. [21]All flesh that moved on the earth perished, birds and cattle and beasts and every swarming thing that swarms upon the earth, and all mankind; [22]of all that was on the dry land, all in whose nostrils was the breath of the spirit of life, died. [23]Thus He blotted out every living thing that was upon the face of the land, from man to animals to creeping things and to birds of the sky, and they were blotted out from the earth; and only Noah was left, together with those that were with him in the ark. [24]The water prevailed upon the earth one hundred and fifty days.

The flood came upon the earth for forty days. The water prevailed and increased greatly upon the earth and the ark floated on the surface of the water. According to verses 19-20 the water prevailed fifteen cubits higher and the mountains were covered. We do not know if the highest mountains in the world today, e.g. Mount Everest at 29,000 feet, were around then or if the flood caused the mountains to grow after the flood. All flesh that moved on the earth perished, human and animal. God blotted out every living thing from the earth and only Noah and those with him in the ark survived. It rained for forty days and night and the prevailed for one hundred and fifty days.

In our day, the fabric of our society can become so rotten, so filled with violence that it can no longer support itself. We cannot demand to wait until some tremendous catastrophe occurs. When God shuts the door to our ark it will be too late. Are you ready to meet God? Are you afraid of Him? Are you within the ark or outside of it? Being inside means you are safe and righteous; being outside means you are perishing like those outside the ark.

CHAPTER EIGHT

The Flood Subsides

¹But God remembered Noah and all the beasts and all the cattle that were with him in the ark; and God caused a wind to pass over the earth, and the water subsided. ² Also the fountains of the deep and the floodgates of the sky were closed, and the rain from the sky was restrained; ³ and the water receded steadily from the earth, and at the end of one hundred and fifty days the water decreased.⁴ In the seventh month, on the seventeenth day of the month, the ark rested upon the mountains of Ararat. ⁵ The water decreased steadily until the tenth month; in the tenth month, on the first day of the month, the tops of the mountains became visible.

Fortunately, God did not forget about Noah and all the animals with him in the ark. God caused a wind to pass over all the earth and the water subsided. God closed the fountains of the deep and the floodgates of the sky. Rain no longer fell and water receded steadily from the earth over one hundred and fifty days. In the seventh month, on the seventeenth day of the month, the ark rested on the mountains of Ararat. The writer intended Noah's Ark to be a genuine historical event, not a myth which is why actually dates on the calendar were given. Ararat is generally understood to be Armenia (eastern Turkey), in which there is a great chain of mountains, like the Alps or the Pyrenees. No one found the ark since its location was never identified and whatever wood was used would have been good for fuel and other needs. The water decreased steadily until the tenth month, on the first day the tops of the mountains became visible. Again, the writer wanted this event to be truly historical and people to believed that it really happened.

⁶ Then it came about at the end of forty days, that Noah opened the window of the ark which he had made; ⁷ and he sent out a raven, and it flew here and there until the water was dried up from the earth. ⁸ Then he sent out a dove from him, to see if the water was abated from the face of the land; ⁹ but the dove found no resting place for the sole of her foot, so she returned to him into the ark, for the water was on the surface of all the earth. Then he put out his hand and took her, and brought her into the ark to himself. ¹⁰ So he waited yet another seven days; and again he sent out the dove from the ark. ¹¹ The dove came to him toward evening, and behold, in her beak was a freshly picked olive leaf. So Noah knew that the water was abated from the earth. ¹² Then he waited yet another seven days, and sent out the dove; but she did not return to him again.

Noah sent out a raven that flew from here and there until the water was dried from the earth. The raven did not return. Then he sent out a dove, but the dove returned since water was still on the surface of the earth. Water still lied on the earth. Noah waited another seven days and sent out the dove again. The dove returned that evening and in her beak was a freshly picked olive leaf. This meant that water has disappeared from the earth. Noah still waited another seven days, sent out the dove again and the dove did not return. Noah must have been thrilled that land was on the earth again. Indeed, how bored Noah and his family would be by now to be in that ark for nearly a year.

¹³ Now it came about in the six hundred and first year, in the first month, on the first of the month, the water was dried up from the earth. Then Noah removed the covering of the ark, and looked, and behold, the surface of the ground was dried up. ¹⁴ In the second month, on the twenty-seventh day of the month, the earth was dry. ¹⁵ Then God spoke to Noah, saying, ¹⁶ "Go out of the ark, you and your wife and your sons and your sons' wives with you. ¹⁷ Bring out with you every living thing of all flesh that is with you, birds and animals and every creeping thing that creeps on the earth, that they may breed abundantly on the earth, and be fruitful and multiply on the earth." ¹⁸ So Noah went out, and his sons and his wife and his sons' wives with him. ¹⁹ Every beast, every creeping thing, and every bird, everything that moves on the earth, went out by their families from the ark. ²⁰ Then Noah built an altar to the Lord, and took of every clean animal and of every clean bird and offered burnt offerings on the altar. ²¹ The Lord smelled the soothing aroma; and the Lord

said to Himself, "I will never again curse the ground on account of man, for the intent of man's heart is evil from his youth; and I will never again destroy every living thing, as I have done. [22] *"While the earth remains,*
Seedtime and harvest,
And cold and heat,
And summer and winter,
And day and night
Shall not cease."

In the 601st year of Noah's life, the first day of the month, Noah saw that the ground was dry. He removed the covering from the ark although we don't know what the covering was. The land was ready him, his family and the animals. They were in the ark for approximately one year and a few days. In verse 15 God spoke to Noah, telling him to go out of the ark with his family and bring out all the animals with him. Humans and animals are now to breed abundantly on the earth, be fruitful and multiply on the earth. Everyone left the ark, then Noah built an altar to the Lord and took every clean animal and bird and offered burnt offerings on the altar. Noah's offerings are what Israel would later practice, that the whole animal is burned and fully consumed by fire on the altar. The animals that were sacrificed were costly to Noah and his family, yet the act of worship to God revealed that Noah continued to be faithful to God even after the flood. In verses 21-22 after God smelled the soothing aroma of the sacrifice and greatly pleased, make a commitment that He would never again curse the ground because of man. He knows the intend of man's heart is evil from his youth. Even we humans know that our hearts are naturally wicked (Genesis 8:21, Ecclesiastes 8:11) and must be changed before anyone can obey the Lord (Psalm 51:10-14). God's original curse still applies (Genesis 3:17-19). God's decision here is that He will not annihilate the earth as He did before the flood. Throughout the rest of our history on earth the patterns of nature will remind as God created them. Verse 22 writes that the earth remains as God created them, seasons upon seasons, cold and hot weather, summer and winter, and day and night will not cease. However, we know that God will not all allow earth to remain like this forever. Someday He will re-do heaven and earth (Revelation 21:1).

CHAPTER NINE

Covenant of the Rainbow

¹And God blessed Noah and his sons and said to them, "Be fruitful and multiply, and fill the earth. ²"The fear of you and the terror of you will be on every beast of the earth and on every bird of the sky; with everything that creeps on the ground, and all the fish of the sea, into your hand they are given. ³"Every moving thing that is alive shall be food for you; I give all to you, as I gave the green plant. ⁴"Only you shall not eat flesh with its life, that is, its blood. ⁵"Surely I will require your lifeblood; from every beast I will require it. And from every man, from every man's brother I will require the life of man. ⁶"Whoever sheds man's blood, by man his blood shall be shed, for in the image of God He made man. ⁷"As for you, be fruitful and multiply; populate the earth abundantly and multiply in it."

God blessed Noah and his sons. Be fruitful and multiply and fill the earth. God repeated this in verse 7. All animals will fear man and the terror of man will be on every beast of the earth and bird in the sky, on everything that creeps on the ground and fish of the sea, they all fearful of man. I do wonder if sharks are fearful of man? Every moving thing that is alive shall be food for man as well as plants only do not eat flesh with its blood. In verses 5-6 it is unlawful to kill another man. Every person is made in the image of God. Anyone who kills another man must be accountable. Whoever sheds man's blood, by man his blood shall be shed.

⁸Then God spoke to Noah and to his sons with him, saying, ⁹"Now behold, I Myself do establish My covenant with you, and with your descendants after you; ¹⁰and with every living creature that is with you, the birds, the cattle, and every beast of the earth with you; of all that comes out of the ark, even every beast of the earth. ¹¹"I establish My covenant with you; and all flesh shall never again be cut off by the water of the flood, neither shall there again be a flood to destroy the earth." ¹²God said, "This is the sign of the covenant which I am making between Me and you and every living creature that is with you, for all successive generations; ¹³I set My bow in the cloud, and it shall be for a sign of a covenant between Me and the earth. ¹⁴"It shall come about, when I bring a cloud over the earth, that the bow will be seen in the cloud, ¹⁵and I will remember My covenant, which is between Me and you and every living creature of all flesh; and never again shall the water become a flood to destroy all flesh. ¹⁶"When the bow is in the cloud, then I will look upon it, to remember the everlasting covenant between God and every living creature of all flesh that is on the earth." ¹⁷And God said to Noah, "This is the sign of the covenant which I have established between Me and all flesh that is on the earth."

God established His covenant (alliance, pledge) with Noah and his sons and all their descendants after them. Imagine how they must have felt every time stormy weather came along. They will never again be cut off by water of the flood. No flood will destroy the earth again. In verse 13 He set His bow in the cloud that is a sign of the covenant between God and the earth. This is today's rainbow. This reminds God never to drown the earth with a flood again. Yet someday, earth and heaven will be destroyed by fire (II Peter 3:10-13). The Lord repeats (covenant mentioned seven times in Genesis 9) His faith to Noah. He gave us the repeated sign of the rainbow to declare an end to His wrath on all flesh. We are safe when we give our lives to Jesus Christ.

¹⁸Now the sons of Noah who came out of the ark were Shem and Ham and Japheth; and Ham was the father of Canaan. ¹⁹These three were the sons of Noah, and from these the whole earth was populated. ²⁰Then Noah began farming and planted a vineyard. ²¹He drank of the wine and became drunk, and uncovered himself inside his tent. ²²Ham, the father of Canaan, saw the nakedness of his father, and told his two brothers outside. ²³But Shem and Japheth took a garment and laid it upon both their shoulders and walked backward and covered the nakedness of their father; and their faces were turned away, so that they did not see their father's nakedness.

²⁴When Noah awoke from his wine, he knew what his youngest son had done to him. ²⁵So he said, "Cursed be Canaan; A servant of servants. He shall be to his brothers." ²⁶He also said, "Blessed be the LORD, The God of Shem; And let Canaan be his servant.²⁷"May God enlarge Japheth, And let him dwell in the tents of Shem; And let Canaan be his servant."

²⁸Noah lived three hundred and fifty years after the flood. ²⁹So all the days of Noah were nine hundred and fifty years, and he died.

After starting their new lives the three sons of Noah began populating the whole earth again. Noah began farming and planted a vineyard. One day he drank his wine and became drunk. He fell asleep naked inside his tent. Ham, the father of Canaan, saw the nakedness of his father and then told Shem and Japheth outside the tent. The two older brothers took a garment, walked in backwards and covered the nakedness of their father. They did not see their father's nakedness but Ham did. Noah replied in verse 24 that he knew what his youngest son had done to him. Read two paragraphs down, did Ham just look or had he done something worse?

How could it be that the only man on earth who found favor with God and kept God from destroying every single living creature on earth proceeded to get drunk after the great flood? Incredulous! Yet, it is equally amazing that the Bible does not hold back the truth, no matter how ugly it is. If the Bible were a fake, do you think that it would contain this story of Noah getting drunk? I don't think so. Noah's drunkenness points out that even the very best man on the earth, even one favored by God, still has his weaknesses. Even though Genesis 6:8-9 tells of Noah being righteous and blameless, he still was vulnerable against sin and it finally caught him after the flood. Paul wrote that "all have sinned and fall short of the glory of God" (Romans 3:23), even a righteous and blameless man can become a sinner.

What was the sin of Ham? He saw his father naked, but why was that a sin? Some have speculated that since Genesis 9:24 states that "he knew what his youngest son had done to him" (the action verb being "done", not "look") Ham did more than look. We don't know. Others have pointed to Leviticus 20:11 where it reads; "The man who lies with his father's wife has uncovered his father's nakedness". Therefore, could Ham have had sex with Noah's wife. Yet, that cannot be true because Ham's brothers walked in after Ham. The most plausible explanation is simply that Ham did not show respect for his father, did not try covering his nakedness, and even may have mocked his father when telling his brothers.

Noah cursed Ham's son, Canaan, not Ham. Why? The Bible doesn't tell us why. The only clue is that Canaan was Ham's youngest son as Ham was to Noah. Could it have been a precursor to Exodus 20:5 that speaks of the sins of the father being visited on the children even to the third and fourth generation? We just don't know.

The curse of Canaan has been used for thousands of years by white supremacists as justification why Negroes were to be slaves ("May Canaan be the slave of Shem", Genesis 9:26) since descendants of Ham mostly ended up in Africa. Yet this is a horrible lie as the Canaanites were not black but wicked people who lived in ancient Palestine, Phoenicia, and Carthage and were part of the tribes defeated by Joshua (e.g. Numbers 14:43, Joshua 9:1). Ham's other two sons were not cursed.

What is the main learning point from this passage? What do you learn about Noah's sin that might keep you from committing similar sin?

CHAPTER TEN

Descendants of Noah

¹Now these are the records of the generations of Shem, Ham, and Japheth, the sons of Noah; and sons were born to them after the flood.

The Bible loves to provide genealogies at least through Jesus Christ. Chapter 10 presents the genealogies of Japheth, Ham, and Shem. They start with Japheth and include sons and grandsons.

²The sons of Japheth were Gomer and Magog and Madai and Javan and Tubal and Meshech and Tiras. ³The sons of Gomer were Ashkenaz and Riphath and Togarmah. ⁴The sons of Javan were Elishah and Tarshish, Kittim and Dodanim. ⁵From these the coastlands of the nations were separated into their lands, every one according to his language, according to their families, into their nations.

Japheth has seven sons, plus likely many daughter too although not named. The first son, Gomer, has three sons. The fourth son, Javan, had four sons. Genesis 10, often called "the Table of Nations," traces the origins of nations and people groups as they dispersed around the world after the Flood. They were dispersed into different lands (most far north) of everyone according to his own language, (this would have happened after Tower of Babel in Genesis 11), according to their families, into their nations (some sons started new nations likely throughout Europe).

⁶The sons of Ham were Cush and Mizraim and Put and Canaan. ⁷The sons of Cush were Seba and Havilah and Sabtah and Raamah and Sabteca; and the sons of Raamah were Sheba and Dedan. ⁸Now Cush became the father of Nimrod; he became a mighty one on the earth. ⁹He was a mighty hunter before the LORD; therefore it is said, "Like Nimrod a mighty hunter before the LORD." ¹⁰The beginning of his kingdom was Babel and Erech and Accad and Calneh, in the land of Shinar. ¹¹From that land he went forth into Assyria, and built Nineveh and Rehoboth-Ir and Calah, ¹²and Resen between Nineveh and Calah; that is the great city. ¹³Mizraim became the father of Ludim and Anamim and Lehabim and Naphtuhim ¹⁴and Pathrusim and Casluhim (from which came the Philistines) and Caphtorim.

Ham bore Cush and Canaan and two other sons. Cush had five sons and one of his sons, Raamah, had two sons. Also Cush had another son, Nimrod, who became a mighty one on the earth. He was a mighty hunter before the Lord. Nimrod[5] in the Bible was the great-grandson of Noah through the line of Cush. Previous to the flood, there had been giants and mighty men on the earth, and "also afterward" (Genesis 6:4). Nimrod established a great kingdom that included "Babel, Erech, Accad, and Calneh, in the land of Shinar" (Genesis 10:9–10). He later extended his kingdom into Assyria, where he built the cities of "Ninevah, Rehoboth Ir, Calah and Resen" (verses 11–12). Nimrod was obviously a skilled man and an ambitious leader. Besides being the founder of the infamous Babel and many other cities, Nimrod was a mighty man with great physical strength and great strength of will. If he was also of giant stature, then that would be another reason why the people of his time would follow him—and why so many legends would spring up around him.

As the leader of the kingdom of Babel, Nimrod is also connected with the Tower of Babel. According to the historian Josephus, Nimrod "said he would be revenged on God, if he should have a mind to drown the world again; for that he would build a tower too high for the waters to reach. And that he would avenge himself on God for destroying their forefathers" (*Antiquities of the Jews*, Book 1, Chapter 4). The motive, according to Josephus, for building the Tower of Babel was to protect humanity against another flood. But the reason for the first flood was humanity's wickedness and rebellion (Genesis 6:5–6), from which humanity refused to repent.

---

5   https://www.gotquestions.org/Nimrod-in-the-Bible.html

Nimrod was rebellious against God, just like his antediluvian forebears, and, according to Josephus, he "persuaded [his subjects] not to ascribe [their strength] to God, as if it were through his means they were happy, but to believe that it was their own courage which procured that happiness". Construction of the Tower of Babel ended with a show of God's power: the Lord confused the languages of the people, making it impossible for them to communicate effectively enough to finish the construction of the tower. So, Nimrod was proved wrong—all of man's strength and ability, even the strength of the mightiest of men, is a gift from God that He can choose to revoke at any time.

[15]Canaan became the father of Sidon, his firstborn, and Heth [16]and the Jebusite and the Amorite and the Girgashite [17]and the Hivite and the Arkite and the Sinite [18]and the Arvadite and the Zemarite and the Hamathite; and afterward the families of the Canaanite were spread abroad. [19]The territory of the Canaanite extended from Sidon as you go toward Gerar, as far as Gaza; as you go toward Sodom and Gomorrah and Admah and Zeboiim, as far as Lasha. [20]These are the sons of Ham, according to their families, according to their languages, by their lands, by their nations.

Canaan, brother of Cush, became the father of Sidon and Heth. All these sons will become the Canaanites, people who occupied the Promised Land. The Canaanites were especially evil such that God sent Israel to judge them (Deuteronomy (9:3-6). This occurred because Canaan was cursed by Noah because of Ham's dishonoring him (Genesis 9:20-25). The Canaanites included the Jebusite, Amorites, Girgashites, Hivites, Arkites and the Sinites, Arvadites, Zemarite and the Hamathites. The Jebusites settled in where later became the site of Jerusalem (Judges 1:21, I Chronicles 11:4). I used to listen to Charles Swindoll sermons when I worked full time and whenever he was talking about all the Canaanites, he would also add "the termites".

[21]Also to Shem, the father of all the children of Eber, and the older brother of Japheth, children were born. [22]The sons of Shem were Elam and Asshur and Arpachshad and Lud and Aram. [23]The sons of Aram were Uz and Hul and Gether and Mash. [24]Arpachshad became the father of Shelah; and Shelah became the father of Eber. [25]Two sons were born to Eber; the name of the one was Peleg, for and his brother's name was Joktan. [26]Joktan became the father of Almodad and Sheleph and Hazarmaveth and Jerah [27]and Hadoram and Uzal

and Diklah ²⁸*and Obal and Abimael and Sheba* ²⁹*and Ophir and Havilah and Jobab; all these were the sons of Joktan.* ³⁰*Now their settlement extended from Mesha as you go toward Sephar, the hill country of the east.* ³¹*These are the sons of Shem, according to their families, according to their languages, by their lands, according to their nations.*

Shem was the father of all the children of Eber. Sons of Shem were five. The sons of Aram were four. Arpachshad became the father of Shelah and then Shelah became the father of Eber. Two sons were born of Eber, one was Peleg, for in his days the earth was divided. The earth divided signifies the Tower of Babel. The other son of Eber was Joktan. Joktan was the father of thirteen sons. Many of his sons because well known as specific regions or people groups in the Middle East. It is believed that Joktan was the father of the Arabic people, since this family went to the hill country of the east. Shem's ancestry spread throughout the Middle East, according to families, languages, their lands and their nations.

³²*These are the families of the sons of Noah, according to their genealogies, by their nations; and out of these the nations were separated on the earth after the flood.*

These are the families of the sons of Noah, according to their genealogies and their nations. They separated widely after the great flood and settled over the middle east.

CHAPTER ELEVEN

Universal Language, Babel, Confusion

¹Now the whole earth used the same language and the same words. ² It came about as they journeyed east, that they found a plain in the land of Shinar and settled there. ³ They said to one another, "Come, let us make bricks and burn them thoroughly." And they used brick for stone, and they used tar for mortar.⁴ They said, "Come, let us build for ourselves a city, and a tower whose top will reach into heaven, and let us make for ourselves a name, otherwise we will be scattered abroad over the face of the whole earth." ⁵ The Lord came down to see the city and the tower which the sons of men had built. ⁶ The Lord said, "Behold, they are one people, and they all have the same language. And this is what they began to do, and now nothing which they purpose to do will be impossible for them. ⁷ Come, let Us go down and confuse their language, so that they will not understand one another's speech." ⁸ So the Lord scattered them abroad from there over the face of the whole earth; and they stopped building the city. ⁹ Therefore its name was called Babel, because there the Lord confused the language of the whole earth; and from there the Lord scattered them abroad over the face of the whole earth.

The whole earth at that time used the same language and words. We don't know what the original language was although perhaps it was Hebrew. As they journeyed east (Middle East) they settled in the land of Shiner, (Babylon, now modern day Iraq). They said "let's make bricks and burn them thoroughly." They used brick for stone and tar for mortar. They then became arrogant and decided that they could build a tall tower whose top would reach into heaven. They would make for themselves a name, otherwise they would be scattered over the face of the whole earth. They would make a name for themselves so that the people/city could never be defeated. Why would any among them want to leave and because a rival. They believed that glorify themselves would achieve their greatest goals and never asked God for his help. We learn that God would not allow them to achieve their goal The Lord came down to see the city and the tower the sons of men built. They did not need a tower to access God, He was everywhere. Various old stories describe how big the Tower was, perhaps anywhere from 1.6 miles high to 695 feet high. The Lord said that they are one people and have the same language. Nothing will be impossible to them. Come, let Us (God the Father, God the Son, God the Holy Spirit), confuse their language so they cannot understand one another's speech. So the Lord did just that. Of the three sons of Noah, 15 names were Japheth's descendants, 30 for Ham and 27 for Shem, thus making at least 72 different languages. He scattered them abroad over the face of the whole earth. They no longer could build the tower. The name of the tower was Babel that means "to confuse".

Descendants of Shem

10 These are the records of the generations of Shem. Shem was one hundred years old, and became the father of Arpachshad two years after the flood; 11 and Shem lived five hundred years after he became the father of Arpachshad, and he had other sons and daughters.

12 Arpachshad lived thirty-five years, and became the father of Shelah; 13 and Arpachshad lived four hundred and three years after he became the father of Shelah, and he had other sons and daughters.

14 Shelah lived thirty years, and became the father of Eber; 15 and Shelah lived four hundred and three years after he became the father of Eber, and he had other sons and daughters.

16 Eber lived thirty-four years, and became the father of Peleg; 17 and Eber lived four hundred and thirty years after he became the father of Peleg, and he had other sons and daughters.

18 Peleg lived thirty years, and became the father of Reu; 19 and Peleg lived two hundred and nine years after he became the father of Reu, and he had other sons and daughters.

²⁰ *Reu lived thirty-two years, and became the father of Serug;* ²¹ *and Reu lived two hundred and seven years after he became the father of Serug, and he had other sons and daughters.*

²² *Serug lived thirty years, and became the father of Nahor;* ²³ *and Serug lived two hundred years after he became the father of Nahor, and he had other sons and daughters.*

²⁴ *Nahor lived twenty-nine years, and became the father of Terah;* ²⁵ *and Nahor lived one hundred and nineteen years after he became the father of Terah, and he had other sons and daughters.*

²⁶ *Terah lived seventy years, and became the father of Abram, Nahor and Haran.*

²⁷ *Now these are the records of the generations of Terah. Terah became the father of Abram, Nahor and Haran; and Haran became the father of Lot.* ²⁸ *Haran died in the presence of his father Terah in the land of his birth, in Ur of the Chaldeans.* ²⁹ *Abram and Nahor took wives for themselves. The name of Abram's wife was Sarai; and the name of Nahor's wife was Milcah, the daughter of Haran, the father of Milcah and Iscah.* ³⁰ *Sarai was barren; she had no child.*

³¹ *Terah took Abram his son, and Lot the son of Haran, his grandson, and Sarai his daughter-in-law, his son Abram's wife; and they went out together from Ur of the Chaldeans in order to enter the land of Canaan; and they went as far as Haran, and settled there.* ³² *The days of Terah were two hundred and five years; and Terah died in Haran.*

All these descendant from Shem (son of Noah) to children of Terah listed here. Each had one main son, but many other sons and daughter. Notice that no one lived after Shem beyond 500 years. Terah was the son of Nahor. At seventy years (and beyond) Terah was the father of Abram, Nahor, and Haran. Later we will read that Abram name was changed to Abraham and Haran became the father of Lot. They lived in Ur of the Chaldeans. Ur was an ancient city of Sumer located on a former channel of the Euphrates River. Sumer - an area in the southern region of Babylonia in present-day Iraq; site of the Sumerian civilization of city-states that flowered during the third millennium BC. Abram married a woman name Sarai that was later changed to Sarah.

CHAPTER TWELVE

Abram Journeys to Egypt

*¹Now the LORD said to Abram,
"Go forth from your country,
And from your relatives
And from your father's house,
To the land which I will show you;
²And I will make you a great nation,
And I will bless you,
And make your name great;
And so you shall be a blessing;
³And I will bless those who bless you,
And the one who curses you I will curse.
And in you all the families of the earth will be blessed."*

God spoke to Abram, told him to leave his country, leave his relatives, and go from your father's house. Go to the land I will show you and I will make you a great nation. I will bless you and make your name great. You shall be a blessing. I will bless those who bless you and the ones who curses you I will curse. In you all the families of the earth will be blessed. God chose Abram, later Abraham, to be the starting vehicle for the blessing of the world.

One of the greatest promises in the Old Testament, if not the greatest promise, is read in these three verses of Genesis 12. God made three promises to Abraham—

(1) A promise to bring him to a new land (modern day Israel)
(2) A promise that he would be the leader of a great nation, and
(3) A promise that all peoples on earth would be blessed through him.

The land that God promised to Abram (Abraham's original name) was far away from where he was living (land of Ur) when God called him to move. Ur, only a railroad station today, is southeast of Baghdad, 10 miles from the Iraqi city, Nasiriyah. From there, Abraham traveled to the middle of modern-day Israel, to a place now called Tell Balatah on the West Bank, north of Jerusalem, about 870 miles from Ur.

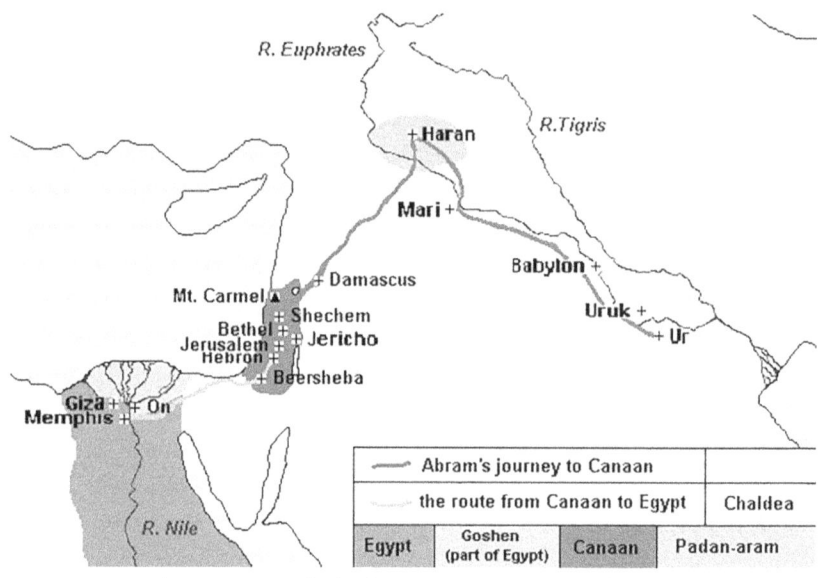

http://www.drshirley.org/geog/geog05.html.

God promised Abram that he would be the start of a great nation and that nation became the Jewish nation through his son, Isaac. However, prior to Isaac's birth, Abram became the father of Ishmael through his wife's maid, Hagar, and Ishmael became the father of the Islamic nation. And, when you read the genealogies of Jesus Christ, Abraham was named first in Matthew 1:2 (father Joseph lineage) and named in mother Mary's lineage in Luke 3:34. So Abraham's name is great and blessed in the world's three major religions—Judaism, Islam, and Christianity.

The third promise from God to Abram was that Abram would be a blessing, that God would bless those who bless Abram and curse those who curse Abram and all people on earth would be blessed because of Abram. Exactly how are people blessed today, you included, because of Abram/Abraham? Because of God's fulfillment of this promise by giving His only begotten Son, Jesus Christ. Read the testimony of Peter in Acts 3 where in verse 25, Peter quotes this passage from Genesis 12:3. Through Abram's faithfulness (Romans 4, the whole chapter), eventually Jesus was brought to earth to be a blessing for all people who believe in Him. Galatians 3:14 says that the blessing of Abraham might come upon the Gentiles (you and me) in Christ Jesus, that we might receive the promise.

What do you learn about faith through a study of Abraham? While God will not call you to establish a nation like He did with Abraham, He calls you to do something for Him and His kingdom. Do you know what your calling is and are you willing to show the kind of faith that Abraham showed when He was called? Faith was the main quality characteristic of Abraham and may the same characteristic be said and named of you.

⁴So Abram went forth as the LORD had spoken to him; and Lot went with him. Now Abram was seventy-five years old when he departed from Haran. ⁵Abram took Sarai his wife and Lot his nephew, and all their possessions which they had accumulated, and the persons which they had acquired in Haran, and they set out for the land of Canaan; thus they came to the land of Canaan. ⁶Abram passed through the land as far as the site of Shechem, to the oak of Moreh. Now the Canaanite was then in the land. ⁷The LORD appeared to Abram and said, "To your descendants I will give this land." So he built an altar there to the LORD who had appeared to him. ⁸Then he proceeded from there to the mountain on the east of Bethel, and pitched his tent, with Bethel on the west and Ai on the east; and there he built an altar to the LORD and called upon the name of the LORD. ⁹Abram journeyed on, continuing toward the Negev.

Abram, his wife, Sarai, and his nephew Lot left Haran (ruins in present Turkey) and they set out for Canaan. This territory is roughly the areas of modern-day Israel, Palestine, Lebanon, western Jordan, and western Syria. Abram passed through the land as far as Shechem, to the oak of Moreh. Moreh is a sacred tree or grove notable for its size and age in the landscape in Shechem in the middle of Israel located between Mt. Gerizim and Mt. Ebal. Canaanites lived in this land, related to Canaan, son of Ham. The Lord appeared to Abram and said, "To your descendants I will give this land". Abram build an altar there to the Lord who had appeared to him. Then he proceeded from there to the mountain on the east side of Bethel and pitched his tent, with Bethel on the west and Ai on the east. Bethel represents the house of God while Ai represents "house of ruins". Are you closer to house of God or house of ruins? Are you faithful to God or are you closer to what is evil in the world? After the Lord appeared to Abram at Shechem, Abram began worshiping the Lord there. He then journeyed on, continuing to the Negev. They went further south in the land of Canaan toward the region of Negev (or Negeb). This area was a dry, desert area with little land for supporting crops. Abram had to keep moving although we do not know the details.

^{10}Now there was a famine in the land; so Abram went down to Egypt to sojourn there, for the famine was severe in the land. ^{11}It came about when he came near to Egypt, that he said to Sarai his wife, "See now, I know that you are a beautiful woman; ^{12}and when the Egyptians see you, they will say, 'This is his wife'; and they will kill me, but they will let you live. ^{13}"Please say that you are my sister so that it may go well with me because of you, and that I may live on account of you." ^{14}It came about when Abram came into Egypt, the Egyptians saw that the woman was very beautiful. ^{15}Pharaoh's officials saw her and praised her to Pharaoh; and the woman was taken into Pharaoh's house. ^{16}Therefore he treated Abram well for her sake; and gave him sheep and oxen and donkeys and male and female servants and female donkeys and camels.

Eventually the famine in the land made Abram and family move to Egypt. When he came near to Egypt, he told Sarai, his wife, that she is beautiful and they will kill Abram but let her live. So Abram asked her to lie, saying she is his sister rather than his wife. This was a half-truth as they both were children of Terah. God would later forbid such marriages but not yet. When Abram came into Egypt, the Egyptians saw that she was very beautiful. Abram put her at great risk saying that she is not his wife. Abram did not trust the Lord to protect him. Despite all God's promises, Abram did not believe Him. The Egyptian people noticed her great beauty. Pharaoh takes Sarai for his wife although she was one of many. We don't know if Pharaoh slept with Sarai or he was prevented by God. Pharaoh made a huge payment to Abram including sheep and oxen animals, male and female servants, and female donkeys and camels. Yet Abram lost his wife for a while. Abram did not consult the Lord, at least the Bible doesn't say. Abram own godless views and actions nearly cost him everything.

[17]But the LORD struck Pharaoh and his house with great plagues because of Sarai, Abram's wife. [18]Then Pharaoh called Abram and said, "What is this you have done to me? Why did you not tell me that she was your wife? [19]"Why did you say, 'She is my sister,' so that I took her for my wife? Now then, here is your wife, take her and go." [20]Pharaoh commanded his men concerning him; and they escorted him away, with his wife and all that belonged to him.

The Lord did not fail Abram even though Abram made a stupid mistake. The Lord struck Pharaoh and his house with great plagues because of Abram considering his wife his sister. Pharaoh came to Abram and demanded, "What have you done to me". Some commentaries believe that the Egyptians were afflicted with plagues of the skin such that they knew something was wrong. Pharaoh soon knew that Sarai was Abram wife, not his sister, plus so many gifts he gave to Abram. Abram does not honorably in any way in this part of his life. Yet the Lord did not give up on him. He promises the same thing to us, but we must believe Him. He does not give up on us even though many times we fail Him. Pharaoh returned Sarai to Abram, telling Abram and all that belonged to him to leave. Abram survived well despite all his failures and silence. God does not leave out stories that show his people flawed. Indeed, most people God uses throughout history are flawed people. Abram eventually learned to trust God and his faith will enable him to trust God later through his son, Isaac.

CHAPTER THIRTEEN

Abram and Lot

¹*So Abram went up from Egypt to the Negev, he and his wife and all that belonged to him, and Lot with him. ²Now Abram was very rich in livestock, in silver and in gold. ³He went on his journeys from the Negev as far as Bethel, to the place where his tent had been at the beginning, between Bethel and Ai, ⁴to the place of the altar which he had made there formerly; and there Abram called on the name of the LORD. ⁵Now Lot, who went with Abram, also had flocks and herds and tents. ⁶And the land could not sustain them while dwelling together, for their possessions were so great that they were not able to remain together. ⁷And there was strife between the herdsmen of Abram's livestock and the herdsmen of Lot's livestock. Now the Canaanite and the Perizzite were dwelling then in the land.*

Abram went back to Negev from Egypt along with Sarai, all that belonged to him and Lot and his family. Abram was very rich with livestock, silver, and gold. He sent from Negev back to Bethel to where his tent had been placed when he was there the first time. He was again between Bethel and Ai, between loving God and loving the world. He returned to the altar he built and there Abram called on the name of the Lord. In both Genesis 13:4 and back at Genesis 12:8, Abram called on the name of the Lord in the context of building an altar to Him. Lot who went with Abram also was wealthy with flocks and herds and tents. They realize that the land could not sustain both as their possessions were so great. And there was strife between the herdsmen of Abrams livestock and the herdsmen of Lot's livestock. The herdsmen were quarreling over resources like grazing and water for the livestock. It was not like the area was empty and many other people like the Canaanites and Perizzites lived there too

⁸So Abram said to Lot, "Please let there be no strife between you and me, nor between my herdsmen and your herdsmen, for we are brothers. ⁹"Is not the whole land before you? Please separate from me; if to the left, then I will go to the right; or if to the right, then I will go to the left." ¹⁰Lot lifted up his eyes and saw all the valley of the Jordan, that it was well watered everywhere—this was before the LORD destroyed Sodom and Gomorrah—like the garden of the LORD, like the land of Egypt as you go to Zoar. ¹¹So Lot chose for himself all the valley of the Jordan, and Lot journeyed eastward. Thus they separated from each other. ¹²Abram settled in the land of Canaan, while Lot settled in the cities of the valley, and moved his tents as far as Sodom. ¹³Now the men of Sodom were wicked exceedingly and sinners against the LORD.

¹⁴The LORD said to Abram, after Lot had separated from him, "Now lift up your eyes and look from the place where you are, northward and southward and eastward and westward; ¹⁵for all the land which you see, I will give it to you and to your descendants forever. ¹⁶"I will make your descendants as the dust of the earth, so that if anyone can number the dust of the earth, then your descendants can also be numbered. ¹⁷"Arise, walk about the land through its length and breadth; for I will give it to you." ¹⁸Then Abram moved his tent and came and dwelt by the oaks of Mamre, which are in Hebron, and there he built an altar to the LORD.

Abram did not want any strife between his family and Lot's family. He said that he and Lot were like brothers so he gave Lot the first choice where he would settle. If Lot went to the left, then Abram would go to the right or vice versa. Abram valued Lot over the land; valued his family more than his possessions. Are you today valuing possessions more than people? Lot saw the valley of the Jordan, well-watered everywhere, like the garden of the Lord, like the land of Egypt. So Lot chose all the valley of the Jordan and he journeyed eastward. Abram settled in the land of Canaan while Lot settled in the cities of the valley and moved his tents as far as Sodom. Unfortunately, the men of Sodom were wicked exceedingly and sinners against the Lord. We learn much more about Sodom and Gomorrah in Genesis 19. Lot made a wrong decision eventually. He was not as wise as Abram.

The Lord said to Abram after Lot separated from him, "Now lift up your eyes and look in every direction. For all the land which you see I will give to you and your descendants forever. Your descendants will be as the dust of the earth, too numerous to count. Arise, Abram, walk about the land I have given to you." Then Abram moved his tent and came and dwelt by the oaks of Mamre and he built an altar to the Lord. Mamre located just south of Bethlehem and Jerusalem. Mamre is where Abram and his immediate family lived the rest of their lives.

CHAPTER FOURTEEN

War of Kings and God's Promise to Abram

¹And it came about in the days of Amraphel king of Shinar, Arioch king of Ellasar, Chedorlaomer king of Elam, and Tidal king of Goiim, ²that they made war with Bera king of Sodom, and with Birsha king of Gomorrah, Shinab king of Admah, and Shemeber king of Zeboiim, and the king of Bela (that is, Zoar). ³All these came as allies to the valley of Siddim (that is, the Salt Sea). ⁴Twelve years they had served Chedorlaomer, but the thirteenth year they rebelled. ⁵In the fourteenth year Chedorlaomer and the kings that were with him, came and defeated the Rephaim in Ashteroth-karnaim and the Zuzim in Ham and the Emim in Shaveh-kiriathaim, ⁶and the Horites in their Mount Seir, as far as El-paran, which is by the wilderness. ⁷Then they turned back and came to En-mishpat (that is, Kadesh), and conquered all the country of the Amalekites, and also the Amorites, who lived in Hazazon-tamar. ⁸And the king of Sodom and the king of Gomorrah and the king of Admah and the king of Zeboiim and the king of Bela (that is, Zoar) came out; and they arrayed for battle against them in the valley of Siddim, ⁹against Chedorlaomer king of Elam and Tidal king of Goiim and Amraphel king of Shinar and Arioch king of Ellasar—four kings against five. ¹⁰Now the valley of Siddim was full of tar pits; and the kings of Sodom and Gomorrah fled, and they fell into them. But those who survived fled to the hill country. ¹¹Then they took all the goods of Sodom and Gomorrah and all their food supply, and departed. ¹²They also took Lot, Abram's nephew, and his possessions and departed, for he was living in Sodom.

Four Mesopotamian kings made war with five kings of Canaan including kings from Sodom and Gomorrah. The four kings won around the Dead

Sea (Salt Sea). All kings had once served Chedorlaomer, king of Elam (Iran today), but in the thirteenth year they rebelled. In the fourteenth year Chedorlaomer and the kings with him defeated the Canaanite kings. Eventually, Abram would defeat Chedorlaomer (Genesis 14:17). The four kings defeated the five kings in the valley called Siddim (verse 8). Later the Dead Sea flooded that valley. The valley of Siddom was full of tar pit and many people, including the kings of Sodom and Gomorrah fell into them. Others made it to the hill country. They took Lot and his possessions. Abram would have to rescue Lot.

[13] Then a fugitive came and told Abram the Hebrew. Now he was living by the oaks of Mamre the Amorite, brother of Eshcol and brother of Aner, and these were allies with Abram. [14] When Abram heard that his relative had been taken captive, he led out his trained men, born in his house, three hundred and eighteen, and went in pursuit as far as Dan. [15] He divided his forces against them by night, he and his servants, and defeated them, and pursued them as far as Hobah, which is north of Damascus. [16] He brought back all the goods, and also brought back his relative Lot with his possessions, and also the women, and the people.

Abram is called the "Hebrew" in verse 13, only time he was called a Hebrew. Abram defeated Chedorlaomer and rescued the prisoners. He defeated them at night. He pursued them as far as Hobah, north of Damascus. Abram brought back all the good and his relative Lot with his possessions and the captive woman and the people.

[17] Then after his return from the defeat of Chedorlaomer and the kings who were with him, the king of Sodom went out to meet him at the valley of Shaveh (that is, the King's Valley). [18] And Melchizedek king of Salem brought out bread and wine; now he was a priest of God Most High. [19] He blessed him and said, "Blessed be Abram of God Most High, Possessor of heaven and earth; [20] And blessed be God Most High, Who has delivered your enemies into your hand." He gave him a tenth of all.

After Abram's return from the defeat of Chedorlaomer and the other kings with him, the king of Sodom went out to meet him in the valley of Shaveh on the north side of Jerusalem. Yet it seems providential that it was not the king of Sodom, but the king of Salem, Melchizedek, who brought out bread and wine. His name means a righteous king, see Hebrews 7:2. Salem likely was the early name for Jerusalem. Melchizedek is the first priest mentioned in Genesis. He blessed the meal and said to Abram, "Blessed be Abram of God Most High, Possessor of heaven and earth." He was both a priest and a king. Melchizedek also blessed the Lord, who delivered enemies into Abram's hand. Abram showed honor to Melchizedek by given him a tenth of all. Abram response was a testimony to his faith in his God that both he and Melchizedek worshipped. God deserved the glory for Abram victories. Although some disagree, I think that this is where the tithe of 10% comes from.

²¹The king of Sodom said to Abram, "Give the people to me and take the goods for yourself." ²²Abram said to the king of Sodom, "I have sworn to the LORD God Most High, possessor of heaven and earth, ²³that I will not take a thread or a sandal thong or anything that is yours, for fear you would say, 'I have made Abram rich.' ²⁴"I will take nothing except what the young men have eaten, and the share of the men who went with me, Aner, Eshcol, and Mamre; let them take their share."

Then the king of Sodom (Bera, verse 2) said to Abram, "Give the people to me and take the goods for yourself." Yet Abram did not agree to keep the possessions. I remembered his swearing to the Lord God Most High that he will not take anything of Sodom that would make him rich. Only God can make him rich. He would never take anything from Sodom, already know as a wicked city. Abram was fair to the men who fought with him---Aner, Eshcol, and Mamre; let them take their share. We know that God helped Abram and granted him success. Abram was able to defeat a larger army because of the Lord God on his side.

CHAPTER FIFTHTEEN

Abram Promised A Son

¹After these things the word of the LORD came to Abram in a vision, saying,
"Do not fear, Abram,
I am a shield to you;
Your reward shall be very great."

The word of the Lord came to Abram in a vision. No words of the bible existed yet so this how the Lord communicated with special people. The Lord said "Do no fear, Abram, I am a shield to you; Your reward shall be very great". Describing God as a shield to us is mentioned a lot in Psalms, e.g. 3:3, 18:2, 28:7, 33:20, 84:11, and 115:9. God protects His people and will reward us in many ways, but we must trust Him.

²Abram said, "O Lord GOD, what will You give me, since I am childless, and the heir of my house is Eliezer of Damascus?" ³And Abram said, "Since You have given no offspring to me, one born in my house is my heir." ⁴Then behold, the word of the LORD came to him, saying, "This man will not be your heir; but one who will come forth from your own body, he shall be your heir." ⁵And He took him outside and said, "Now look toward the heavens, and count the stars, if you are able to count them." And He said to him, "So shall your descendants be." ⁶Then he believed in the LORD; and He reckoned it to him as righteousness. ⁷And He said to him, "I am the LORD who brought you out of Ur of the Chaldeans, to give you this land to possess it." ⁸He said, "O Lord GOD, how may I know that I will possess it?" ⁹So He said to him, "Bring Me a three year old heifer, and a three year old female goat, and a three year old ram, and a turtledove, and a young pigeon." ¹⁰Then he brought all these to Him and cut them in two, and laid each half opposite the other; but he did not cut the birds. ¹¹The birds of prey came down upon the carcasses, and Abram drove them away.

Abram responded, "O Lord God, what will You give me, since I am childless, and the heir of my house is Eliezer of Damascus?" Eliezer of Damascus, who would have inherited Abraham's fortune if Ishmael and Isaac had not been born. He is thought to be a son of Nimrod. A common custom in those days was for couples with no children to adopt a servant as an heir to take the place of a firstborn son. Eliezer of Damascus was likely the same "senior servant" in charge of all Abraham's possessions who, many years later, was commissioned by Abraham to go and find a wife for his son, Isaac, from among Abraham's own relatives in his native land (Genesis 24:1–9). And Abram said, "Since You have given no offspring to me, one born in my house is my heir" (Eliezer of Damascus). Then the word of the Lord came to him, saying, "This man will not be your heir, but one who will come forth from your own body, he shall be your heir.". God took Abram outside and said, "Look toward the heavens and count the stars, if you can. So your descendants be." God is speaking and He does not say "your descendants will be", but your descendants be. God never lies (Numbers 23:19); Abram's descendants are like the stars in heaven.

Abram believed in the Lord and He reckoned it to him as righteousness. The apostle Paul reminded his readers in Romans (4:3, 4:9, 4:22) that God reckoned Abram's faith as righteousness. It was not works that saved Abram, but faith in the Lord. God said to Abram, "I am the Lord who brought you out of Ur of the Chaldeans, to give you this land to possess." Abram replied, "Oh Lord God, how may I know that I will possess it?" God told him to bring a heifer, goat, ram and a young pigeon. Abram brought all these to God and cut them in two, laid each half opposite the other, but Abram did not cut the birds. Birds of prey came down upon the carcasses and Abram drove them away. The agreement between God and Abram was a covenant that was sealed by the dividing of animals. This was not an animal sacrifice but a legal act of making a binding agreement.

¹²Now when the sun was going down, a deep sleep fell upon Abram; and behold, terror and great darkness fell upon him. ¹³God said to Abram, "Know for certain that your descendants will be strangers in a land that is not theirs, where they will be enslaved and oppressed four hundred years. ¹⁴"But I will *also judge the nation whom they will serve, and afterward they will come out with many possessions. *¹⁵*"As for you, you shall go to your fathers in peace; you will be buried at a good old age. *¹⁶*"Then in the fourth generation they will return here, for the iniquity of the Amorite is not yet complete."*

A deep sleep fell upon Abram and, behold, terror and great darkness fell upon him. God told Abram that Abram's descendants will be in slavery in Egypt for four hundred years, then their exodus from Egypt and their conquest of the sinful nations resident in Canaan. God will keep His promise to Abram but it will be over four hundred years before his family returns to Israel. Abram will not see the return from Egypt but his ancestors will. God predicts that Abram will go to his fathers in peace and he will be buried at a good old age. The four hundred plus years (Exodus 12:40 say it was four hundred and thirty years) was because of the iniquity of the Amorite people was not yet complete. The returning Israelites were a judgment on the Amorite people. The term *Amorites* is used in the bible to refer to certain highland mountaineers who inhabited the land of Canaan described in Genesis 10:16 as descendants of Canaan the son of Ham. They are described as a powerful people of great stature "like the height of the cedars" (Amos 2:9) who had occupied the land east and west of the Jordan. God did not preemptively judge the Amorites or any other people of Canaan. He allowed them great mercy in allowing much more time for the wicked people in Canaan to see their sin and repent. When they did not, God allow Israel through Joshua to judge the Amorites.

¹⁷It came about when the sun had set, that it was very dark, and behold, there appeared a smoking oven and a flaming torch which passed between these pieces. ¹⁸On that day the LORD made a covenant with Abram, saying,
"To your descendants I have given this land,
From the river of Egypt as far as the great river, the river Euphrates:
¹⁹the Kenite and the Kenizzite and the Kadmonite ²⁰and the Hittite and the Perizzite and the Rephaim ²¹and the Amorite and the Canaanite and the Girgashite and the Jebusite."

And it came about when the sun had set, that it was very dark, and behold, there appeared a smoking oven and a flaming torch which passed between these pieces. On that day, the Lord made a covenant with Abram, saying, 'To your descendants I have given this land, from the river of Egypt as far as the great river, the river Euphrates: the Kenite and the Kenizzite and the Kadmonite and the Hittite and the Perizzite and the Rephaim and the Amorite and the Canaanite and the Girgashite and the Jebusite'. This covenant is distinctive because only God, in the appearance of a smoking oven and a flaming torch, passed between the divided carcasses of animals. This was done to signify that the covenant was unilateral and unconditional. No conditions were placed upon Abram for its fulfillment.

CHAPTER SIXTEEN

Sarai and Hagar

¹Now Sarai, Abram's wife had borne him no children, and she had an Egyptian maid whose name was Hagar. ²So Sarai said to Abram, "Now behold, the LORD has prevented me from bearing children. Please go in to my maid; perhaps I will obtain children through her." And Abram listened to the voice of Sarai. ³After Abram had lived ten years in the land of Canaan, Abram's wife Sarai took Hagar the Egyptian, her maid, and gave her to her husband Abram as his wife. ⁴He went in to Hagar, and she conceived; and when she saw that she had conceived, her mistress was despised in her sight. ⁵And Sarai said to Abram, "May the wrong done me be upon you. I gave my maid into your arms, but when she saw that she had conceived, I was despised in her sight. May the LORD judge between you and me." ⁶But Abram said to Sarai, "Behold, your maid is in your power; do to her what is good in your sight." So Sarai treated her harshly, and she fled from her presence.

Sarai, Abram wife, had borne him no children. She had an Egypt maid names Hagar. It was Sarai's idea for Abram to have children through Hagar. He married Hagar, she conceived, but then Sarai despised her. Abram told Sarai to do with Hagar what she pleased. Sarai treated Hagar harshly and Hagar fled.

It is disappointing that Abram chose to allow his wife, Sarai, to dictate to him. He was unfaithful to God who promised him a son eventually even thought by now Abram probably was in his 90s. Yet he still gave up on God. When Hagar become pregnant, she treated Sarai with contempt because Sarai was childless. Perhaps Hagar believed that the child would belong to Sarai. Although this was Sarai idea in the first place, she now holds Abram responsible for this conflict. And, he agrees with Sarai. Sarai dealt harshly with Hagar, so harshly that Hagar had to flee, she might have even been fearful for her life.

[7]Now the angel of the LORD found her by a spring of water in the wilderness, by the spring on the way to Shur. [8]He said, "Hagar, Sarai's maid, where have you come from and where are you going?" And she said, "I am fleeing from the presence of my mistress Sarai." [9]Then the angel of the LORD said to her, "Return to your mistress, and submit yourself to her authority." [10]Moreover, the angel of the LORD said to her, "I will greatly multiply your descendants so that they will be too many to count." [11] The angel of the LORD said to her further, "Behold, you are with child,
And you will bear a son;
And you shall call his name Ishmael,
Because the LORD has given heed to your affliction.
[12] "He will be a wild donkey of a man,
His hand will be against everyone,
And everyone's hand will be against him;
And he will live to the east of all his brothers."
[13]Then she called the name of the LORD who spoke to her, "You are a God who sees"; for she said, "Have I even remained alive here after seeing Him?" [14]Therefore the well was called Beer-lahai-roi; behold, it is between Kadesh and Bered.

[15]So Hagar bore Abram a son; and Abram called the name of his son, whom Hagar bore, Ishmael. [16]Abram was eighty-six years old when Hagar bore Ishmael to him.

God would not allow Hagar and her child to be forgotten about. The angel of the Lord found her by a spring of water in the wilderness on the way to Shur (a strip of land east of the Nile, connecting Egypt and Canaan across the Sinai). The angel gave Hagar a command and a promise. Hagar replied that she was fleeing Sarai, but the angel told her to return to Sarai and submit yourself to her authority (command). However, the angel also told her that her descendants would greatly multiply so that they would be too many to count (promise). Furthermore, you will bear a son and you shall call his name Ishmael because the Lord has given heed to your affliction. Ishmael will be a wild donkey of a man, his hand will be against everyone and everyone's hand will be against him. He will live to the east of all his brothers. The family and descendants of Ishmael will be in conflict with everyone. More on Ismael in the following paragraph. Hagar called the name of the Lord, "You are a God who sees" for she said, "Have I ever remained alive here after seeing him?" She was located at a well called Beer Lahai Roi, between Kadesh and Bered. Beer Lahai Roi literally means "the well of the vision of life." Hagar named the location thus because the Living God saw her situation and intervened to give her hope and comfort. Beer Lahai Roi is also mentioned other places in Genesis. Moses recorded this event some four hundred years later, but the well was still known to people in Moses's day. The use of the name Beer Lahai Roi would have illustrated to the Hebrews that Abram and his family had been active in the land of Canaan long before the exodus and that God, through Moses, was simply bringing the people back in fulfillment of His promise to Abram.

Later we will read that Ishmael grew up, married an Egyptian woman, and begat twelve sons who became princes over their respective tribes (Genesis 25:12ff) — exactly as prophesied (17:20). These people inhabited the territory between Havilah (probably in NW Arabia) and Shur (near the Egyptian border), and were one of the several peoples who were the ancestors of the Arabians (Genesis 10:7, 25-30; 25:1-4, 13-16). Today, Arab-dominated territories are much more extensive even than in Bible times. Ishmael was characterized as a "wild donkey."

What is the significance of that expression? He and his descendants were nomads, lived friendless existence, great hunters. Today people of the Bedouin are nomadic Arab people who inhabit the area in North Africa, Arabian Peninsula, and Iraq. Wild donkeys are fierce people, hostile, warlike, yet no one has been able to conquer them, even Alexander the Great or the Romans. Only Mohammed in the late sixth century started a religious zealotry that conquered these "wild donkey of people". His movement began the religion of Islam.

CHAPTER SEVENTEEN

Abraham and the Covenant of Circumcision

¹*Now when Abram was ninety-nine years old, the LORD appeared to Abram and said to him,*
"I am God Almighty;
Walk before Me, and be blameless.
²*"I will establish My covenant between Me and you,*
And I will multiply you exceedingly."
³*Abram fell on his face, and God talked with him, saying,*
⁴*"As for Me, behold, My covenant is with you,*
And you will be the father of a multitude of nations.
⁵*"No longer shall your name be called Abram,*
But your name shall be Abraham;
For I have made you the father of a multitude of nations.

Abram was ninety-nine years old, still childless, when the Lord appeared to him and said, "I am God Almighty (El Shaddai); walk with Me and be blameless. Be intimate with God and be blameless (whole-hearted, integrity). It has been thirteen years since God told Abram that he and Sarai would have a son. Indeed, the integrity of Abram to remain faithful. God repeated His covenant between Him and Abram and God said He will multiply you exceedingly. Abram fell on his face (in great reverence) and God talked with him saying that His covenant with Abram and he will be the father of a multitude of nations. Abram's name will be changed to Abraham. Names in ancient times were given by parents to describe the life they hoped their child would fulfill. Abram, named by Terah, meant "exalted father". God's new name, Abraham, means "father of multitude" that will describe what Abraham will become.

[6]"I will make you exceedingly fruitful, and I will make nations of you, and kings will come forth from you. [7]"I will establish My covenant between Me and you and your descendants after you throughout their generations for an everlasting covenant, to be God to you and to your descendants after you. [8]"I will give to you and to your descendants after you, the land of your sojournings, all the land of Canaan, for an everlasting possession; and I will be their God." [9]God said further to Abraham, "Now as for you, you shall keep My covenant, you and your descendants after you throughout their generations. [10]"This is My covenant, which you shall keep, between Me and you and your descendants after you: every male among you shall be circumcised. [11]"And you shall be circumcised in the flesh of your foreskin, and it shall be the sign of the covenant between Me and you. [12]"And every male among you who is eight days old shall be circumcised throughout your generations, a servant who is born in the house or who is bought with money from any foreigner, who is not of your descendants. [13]"A servant who is born in your house or who is bought with your money shall surely be circumcised; thus shall My covenant be in your flesh for an everlasting covenant. [14]"But an uncircumcised male who is not circumcised in the flesh of his foreskin, that person shall be cut off from his people; he has broken My covenant."

God promised to make Abraham exceedingly fruitful. God said that He will make nations of you and kings will come forth from you. Abraham eventually became the father of Jews, Muslins, and Christians. God said, "I will establish My covenant between Me and you and your descendants after you throughout their generations for an everlasting covenant, to be God to you and to your descendants after you. God simply asks that Abraham and his descendants to keep His covenant. As a sign of keeping His covenant, every male in your family will be circumcised. This is a ritual of removing the foreskin above their penis. Those who are not circumcised will not be included in the covenant between God and Abraham's people.

Circumcision mentioned over 100 times in the bible, but it began in Genesis 17. The miraculous nature of Isaac's birth is the key to understanding circumcision as the sign of the covenant. Everyone in Abraham's household witnessed the miracle of Isaac's birth. From that point on, every male understood why they had been circumcised: Their entire race—their very existence—began with a miraculous act of God. Every woman was reminded of this when she had sexual relations with her Israelite husband, and when her sons were circumcised. Circumcision was a visible, continuous reminder that Israel owed its existence to Yahweh, who created them out of nothing.

[15] Then God said to Abraham, "As for Sarai your wife, you shall not call her name Sarai, but Sarah shall be her name. [16] "I will bless her, and indeed I will give you a son by her. Then I will bless her, and she shall be a mother of nations; kings of peoples will come from her." [17] Then Abraham fell on his face and laughed, and said in his heart, "Will a child be born to a man one hundred years old? And will Sarah, who is ninety years old, bear a child?" [18] And Abraham said to God, "Oh that Ishmael might live before You!" [19] But God said, "No, but Sarah your wife will bear you a son, and you shall call his name Isaac; and I will establish My covenant with him for an everlasting covenant for his descendants after him. [20] "As for Ishmael, I have heard you; behold, I will bless him, and will make him fruitful and will multiply him exceedingly. He shall become the father of twelve princes, and I will make him a great nation. [21] "But My covenant I will establish with Isaac, whom Sarah will bear to you at this season next year." [22] When He finished talking with him, God went up from Abraham.

God not only introduced circumcision as a sign of the covenant between Him and Abraham family, He also told Abraham that Sarai's name would be changed to Sarah (noblewoman). She and Abraham will have a son after all after being childless for many years (he was approached 100 and she was 90). Abraham, upon hearing this news from God, falls facedown and laughs. He was shocked that Sarah would have a child at this age. Sarah will be a mother of nations, kings of peoples will come from her.

Abraham had another thought. What about Ishmael? But God said, "No, Sarah your wife will bear you a son and you will call his name Isaac ('he laughs'), and God will establish His covenant with him for an everlasting covenant for his descendants after him. Yet what about Ishmael? God will bless him and make him fruitful and multiply him exceedingly; he will become the father of twelve princes (listed in Genesis 25) and I will make him a great nation. But, God said, "My covenant I will establish with Isaac who Sarah will bear to you next year." Then God left Abraham with these thoughts.

²³*Then Abraham took Ishmael his son, and all the servants who were born in his house and all who were bought with his money, every male among the men of Abraham's household, and circumcised the flesh of their foreskin in the very same day, as God had said to him.* ²⁴*Now Abraham was ninety-nine years old when he was circumcised in the flesh of his foreskin.* ²⁵*And Ishmael his son was thirteen years old when he was circumcised in the flesh of his foreskin.* ²⁶*In the very same day Abraham was circumcised, and Ishmael his son.* ²⁷*All the men of his household, who were born in the house or bought with money from a foreigner, were circumcised with him.*

Abraham took his son, Ishmael, all the servants who were born in his house and all those bought with his money, every male among the men is his household and circumcised the flesh of their foreskin as God commended him, including himself that very same day. Abraham was nighty-nine years old when he did this as immediate obedience to the Lord. Abraham chose to trust the Lord and accept His word.

CHAPTER EIGHTEEN

Birth of Isaac Promised

¹Now the LORD appeared to him by the oaks of Mamre, while he was sitting at the tent door in the heat of the day. ²When he lifted up his eyes and looked, behold, three men were standing opposite him; and when he saw them, he ran from the tent door to meet them and bowed himself to the earth, ³and said, "My Lord, if now I have found favor in Your sight, please do not pass Your servant by. ⁴"Please let a little water be brought and wash your feet, and rest yourselves under the tree; ⁵and I will bring a piece of bread, that you may refresh yourselves; after that you may go on, since you have visited your servant." And they said, "So do, as you have said." ⁶So Abraham hurried into the tent to Sarah, and said, "Quickly, prepare three measures of fine flour, knead it and make bread cakes." ⁷Abraham also ran to the herd, and took a tender and choice calf and gave it to the servant, and he hurried to prepare it. ⁸He took curds and milk and the calf which he had prepared, and placed it before them; and he was standing by them under the tree as they ate.

In chapter 18 the Lord again appeared to Abraham by the oaks of Mamre, where Abraham and his family lived. However, in the heat of the day, the Lord appeared as three men standing opposite of Abraham. Not sure if Abraham, at first, knew these three men, who were the Lord and two angels in human form. Abraham ran from the tent door to meet them and bowed himself to the earth. Abraham said, "My Lord, if now I have found favor in your sight, please do not pass by your servant. Abraham runs to show them deep respect and hospitality and tell Sarah to bake them bread and has a young calf slaughtered for them to eat under the tree.

⁹Then they said to him, "Where is Sarah your wife?" And he said, "There, in the tent." ¹⁰He said, "I will surely return to you at this time next year; and behold, Sarah your wife will have a son." And Sarah was listening at the tent door, which was behind him. ¹¹Now Abraham and Sarah were old, advanced in age; Sarah was past childbearing. ¹²Sarah laughed to herself, saying, "After I have become old, shall I have pleasure, my lord being old also?" ¹³And the LORD said to Abraham, "Why did Sarah laugh, saying, 'Shall I indeed bear a child, when I am so old?' ¹⁴"Is anything too difficult for the LORD? At the appointed time, I will return to you, at this time next year, and Sarah will have a son." ¹⁵Sarah denied it however, saying, "I did not laugh"; for she was afraid. And He said, "No, but you did laugh."

After eating the men asked, "Where is Sarah your wife?" "She is in the tent", Abraham answered. One man (the Lord) said, "I will surely return to you at this time next year and behold, Sarah your wife will have a son." Sarah was listening at the tent door. Both Sarah and Abraham were well past child bearing so she laughed to herself. The phrasing here might suggest the idea of menopause: Sarah is literally "beyond" a woman's normal ability to conceive. She describes herself and her husband as old. She cannot imagine having a child at this stage of her life. He asks Abraham why she laughed. "Is anything too hard for the LORD?" Then He repeats the promise of a son at the appointed time. She lies and says that she did not laugh. The Lord corrects again, said that she did laugh, but He lets it go. Indeed, the baby coming has the name "Isaac" and that name literally means "laughter".

¹⁶Then the men rose up from there, and looked down toward Sodom; and Abraham was walking with them to send them off. ¹⁷The LORD said, "Shall I hide from Abraham what I am about to do, ¹⁸since Abraham will surely become a great and mighty nation, and in him all the nations of the earth will be blessed? ¹⁹"For I have chosen him, so that he may command his children and his household after him to keep the way of the LORD by doing righteousness and justice, so that the LORD may bring upon Abraham what He has spoken about him." ²⁰And the LORD said, "The outcry of Sodom and Gomorrah is indeed great, and their sin is exceedingly grave. ²¹"I will go down now, and see if they have done entirely according to its outcry, which has come to Me; and if not, I will know."

The Book of Genesis

The three men then set out on their journey, leaving Abraham's home and walking toward the city of Sodom. From there, the Lord reveals to Abraham what He is about to do with Sodom and Gomorrah. God will bring judgment on those people if their sins were as wicked as He already knows. The reason for this human perspective is revealed in the conversation with Abraham. Just how wicked are the cities and their people that will deserve God's wrath.

[22]Then the men turned away from there and went toward Sodom, while Abraham was still standing before the LORD. [23]Abraham came near and said, "Will You indeed sweep away the righteous with the wicked? [24]"Suppose there are fifty righteous within the city; will You indeed sweep it away and not spare the place for the sake of the fifty righteous who are in it? [25]"Far be it from You to do such a thing, to slay the righteous with the wicked, so that the righteous and the wicked are treated alike. Far be it from You! Shall not the Judge of all the earth deal justly?" [26]So the LORD said, "If I find in Sodom fifty righteous within the city, then I will spare the whole place on their account." [27]And Abraham replied, "Now behold, I have ventured to speak to the Lord, although I am but dust and ashes. [28]"Suppose the fifty righteous are lacking five, will You destroy the whole city because of five?" And He said, "I will not destroy it if I find forty-five there." [29]He spoke to Him yet again and said, "Suppose forty are found there?" And He said, "I will not do it on account of the forty." [30]Then he said, "Oh may the Lord not be angry, and I shall speak; suppose thirty are found there?" And He said, "I will not do it if I find thirty there." [31]And he said, "Now behold, I have ventured to speak to the Lord; suppose twenty are found there?" And He said, "I will not destroy it on account of the twenty." [32]Then he said, "Oh may the Lord not be angry, and I shall speak only this once; suppose ten are found there?" And He said, "I will not destroy it on account of the ten." [33]As soon as He had finished speaking to Abraham the LORD departed, and Abraham returned to his place.

The men turned away and went toward Sodom while Abraham was still standing before the Lord. Abraham came near to the Lord and asked, "will You sweep away the righteous with the wicked?" Then Abraham started negotiation with the Lord, especially with his nephew Lot and family living in Sodom. Would destroying the righteous with the wicked be consistent with the Lord's character? The Lord shows patience with

Abraham if the Lord might find 50 righteous people there? The Lord answers that He would not. Then Abraham keeps asking the Lord if He only found 45, 40, 30, 20 and only 10 righteous people in Sodom and each time the Lord responded that He would not destroy the city. Abraham was satisfied with the Lord's responses and returned home.

CHAPTER NINETEEN

The Doom of Sodom

¹Now the two angels came to Sodom in the evening as Lot was sitting in the gate of Sodom. When Lot saw them, he rose to meet them and bowed down with his face to the ground. ²And he said, "Now behold, my lords, please turn aside into your servant's house, and spend the night, and wash your feet; then you may rise early and go on your way." They said however, "No, but we shall spend the night in the square." ³Yet he urged them strongly, so they turned aside to him and entered his house; and he prepared a feast for them, and baked unleavened bread, and they ate. ⁴Before they lay down, the men of the city, the men of Sodom, surrounded the house, both young and old, all the people from every quarter; ⁵and they called to Lot and said to him, "Where are the men who came to you tonight? Bring them out to us that we may have relations with them." ⁶But Lot went out to them at the doorway, and shut the door behind him, ⁷and said, "Please, my brothers, do not act wickedly. ⁸"Now behold, I have two daughters who have not had relations with man; please let me bring them out to you, and do to them whatever you like; only do nothing to these men, inasmuch as they have come under the shelter of my roof." ⁹But they said, "Stand aside." Furthermore, they said, "This one came in as an alien, and already he is acting like a judge; now we will treat you worse than them." So they pressed hard against Lot and came near to break the door. ¹⁰But the men reached out their hands and brought Lot into the house with them, and shut the door. ¹¹They struck the men who were at the doorway of the house with blindness, both small and great, so that they wearied themselves trying to find the doorway.

Chapter 19 is one of the most shocking chapters in Genesis. The people of Sodom, except for Lot and family, are wicked beyond belief. Lot met the two angels as he was sitting in the gate of Sodom (burning city). Lot bowed down with his face to the ground. Apparently, Lot knew who these men were. He asked them to spend the night, to wash their feet so that they could rise early and be on their way. They initially declined, but Lot urged them strongly so they entered his house and he prepared a feast for them. Staying inside Lot's home still did not dissuade the men of the city to surround the Lot's house and told Lot to bring the men outside. Why? Lot knew that the men of the city were evil and what they wanted to do with the strangers was to have homosexual sex with them. He offers them his virgin daughters instead. How awful it was the Lot would offer his virgin daughters to these vile men. The awful men of Sodom will not relent. The angels intervened and brought Lot and his family outside from the city. They struck the men at the doorway with blindness so they could not even find the doorway.

12 Then the two men said to Lot, "Whom else have you here? A son-in-law, and your sons, and your daughters, and whomever you have in the city, bring them out of the place; 13 for we are about to destroy this place, because their outcry has become so great before the LORD that the LORD has sent us to destroy it." 14 Lot went out and spoke to his sons-in-law, who were to marry his daughters, and said, "Up, get out of this place, for the LORD will destroy the city." But he appeared to his sons-in-law to be jesting.

The angels said to Lot, who else lives with you? Bring them out of this place for we are about the destroy this place. Their outcry has become so great before the Lord that the Lord sent us here to destroy Sodom. Lot spoke to his sons-in-law, who were to marry his daughters and told them to leave Sodom. But, the sons-in-law thought that Lot was joking. Thus, when Lot left Sodom with his wife and two daughters, the sons-in-law (not married to Lot's daughters yet) did not leave with them because they did not believe that he was serious. Some scholars believe that the sons-in-law were homosexual as were the other men in Sodom.

15 When morning dawned, the angels urged Lot, saying, "Up, take your wife and your two daughters who are here, or you will be swept away in the punishment of the city." 16 But he hesitated. So the men seized his hand and the hand of his wife and the hands of his two daughters, for the compassion of the LORD was upon him; and they brought him out, and put him outside the city. ¹⁷When they had brought them outside, one said, "Escape for your life! Do not look behind you, and do not stay anywhere in the valley; escape to the mountains, or you will be swept away." ¹⁸But Lot said to them, "Oh no, my lords! ¹⁹"Now behold, your servant has found favor in your sight, and you have magnified your lovingkindness, which you have shown me by saving my life; but I cannot escape to the mountains, for the disaster will overtake me and I will die; ²⁰now behold, this town is near enough to flee to, and it is small. Please, let me escape there (is it not small?) that my life may be saved." ²¹He said to him, "Behold, I grant you this request also, not to overthrow the town of which you have spoken. ²²"Hurry, escape there, for I cannot do anything until you arrive there." Therefore the name of the town was called Zoar.

Early in the morning the angels urged Lot to leave what was about to happen to Sodom. He needs to take his wife and two daughters and escape the punishment of the city. Lot hesitated so the men (angels) seized his hand, his wife's hand, and the hands of his two daughters and took them outside the city. God's compassion was upon Lot's immediate family. The angels told Lot's family to escape for their lives. Do not look behind you, do not stay anywhere in the valley, escape to the mountains or you will be burned up like everyone else. Lot replied, "Oh no, my lords! Behold, your servant has found favor in your sight and you have magnified your lovingkindness by saving my life (from the men of the city); but I cannot escape to the mountains as disaster will overtake me and I will die. The angels allow Lot and his family to flee to a town called Zoar. Zoar, previously called Bela (Genesis 14:8), was one of the five "cities of the plain" –located along the lower Jordan Valley and the Dead Sea plains. It was said to have been spared the "brimstone and fire" which destroyed Sodom and Gomorrah in order to provide a refuge for Lot and his daughters.

²³The sun had risen over the earth when Lot came to Zoar. ²⁴Then the LORD rained on Sodom and Gomorrah brimstone and fire from the LORD out of heaven, ²⁵and He overthrew those cities, and all the valley, and all the inhabitants of the cities, and what grew on the ground. ²⁶But his wife, from behind him, looked back, and she became a pillar of salt.

When Lot and family made it to Zoar, the Lord rained on Sodom and Gomorrah with brimstone (sulfur) and fire.. God destroys Sodom, Gomorrah, the region around it, all the people, and all the vegetation.

Lot's wife disobeys, looks back, and is turned into a pillar of salt. Jesus reminded his listeners of Lot in Luke 17:32. Lot and his two daughters have been spared, but they have lost everything. The following morning, Abraham sees the smoke rising from all the land of the valley as from a furnace, everything utterly destroyed. Though they are safe in Zoar, Lot is afraid to stay there. He takes his daughters and runs for the hills, settling in a cave. Why didn't he and family go to the house of Abraham?

³⁰Lot went up from Zoar, and stayed in the mountains, and his two daughters with him; for he was afraid to stay in Zoar; and he stayed in a cave, he and his two daughters. ³¹Then the firstborn said to the younger, "Our father is old, and there is not a man on earth to come in to us after the manner of the earth. ³²"Come, let us make our father drink wine, and let us lie with him that we may preserve our family through our father." ³³So they made their father drink wine that night, and the firstborn went in and lay with her father; and he did not know when she lay down or when she arose. ³⁴On the following day, the firstborn said to the younger, "Behold, I lay last night with my father; let us make him drink wine tonight also; then you go in and lie with him, that we may preserve our family through our father." ³⁵So they made their father drink wine that night also, and the younger arose and lay with him; and he did not know when she lay down or when she arose. ³⁶Thus both the daughters of Lot were with child by their father. ³⁷The firstborn bore a son, and called his name Moab; he is the father of the Moabites to this day. ³⁸As for the younger, she also bore a son, and called his name Ben-ammi; he is the father of the sons of Ammon to this day.

Lot and his two daughters were too afraid to stay in Zoar so they moved to a cave in the mountains. In one of Scripture's most tragic embarrassments, Lot's daughters decide they have lost all hope of ever being married or having children. They were raised in the Sodomite culture where they had no personal values so they decided to do things for themselves. They decided to get their father blindly drunk on two consecutive nights, each having sex with him in his drunkenness. Both daughters became pregnant with their father. Both had sons that grew up to be the fathers/leaders of the Moabites and the Ammonites. Lot's life was never revealed again, we don't know what happened to him.

CHAPTER TWENTY

Abraham Treachery

¹Now Abraham journeyed from there toward the land of the Negev, and settled between Kadesh and Shur; then he sojourned in Gerar. ²Abraham said of Sarah his wife, "She is my sister." So Abimelech king of Gerar sent and took Sarah. ³But God came to Abimelech in a dream of the night, and said to him, "Behold, you are a dead man because of the woman whom you have taken, for she is married." ⁴Now Abimelech had not come near her; and he said, "Lord, will You slay a nation, even though blameless? ⁵ "Did he not himself say to me, 'She is my sister'? And she herself said, 'He is my brother.' In the integrity of my heart and the innocence of my hands I have done this." ⁶Then God said to him in the dream, "Yes, I know that in the integrity of your heart you have done this, and I also kept you from sinning against Me; therefore I did not let you touch her. ⁷ "Now therefore, restore the man's wife, for he is a prophet, and he will pray for you and you will live. But if you do not restore her, know that you shall surely die, you and all who are yours."

Abraham journeyed to the land of Negev, southern-most part of Israel. Gerar was in the Northwestern part of the Negev where the Abimelech was king. Again, Abraham lied, like he did with the pharaoh of Egypt (Genesis 12:10-18), saying that Sarah was his sister.

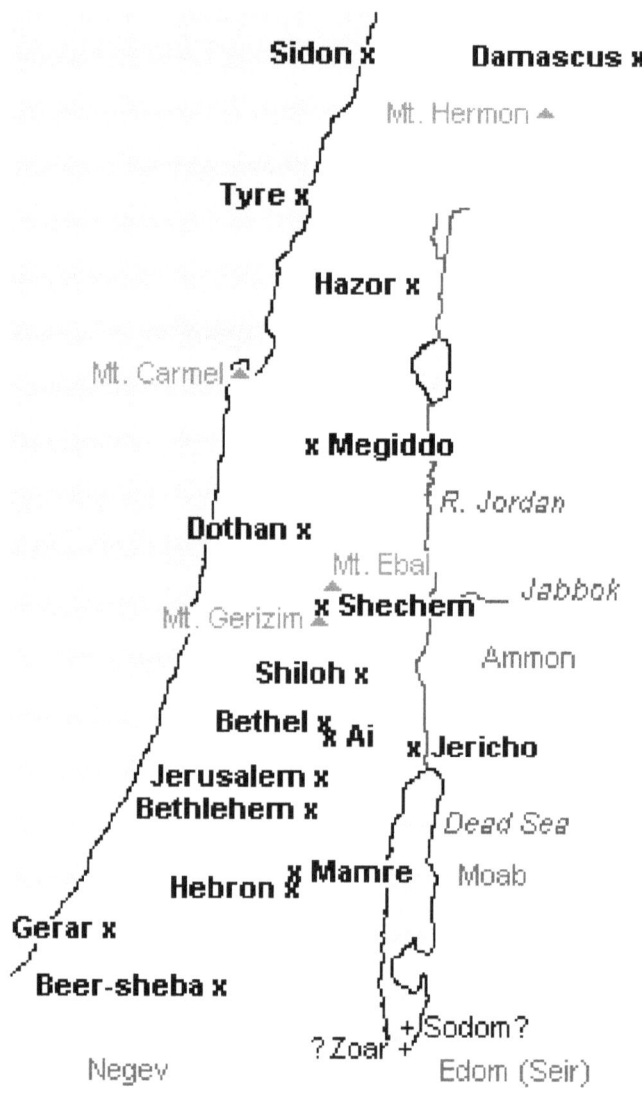

Created and approved by Sarah Rollinson

Abimelech took Sarah, but then God came to Abimelech in a dream of the night and said to him, "Behold, you are a dead man because the woman you have taken is married to Abraham. Fortunately, Abimelech had not come near her and said, "Lord, will you slay a nation even though blameless? Did he not himself say to me, 'She is my sister'?" And she herself said, "He is my brother. Abimelech claims to God that he is innocent. He and his city should not die for a sin that he did not do.

⁸So Abimelech arose early in the morning and called all his servants and told all these things in their hearing; and the men were greatly frightened. ⁹Then Abimelech called Abraham and said to him, "What have you done to us? And how have I sinned against you, that you have brought on me and on my kingdom a great sin? You have done to me things that ought not to be done." ¹⁰And Abimelech said to Abraham, "What have you encountered, that you have done this thing?" ¹¹Abraham said, "Because I thought, surely there is no fear of God in this place, and they will kill me because of my wife. ¹²"Besides, she actually is my sister, the daughter of my father, but not the daughter of my mother, and she became my wife; ¹³and it came about, when God caused me to wander from my father's house, that I said to her, 'This is the kindness which you will show to me: everywhere we go, say of me, "He is my brother."'" ¹⁴Abimelech then took sheep and oxen and male and female servants, and gave them to Abraham, and restored his wife Sarah to him. ¹⁵Abimelech said, "Behold, my land is before you; settle wherever you please." ¹⁶To Sarah he said, "Behold, I have given your brother a thousand pieces of silver; behold, it is your vindication before all who are with you, and before all men you are cleared." ¹⁷Abraham prayed to God, and God healed Abimelech and his wife and his maids, so that they bore children. ¹⁸For the LORD had closed fast all the wombs of the household of Abimelech because of Sarah, Abraham's wife.

Abimelech arose early the next morning after his dream and called all his servants and told them all things in their hearing. They were so frightened. They knew what had happened to Sodom and Gomorrah. Then Abimelech asked Abraham, "What have you done to us? What have I done to you that you have brought to me and his kingdom a great sin? You have done to me things that ought not to be done". Abraham replied, "Because I thought that there is surely no fear of God in this place and they will kill me because of my wife." Why did Abraham come to this conclusion about Gerar? Then Abraham admitted that Sarah was his sister, same father, different mothers. Sarah became his wife and it came about that God caused me to wander from my father's house, asking her to admit that he was her brother. Abimelech took sheep, oxen, human servants and gave them to Abraham and restored his wife to him. Abimelech asked Abraham to settle where he pleased and gave Abraham a thousand pieces of silver, maybe worth about $3,000 today. Abraham prayed to God and God healed Abimelech, his wife, and his maids so that they bore children again. For we learned in Genesis 20:18 that the Lord had closed all the wombs of the household of Abimelech because of Sarah. Again, we learned from this story that Abraham lacked confidence in God to protect him and Sarah in a different part of Israel, despite all God had done to show faithfulness.

CHAPTER TWENTY-ONE

Isaac Is Born

¹Then the LORD took note of Sarah as He had said, and the LORD did for Sarah as He had promised. ²So Sarah conceived and bore a son to Abraham in his old age, at the appointed time of which God had spoken to him. ³Abraham called the name of his son who was born to him, whom Sarah bore to him, Isaac. ⁴Then Abraham circumcised his son Isaac when he was eight days old, as God had commanded him. ⁵Now Abraham was one hundred years old when his son Isaac was born to him. ⁶Sarah said, "God has made laughter for me; everyone who hears will laugh with me." ⁷And she said, "Who would have said to Abraham that Sarah would nurse children? Yet I have borne him a son in his old age." ⁸The child grew and was weaned, and Abraham made a great feast on the day that Isaac was weaned.

The Lord, as He promised, allowed Sarah to become pregnant and she bore a son to Abraham in his old age at the appointed time that God had spoken to him. Abraham named his son, Isaac (he laughs). When Isaac was eight days old, Abraham circumcised as God commanded him. Abraham was one hundred years old when Isaac was born to him. Sarah said, "God has made laughter for me, everyone who hears will laugh with me." Of course, she is referring to Isaac's name, he laughs. Others will laugh with her, not against her. She remarked that "who would have said to Abraham that Sarah would nurse children at ninety years old?" Yet, she has borne him a son in his old age. The children grew and was weaned (no longer a child) and Abraham made a great feast great feast on the day that Isaac was weaned.

9Now Sarah saw the son of Hagar the Egyptian, whom she had borne to Abraham, mocking. 10Therefore she said to Abraham, "Drive out this maid and her son, for the son of this maid shall not be an heir with my son Isaac." 11The matter distressed Abraham greatly because of his son. 12But God said to Abraham, "Do not be distressed because of the lad and your maid; whatever Sarah tells you, listen to her, for through Isaac your descendants shall be named. 13"And of the son of the maid I will make a nation also, because he is your descendant." 14So Abraham rose early in the morning and took bread and a skin of water and gave them to Hagar, putting them on her shoulder, and gave her the boy, and sent her away. And she departed and wandered about in the wilderness of Beersheba.

Sarah saw Hagar and subsequently asked Abraham to get rid of Hagar and her son. Ishmael, Hagar's son, shall not be an heir with Sarah's son Isaac. Abraham was distressed, but God said to Abraham, do not be distressed because of the lad and his mother, Hagar. Whatever Sarah tells you, listen to her, for through her son, Isaac, your descendants shall be named. Abraham rose early in the morning and took bread and a skin of water and gave them to Hagar and sent her and her son away. Hagar departed and wandered about in the wilderness of Beersheba (see map above).

15When the water in the skin was used up, she left the boy under one of the bushes. 16Then she went and sat down opposite him, about a bowshot away, for she said, "Do not let me see the boy die." And she sat opposite him, and lifted up her voice and wept. 17God heard the lad crying; and the angel of God called to Hagar from heaven and said to her, "What is the matter with you, Hagar? Do not fear, for God has heard the voice of the lad where he is. 18"Arise, lift up the lad, and hold him by the hand, for I will make a great nation of him." 19Then God opened her eyes and she saw a well of water; and she went and filled the skin with water and gave the lad a drink. 20God was with the lad, and he grew; and he lived in the wilderness and became an archer. 21He lived in the wilderness of Paran, and his mother took a wife for him from the land of Egypt.

Hagar and Ishmael soon run out of water. Hagar put Ishmael in one of the bushes to die. An angel of God calls to her from heaven and asked what is the matter with Hagar? God heard Ishmael's voice in the bush and He will make Ishmael and his ancestry into a great nation. Hagar was asked to "arise, lift up the lad and hold him by the hand". Literally,

God is telling Hagar to grab his hand, give him support now, and take care of him until he reaches manhood. Water was provided, Hagar and Ishmael survive, Ishmael grows up in the wilderness, became a great archer and, from his mother, eventually married an Egyptian woman. Ishmael lived in Paran. The wilderness of Paran entirely transjordan, east of the Arabah Valley. The wilderness of Paran is adjacent to the land of Midian (1 Kings 11:18). The land of Midian is located at modern Al Bad in North Saudi Arabia.

[22]Now it came about at that time that Abimelech and Phicol, the commander of his army, spoke to Abraham, saying, "God is with you in all that you do; [23]now therefore, swear to me here by God that you will not deal falsely with me or with my offspring or with my posterity, but according to the kindness that I have shown to you, you shall show to me and to the land in which you have sojourned." [24]Abraham said, "I swear it." [25]But Abraham complained to Abimelech because of the well of water which the servants of Abimelech had seized. [26]And Abimelech said, "I do not know who has done this thing; you did not tell me, nor did I hear of it until today." [27]Abraham took sheep and oxen and gave them to Abimelech, and the two of them made a covenant. [28]Then Abraham set seven ewe lambs of the flock by themselves. [29]Abimelech said to Abraham, "What do these seven ewe lambs mean, which you have set by themselves?" [30]He said, "You shall take these seven ewe lambs from my hand so that it may be a witness to me, that I dug this well." [31]Therefore he called that place Beersheba, because there the two of them took an oath. [32]So they made a covenant at Beersheba; and Abimelech and Phicol, the commander of his army, arose and returned to the land of the Philistines. [33]Abraham planted a tamarisk tree at Beersheba, and there he called on the name of the LORD, the Everlasting God. [34]And Abraham sojourned in the land of the Philistines for many days.

Abimelech, king of Gerar, and Phicol, commander of Abimelech's army, spoke with Abraham about God being with Abraham in all that he does. Abimelech has respect for God's power and His blessing with Abraham. Abimelech asked that Abraham swear by God that he will not deal falsely with him, as he did before, but he will instead kindness to Abimelech and the land that he has sojourned. Abraham promised that he would. Abraham insisted on including in their agreement the resolution of the ownership of the disputed well, one that Abraham has had built. Abraham gave Abimelech sheep and oxen and they made a covenant. In verses 28-30 he gives seven additional lambs to Abimelech as a sign that the well does indeed belong to Abraham. After they both swear their oaths to bind the agreement, the place where they met is called Beersheba. All that God has promised him has come true.

CHAPTER TWENTY-TWO

The Offering of Isaac

¹Now it came about after these things, that God tested Abraham, and said to him, "Abraham!" And he said, "Here I am." ²He said, "Take now your son, your only son, whom you love, Isaac, and go to the land of Moriah, and offer him there as a burnt offering on one of the mountains of which I will tell you." ³So Abraham rose early in the morning and saddled his donkey, and took two of his young men with him and Isaac his son; and he split wood for the burnt offering, and arose and went to the place of which God had told him. ⁴On the third day Abraham raised his eyes and saw the place from a distance. ⁵Abraham said to his young men, "Stay here with the donkey, and I and the lad will go over there; and we will worship and return to you." ⁶Abraham took the wood of the burnt offering and laid it on Isaac his son, and he took in his hand the fire and the knife. So the two of them walked on together. ⁷Isaac spoke to Abraham his father and said, "My father!" And he said, "Here I am, my son." And he said, "Behold, the fire and the wood, but where is the lamb for the burnt offering?" ⁸Abraham said, "God will provide for Himself the lamb for the burnt offering, my son." So the two of them walked on together.

Genesis 22 tells of Abraham's near-sacrifice of his son, Isaac. How many of us would attempt to do what Abraham almost did because of his trust in God? We do not really know how old Isaac was when he was to follow his father to be sacrificed. Of course, at first Isaac did not know why Abraham was taking him to the land of Moriah. God commanded Abraham to sacrifice his only son, Isaac, in the region of Moriah. God makes the command especially poignant by acknowledging up front that Abraham loves Isaac, his only son.

Abraham doesn't hesitate. He loads his donkey with enough wood for a sacrifice. How old is Isaac is at this point, we don't know. The small group immediately heads out on the three-day trip to Moriah. Abraham leaves the servants and donkey behind and heads to the top of Moriah with Isaac and the wood (Genesis 22:3–6).

Does Abraham expect God to stop him before he kills Isaac? Perhaps, but perhaps not. Hebrews 11:19 gives us a clue: "Abraham reasoned that God could even raise the dead." In any case, Abraham doesn't slow down even when Isaac asks where the lamb is. Abraham simply replies that the God will provide the lamb. Isaac, for his part, seems willing to cooperate with his father (Genesis 22:6–8).

⁹Then they came to the place of which God had told him; and Abraham built the altar there and arranged the wood, and bound his son Isaac and laid him on the altar, on top of the wood. ¹⁰Abraham stretched out his hand and took the knife to slay his son. ¹¹But the angel of the LORD called to him from heaven and said, "Abraham, Abraham!" And he said, "Here I am." ¹²He said, "Do not stretch out your hand against the lad, and do nothing to him; for now I know that you fear God, since you have not withheld your son, your only son, from Me." ¹³Then Abraham raised his eyes and looked, and behold, behind him a ram caught in the thicket by his horns; and Abraham went and took the ram and offered him up for a burnt offering in the place of his son. ¹⁴Abraham called the name of that place The LORD Will Provide, as it is said to this day, "In the mount of the LORD it will be provided."

They came to the place God has told Abraham, Abraham built an altar there, arranged the wood and then bound his son, Isaac, and laid him on the altar. We do not know if Isaac realized what was happening and screamed bloody murder! Abraham stretched out his hand and took the knife to slay his son. I recall a movie where Isaac indeed protested what his father was about to do and it was very scary. What God-fearing father would ever do this?

Before he can kill his son, though, the Lord's tells Abraham not to harm Isaac. Abraham has passed: "…now I know that you fear God, seeing you have not withheld your son, your only son, from me" (Genesis 22:12). Abraham looked and saw behind him a ram caught in the thicket by his horns. The ram was the burnt offering instead of his son. Abraham called this place "The Lord Will Provide" and the name remains to this day. How did Abraham and Isaac reconcile this incident the rest of their lives?

[15] Then the angel of the LORD called to Abraham a second time from heaven, [16] and said, "By Myself I have sworn, declares the LORD, because you have done this thing and have not withheld your son, your only son, [17] indeed I will greatly bless you, and I will greatly multiply your seed as the stars of the heavens and as the sand which is on the seashore; and your seed shall possess the gate of their enemies. [18] "In your seed all the nations of the earth shall be blessed, because you have obeyed My voice." [19] So Abraham returned to his young men, and they arose and went together to Beersheba; and Abraham lived at Beersheba.

The Lord renewed and emphasized His promises to Abraham once more, swearing by Himself. Because of Abraham's obedience, the Lord promises to bless Abraham, to multiply his offspring, and to give Abraham's offspring victory over their enemies (Genesis 22:15–17). The Lord adds another promise: All the nations of the earth will be blessed through Abraham's offspring, something that happens unequivocally when Abraham's descendant, Jesus, becomes God's blessing to all. Abraham's faith allowed him to be part of the lineage of Jesus Christ. He obeyed God's voice. Abraham returned to Beersheba. [20] Now it came about after these things, that it was told Abraham, saying, "Behold, Milcah also has borne children to your brother Nahor: [21] Uz his firstborn and Buz his brother and Kemuel the father of Aram [22] and Chesed and Hazo and Pildash and Jidlaph and Bethuel." [23] Bethuel became the father of Rebekah; these eight Milcah bore to Nahor, Abraham's brother. [24] His concubine, whose name was Reumah, also bore Tebah and Gaham and Tahash and Maacah.

Genesis 22 ends with twelve children born through Abraham's brother Nahor. One of those children, Bethuel, became the father of Rebekah. Abraham's son, Isaac, will eventually marry Rebekah (Genesis 24) and they will give birth to Jacob who had twelve children also and these children will be the leaders of the twelves tribes of Israel

CHAPTER TWENTY-THREE

Death and Burial of Sarah

¹*Now Sarah lived one hundred and twenty-seven years; these were the years of the life of Sarah.* ²*Sarah died in Kiriath-arba (that is, Hebron) in the land of Canaan; and Abraham went in to mourn for Sarah and to weep for her.* ³*Then Abraham rose from before his dead, and spoke to the sons of Heth, saying,* ⁴*"I am a stranger and a sojourner among you; give me a burial site among you that I may bury my dead out of my sight."* ⁵*The sons of Heth answered Abraham, saying to him,* ⁶*"Hear us, my lord, you are a mighty prince among us; bury your dead in the choicest of our graves; none of us will refuse you his grave for burying your dead."* ⁷*So Abraham rose and bowed to the people of the land, the sons of Heth.* ⁸*And he spoke with them, saying, "If it is your wish for me to bury my dead out of my sight, hear me, and approach Ephron the son of Zohar for me,* ⁹*that he may give me the cave of Machpelah which he owns, which is at the end of his field; for the full price let him give it to me in your presence for a burial site."*

Sarah lived for 127 years then died at Hebron in the land of Canaan. Abraham wept over her death. He was 10 years older at 137. Their son, Isaac, would have been 37 years old. They lived in in Hebron, near the familiar area of Mamre. He spoked to the sons of Heth (one of Canaan sons, chapter 10) and rose before his dead, saying "I am a stranger and sojourner among you. Sell me some property as a burial site among you." The sons of Heth replied, "Hear us, my lord, you are a mighty prince among us; bury your dead in the choices of our graves; none of us will refuses you his grave for burying your dead." The Hittites regarded Abraham as a friend. Abraham rose and bowed to the people of the land, the sons of Heth. Abraham said "If it is your wish for me to bury my dead out of my sight, hear me and approach Ephron the son of Zohar for me, that he may give me the cave of Machpelah (east of Mamre) that he owns, the end of his field; for the full price let him give it to me in your presence for a burial site." Abraham wishes to acquire a piece of property that will belong to him and only him.

[10]Now Ephron was sitting among the sons of Heth; and Ephron the Hittite answered Abraham in the hearing of the sons of Heth; even of all who went in at the gate of his city, saying, [11]"No, my lord, hear me; I give you the field, and I give you the cave that is in it. In the presence of the sons of my people I give it to you; bury your dead." [12]And Abraham bowed before the people of the land. [13]He spoke to Ephron in the hearing of the people of the land, saying, "If you will only please listen to me; I will give the price of the field, accept it from me that I may bury my dead there." [14]Then Ephron answered Abraham, saying to him, [15]"My lord, listen to me; a piece of land worth four hundred shekels of silver, what is that between me and you? So bury your dead." [16]Abraham listened to Ephron; and Abraham weighed out for Ephron the silver which he had named in the hearing of the sons of Heth, four hundred shekels of silver, commercial standard. [17]So Ephron's field, which was in Machpelah, which faced Mamre, the field and cave which was in it, and all the trees which were in the field, that were within all the confines of its border, were deeded over [18]to Abraham for a possession in the presence of the sons of Heth, before all who went in at the gate of his city.

A negotiation of sorts takes place with Ephron offers to give the cave to Abraham, along with the field attached to it. Abraham insists on paying for it (so there can be no future dispute about who owns it). Ephron dismissively mentions a price of 400 shekels of silver for the cave and field. Abraham immediately agrees, paying out the price on the spot, and the transaction is concluded and signed off by the Hittite elders (Genesis 23:7–18).

[19]After this, Abraham buried Sarah his wife in the cave of the field at Machpelah facing Mamre (that is, Hebron) in the land of Canaan. [20]So the field and the cave that is in it, were deeded over to Abraham for a burial site by the sons of Heth.

Finally, Abraham buries Sarah in the cave he now owns in the promised land of Canaan. The field and the cave in it were deeded to Abraham for Sarah's burial site and will someday be the burial site for Abraham and others in his family.

CHAPTER TWENTY-FOUR

A Bride for Isaac

¹Now Abraham was old, advanced in age; and the LORD had blessed Abraham in every way. ²Abraham said to his servant, the oldest of his household, who had charge of all that he owned, "Please place your hand under my thigh, ³and I will make you swear by the LORD, the God of heaven and the God of earth, that you shall not take a wife for my son from the daughters of the Canaanites, among whom I live, ⁴but you will go to my country and to my relatives, and take a wife for my son Isaac." ⁵The servant said to him, "Suppose the woman is not willing to follow me to this land; should I take your son back to the land from where you came?" ⁶Then Abraham said to him, "Beware that you do not take my son back there! ⁷"The LORD, the God of heaven, who took me from my father's house and from the land of my birth, and who spoke to me and who swore to me, saying, 'To your descendants I will give this land,' He will send His angel before you, and you will take a wife for my son from there. ⁸"But if the woman is not willing to follow you, then you will be free from this my oath; only do not take my son back there." ⁹So the servant placed his hand under the thigh of Abraham his master, and swore to him concerning this matter.

Abraham was getting very old, although he will live another 35 years, yet the Lord has blessed him in every way. Abraham asked his oldest servant of his household who had changed of all that he owned, to please his hand under his thigh. Then Abraham made him swear by the Lord, God of heaven and God of earth, that he will not take a wife for Isaac from the daughters of the Canaanites, but the servant would return to Abraham's country (Mesopotamia, today's Iraq) and to his relatives and find his wife there. Also the servant must not allow Isaac to return to

Canaan. Abraham then said, "The LORD, the God of heaven, who took me from my father's house and from the land of my birth, and who spoke to me and who swore to me, saying, 'To your descendants I will give this land,' He will send His angel before you, and you will take a wife for my son from there. But if the woman is not willing to follow you, then you will be free from this my oath; only do not take my son back there." The servant receives a caveat from Abraham-- If he cannot find a woman willing to return to Canaan to marry Isaac, the servant will be released from his oath.

10 Then the servant took ten camels from the camels of his master, and set out with a variety of good things of his master's in his hand; and he arose and went to Mesopotamia, to the city of Nahor. 11 He made the camels kneel down outside the city by the well of water at evening time, the time when women go out to draw water. 12 He said, "O LORD, the God of my master Abraham, please grant me success today, and show lovingkindness to my master Abraham. 13 "Behold, I am standing by the spring, and the daughters of the men of the city are coming out to draw water; 14 now may it be that the girl to whom I say, 'Please let down your jar so that I may drink,' and who answers, 'Drink, and I will water your camels also'—may she be the one whom You have appointed for Your servant Isaac; and by this I will know that You have shown lovingkindness to my master."

The servant arrives in Mesopotamia at the town of Nahor. Eager not to fail in his mission, the servant prays to Abraham's God and asks that if any of the young women coming to draw water at the town well offer to water his ten camels, she will be the one God has appointed for Isaac (Genesis 24:10–14).

15 Before he had finished speaking, behold, Rebekah who was born to Bethuel the son of Milcah, the wife of Abraham's brother Nahor, came out with her jar on her shoulder. 16 The girl was very beautiful, a virgin, and no man had had relations with her; and she went down to the spring and filled her jar and came up. 17 Then the servant ran to meet her, and said, "Please let me drink a little water from your jar." 18 She said, "Drink, my lord"; and she quickly lowered her jar to her hand, and gave him a drink. 19 Now when she had finished giving him a drink, she said, "I will draw also for your camels until they have finished drinking." 20 So she quickly emptied her jar into the trough, and ran back to the well to draw, and she drew for all his camels. 21 Meanwhile, the man was gazing at her in silence, to know whether the LORD had made his journey successful or not.*

Before the servant has finished his prayer, Rebekah enters the scene and does exactly as the servant had asked. Rebekah was beautiful, a virgin, she went down to the spring and filled her jar. The servant ran to meet her, asked for some water from her jar and she then said that she would draw water for his camels. The servant was gazing at her in silence and wondering if the Lord as made his journal successful or not.

²²When the camels had finished drinking, the man took a gold ring weighing a half-shekel and two bracelets for her wrists weighing ten shekels in gold, ²³and said, "Whose daughter are you? Please tell me, is there room for us to lodge in your father's house?" ²⁴She said to him, "I am the daughter of Bethuel, the son of Milcah, whom she bore to Nahor." ²⁵Again she said to him, "We have plenty of both straw and feed, and room to lodge in." ²⁶Then the man bowed low and worshiped the LORD. ²⁷He said, "Blessed be the LORD, the God of my master Abraham, who has not forsaken His lovingkindness and His truth toward my master; as for me, the LORD has guided me in the way to the house of my master's brothers."

The servant immediately gave expensive jewelry to Rebekah. He asked if her family has room to accommodate a visit from himself and his company, including their camels. He also asks who her father is. When Rebekah names her father, the servant knows exactly who she is. She is the granddaughter of Abraham's own brother Nahor. This is better even than the servant had hoped. He knows now that the Lord has led him to the exact young lady intended for Isaac. As Abraham has requested, he has found Abraham's kinsmen and identified a bride for Isaac. He immediately worships the Lord right in front of Rebekah (Genesis 24:24–27).

²⁸Then the girl ran and told her mother's household about these things. ²⁹Now Rebekah had a brother whose name was Laban; and Laban ran outside to the man at the spring. ³⁰When he saw the ring and the bracelets on his sister's wrists, and when he heard the words of Rebekah his sister, saying, "This is what the man said to me," he went to the man; and behold, he was standing by the camels at the spring. ³¹And he said, "Come in, blessed of the LORD! Why do you stand outside since I have prepared the house, and a place for the camels?" ³²So the man entered the house. Then Laban unloaded the camels, and he gave straw and feed to the camels, and water to wash his feet and the feet of the men who were with him. ³³But when food was set before him to eat, he said, "I will not eat until I have told my business." And he said, "Speak on." ³⁴So he said, "I am Abraham's servant. ³⁵"The LORD has greatly blessed my master, so that he has become rich; and He has given him flocks and herds, and silver and gold, and servants and maids, and camels and donkeys. ³⁶"Now Sarah my master's wife bore a son to my master in her old age, and he has given him all that he has. ³⁷"My master made me swear, saying, 'You shall not take a wife for my son from the daughters of the Canaanites, in whose land I live; ³⁸but you shall go to my father's house and to my relatives, and take a wife for my son.' ³⁹"I said to my master, 'Suppose the woman does not follow me.' ⁴⁰"He said to me, 'The LORD, before whom I have walked, will send His angel with you to make your journey successful, and you will take a wife for my son from my relatives and from my father's house; ⁴¹then you will be free from my oath, when you come to my relatives; and if they do not give her to you, you will be free from my oath.'

Rebekah told her mother's household about Abraham and Isaac. Rebekah had a brother, Laban, who ran outside to meet the servant. The servant was standing by the camels at the spring. Laban told the servant to come in since he is blessed of the Lord. The servant entered the house. Laban unloaded the camels, gave them straw and feed, and water to wash the servant's feed and the feet of his men. When food was set before the servant, he could not eat until he shared his reason for being them. He told Rebekah's family about Abraham, being very rich and lots of servants. His wife, Sarah, bore him one son. He promised Abraham not to find a wife from the Canaanites, but travel to Mesopotamia to his relatives and find a wife there. Abraham promised that an angel will make this trip successful and you will find a wife for Isaac from his relatives. If no one can be found, the servant will be free from Abraham's oath.

⁴²"So I came today to the spring, and said, 'O LORD, the God of my master Abraham, if now You will make my journey on which I go successful; ⁴³behold, I am standing by the spring, and may it be that the maiden who comes out to draw, and to whom I say, "Please let me drink a little water from your jar"; ⁴⁴and she will say to me, "You drink, and I will draw for your camels also"; let her be the woman whom the LORD has appointed for my master's son.' ⁴⁵"Before I had finished speaking in my heart, behold, Rebekah came out with her jar on her shoulder, and went down to the spring and drew, and I said to her, 'Please let me drink.' ⁴⁶*"She quickly lowered her jar from her shoulder, and said, 'Drink, and I will water your camels also'; so I drank, and she watered the camels also.* ⁴⁷*"Then I asked her, and said, 'Whose daughter are you?' And she said, 'The daughter of Bethuel, Nahor's son, whom Milcah bore to him'; and I put the ring on her nose, and the bracelets on her wrists.* ⁴⁸*"And I bowed low and worshiped the LORD, and blessed the LORD, the God of my master Abraham, who had guided me in the right way to take the daughter of my master's kinsman for his son.* ⁴⁹*"So now if you are going to deal kindly and truly with my master, tell me; and if not, let me know, that I may turn to the right hand or the left."*

The servant asked the Lord, the God of his master Abraham, to be successful in finding the right maiden for Isaac. Most of what is written in Genesis 24:42-49 was a repeat of what was written in the earlier part of Genesis. In verse 50 Laban and Bethuel, Rebekah's brother and father, agree that the matter comes from the Lord. They gave Rebekah to the servant, take her and go and let her be the wife of Isaac. The Lord has spoken. How carefully Rebekah's brother and father listened to the voice of the Lord.

⁵⁴*Then he and the men who were with him ate and drank and spent the night. When they arose in the morning, he said, "Send me away to my master."* ⁵⁵*But her brother and her mother said, "Let the girl stay with us a few days, say ten; afterward she may go."* ⁵⁶*He said to them, "Do not delay me, since the LORD has prospered my way. Send me away that I may go to my master."* ⁵⁷*And they said, "We will call the girl and consult her wishes."* ⁵⁸*Then they called Rebekah and said to her, "Will you go with this man?" And she said, "I will go."*

Abraham servant bowed himself to the ground before the Lord. The servant brought out articles of silver and gold and garment and gave them to Rebekah. He also gave things to her brother and her mother. What happened to Bethuel? They all ate and drank and spent the night here, but in the morning her brother and mothers asked if the girl could stay another few days. But the servant asked "do no delay me since the Lord has prospered his way. Send me away so that I may go to my master". Rebekah was asked her wished and she replied that she will go now.

*⁵⁹Thus they sent away their sister Rebekah and her nurse with Abraham's servant and his men. ⁶⁰They blessed Rebekah and said to her,
"May you, our sister,
Become thousands of ten thousands,
And may your descendants possess
The gate of those who hate them."
⁶¹Then Rebekah arose with her maids, and they mounted the camels and followed the man. So the servant took Rebekah and departed.*

They sent away their sister Rebekah and her nurse with Abraham's servant and his men. They blessed Rebekah with the following blessing: "May you, our sister, become thousand of ten thousands and may your descendants possess the gate of those who them". This poem may have been a traditional type of wedding blessing for the bride. Refer to Genesis 22:17 to see how this poem was similar to the Lord's promises of blessing to Abraham. We know later that Rebekah would give birth to Jacob, the next in the covenant line of Israel and she will become through all her offspring the mother of God's chosen people, in thousands of ten thousands. Her offspring will conquer their enemies and possess the gates of their cities.

⁶²Now Isaac had come from going to Beer-lahai-roi; for he was living in the Negev. ⁶³Isaac went out to meditate in the field toward evening; and he lifted up his eyes and looked, and behold, camels were coming. ⁶⁴Rebekah lifted up her eyes, and when she saw Isaac she dismounted from the camel. ⁶⁵She said to the servant, "Who is that man walking in the field to meet us?" And the servant said, "He is my master." Then she took her veil and covered herself. ⁶⁶The servant told Isaac all the things that he had done. ⁶⁷Then Isaac brought her into his mother Sarah's tent, and he took Rebekah, and she became his wife, and he loved her; thus Isaac was comforted after his mother's death.

Isaac lived in the Negev, large desert region in southern Israel. He saw the camels coming from the east. Rebekah lifted her eyes and when she saw Isaac she dismounted from the camel. She said to the servant, "who is the man walking in the field to meet us"? The servant replied that he is my master and Rebekah had to assume that it was Isaac. She covered herself with her veil. The servant told Isaac all he had done in following Abraham's orders. Then Isaac brought Rebekah into Sarah's tent and he took Rebekah and she became his wife. He loved her and she so comforted him after the death of his mother, Sarah.

CHAPTER TWENTY-FIVE

Abraham's Death

¹Now Abraham took another wife, whose name was Keturah. ²She bore to him Zimran and Jokshan and Medan and Midian and Ishbak and Shuah. ³Jokshan became the father of Sheba and Dedan. And the sons of Dedan were Asshurim and Letushim and Leummim. ⁴The sons of Midian were Ephah and Epher and Hanoch and Abida and Eldaah. All these were the sons of Keturah. ⁵Now Abraham gave all that he had to Isaac; ⁶but to the sons of his concubines, Abraham gave gifts while he was still living, and sent them away from his son Isaac eastward, to the land of the east.

Genesis 25 records the deaths of both Abraham and Ishmael, as well as the births of Jacob and Esau. Abraham married another woman, Keturah, although she could have been another concubine (see verse 6). Incredible that he could have six more sons, plus perhaps some daughters, Abraham was nearly 140 years old when Sarah died at age 127. One of his sons, Midian, became the father the Midianites who lived in the "the land of the east" (Genesis 25:6). Most scholars believe the land of Midian was officially on both sides of the Gulf of Aqaba, near the Red Sea although the Midianites showed nomadic tendencies later in their history.

⁷These are all the years of Abraham's life that he lived, one hundred and seventy-five years. ⁸Abraham breathed his last and died in a ripe old age, an old man and satisfied with life; and he was gathered to his people. ⁹Then his sons Isaac and Ishmael buried him in the cave of Machpelah, in the field of Ephron the son of Zohar the Hittite, facing Mamre, ¹⁰the field which Abraham purchased from the sons of Heth; there Abraham was buried with Sarah his wife. ¹¹It came about after the death of Abraham, that God blessed his son Isaac; and Isaac lived by Beer-lahai-roi.

Abraham died at age 175, an old man and satisfied with his life. His two sons, Isaac and Ishmael buried him in a cave of Machpelah (Genesis 23:17-20) in the field of Ephron the son of Zohar the Hittite, facing Mamre, the field which Abraham purchased from the sons of Heth. This is where Sarah is buried and later the burial place of Isaac and Rebekah (Genesis 49:31), and Jacob and Leah (Genesis 50:13). Beer Lahai Roi literally mans "the well of him that lives and sees me" or "the well of the vision of life." Regardless of the exact translation, Hagar named the location thus because the Living God saw her situation and intervened to give her hope and comfort. The same location is mentioned two other times as the place where Isaac was living (Genesis 25:62 and Genesis 25:11).

Descendants of Ishmael
¹²Now these are the records of the generations of Ishmael, Abraham's son, whom Hagar the Egyptian, Sarah's maid, bore to Abraham; ¹³and these are the names of the sons of Ishmael, by their names, in the order of their birth: Nebaioth, the firstborn of Ishmael, and Kedar and Adbeel and Mibsam ¹⁴and Mishma and Dumah and Massa, ¹⁵Hadad and Tema, Jetur, Naphish and Kedemah. ¹⁶These are the sons of Ishmael and these are their names, by their villages, and by their camps; twelve princes according to their tribes. ¹⁷These are the years of the life of Ishmael, one hundred and thirty-seven years; and he breathed his last and died, and was gathered to his people. ¹⁸They settled from Havilah to Shur which is east of Egypt as one goes toward Assyria; he settled in defiance of all his relatives.

In Genesis 25:12-18 the chapter lists the 12 sons of Ishmael by birth order. These dozen groups settled to the east of what would become Israel. Ishmael himself lived a good long time, to the age of 137 (Genesis 25:12–18). Remember back in Genesis 16:10-12 that God vowed to make Ishmael and his offspring successful "He will be a wild donkey of a man, his hand will be against everyone, and everyone's hand will be against him; And he will live to the east of all his brothers."

Isaac's Sons

¹⁹Now these are the records of the generations of Isaac, Abraham's son: Abraham became the father of Isaac; ²⁰and Isaac was forty years old when he took Rebekah, the daughter of Bethuel the Aramean of Paddan-aram, the sister of Laban the Aramean, to be his wife. ²¹Isaac prayed to the LORD on behalf of his wife, because she was barren; and the LORD answered him and Rebekah his wife conceived. ²²But the children struggled together within her; and she said, "If it is so, why then am I this way?" So she went to inquire of the LORD. ²³The LORD said to her,
"Two nations are in your womb;
And two peoples will be separated from your body;
And one people shall be stronger than the other;
And the older shall serve the younger."
²⁴When her days to be delivered were fulfilled, behold, there were twins in her womb. ²⁵Now the first came forth red, all over like a hairy garment; and they named him Esau. ²⁶Afterward his brother came forth with his hand holding on to Esau's heel, so his name was called Jacob; and Isaac was sixty years old when she gave birth to them.

Now Isaac is the patriarch. As with his mother, Sarah, Rebekah cannot conceive a child (twenty years, Genesis 25:26) until Isaac prayed about this to the Lord. Another example where good things happen but often we must wait. Rebekah become pregnant but her pregnancy gave her trouble. The children in her womb gave her trouble and she needed to find out why. She went to the Lord and He said to her: "Two nations are in your womb and two peoples will be separate from your body. One will be stronger than the other; the older shall serve the younger." Indeed, the trouble in her womb was because there were twins in her womb. The first child looked, like a hairy garment and they named him Esau, perhaps meaning "red". The second brother was borne with his hand holding on to Esau's heal; they named him Jacob. Jacob means he grasps the heel which is a Hebrew idiom for deceptive behavior.

Esau close to Isaac; Jacob close to Rebekah.
https://tvtropes.org/pmwiki/pmwiki.php/Main/JacobAndEsau

27 When the boys grew up, Esau became a skillful hunter, a man of the field, but Jacob was a peaceful man, living in tents. 28 Now Isaac loved Esau, because he had a taste for game, but Rebekah loved Jacob. 29 When Jacob had cooked stew, Esau came in from the field and he was famished; 30 and Esau said to Jacob, "Please let me have a swallow of that red stuff there, for I am famished." Therefore, his name was called Edom. 31 But Jacob said, "First sell me your birthright." 32 Esau said, "Behold, I am about to die; so of what use then is the birthright to me?" 33 And Jacob said, "First swear to me"; so he swore to him, and sold his birthright to Jacob. 34 Then Jacob gave Esau bread and lentil stew; and he ate and drank, and rose and went on his way. Thus, Esau despised his birthright.

The pair grow into very different sorts of men. Esau was loved by his father for bringing home the meat. Jacob was quiet, loved by his mother (Genesis 25:27–28). Esau returns from the fields exhausted and request a bowl of Jacob's red stew. Jacob demands Esau's birthright in exchange for the stew. Esau foolishly agrees, swearing an oath to seal the deal. Esau shows how careless he was, selling his birthright. Jacob also was displeasing, demanding his brother's birthright. Did Esau consider Jacob's request a joke? The Bible also tells us that Esau's name was also called Edom, the name of his people later. Edom is a word that means "red", the color of Esau's hair or skin at his birth. We know later (Obadiah 1:10-14) that Edom would become a spiteful enemy of Israel.

CHAPTER TWENTY-SIX

Isaac Settles in Gerar

¹Now there was a famine in the land, besides the previous famine that had occurred in the days of Abraham. So Isaac went to Gerar, to Abimelech king of the Philistines. ²The LORD appeared to him and said, "Do not go down to Egypt; stay in the land of which I shall tell you. ³ "Sojourn in this land and I will be with you and bless you, for to you and to your descendants I will give all these lands, and I will establish the oath which I swore to your father Abraham. ⁴ "I will multiply your descendants as the stars of heaven, and will give your descendants all these lands; and by your descendants all the nations of the earth shall be blessed; ⁵ because Abraham obeyed Me and kept My charge, My commandments, My statutes and My laws."

Another famine occurred in Israel when Isaac and family lived there like what occurred in the days of Abraham. Isaac and family traveled west to the Gerar to live in the land of the Philistines under the rule of Abimelech. The Lord told Isaac not to go to Egypt as Abraham had done (Genesis 12), but to go to Gerar. Their king, Abimelech, likely is not the same king that Abraham had interacted with some 90 years before. Could have been a different relative or could have been a title like "Pharoah". The Lord delivers to Isaac a powerful message: I will be with you. I will bless you. I will give all these lands to you and to your offspring. That sounds familiar, since these are the same promises the Lord had given to Isaac's father Abraham (Genesis 12:1–3). In fact, the Lord makes that point: I will establish the same oath with you that I did with your father. In verses 26:4-5 the Lord said, "I will multiply your descendants as the stars of heaven, and will give your descendants all these lands; and by your descendants all the nations of the earth shall be blessed; because Abraham obeyed Me and kept My charge, My commandments, My statutes and My laws." Isaac realized that God blessed him because of his father's obedience to the Lord and to continue as Isaac's example.

⁶So Isaac lived in Gerar. ⁷When the men of the place asked about his wife, he said, "She is my sister," for he was afraid to say, "my wife," thinking, "the men of the place might kill me on account of Rebekah, for she is beautiful." ⁸It came about, when he had been there a long time, that Abimelech king of the Philistines looked out through a window, and saw, and behold, Isaac was caressing his wife Rebekah. ⁹Then Abimelech called Isaac and said, "Behold, certainly she is your wife! How then did you say, 'She is my sister'?" And Isaac said to him, "Because I said, 'I might die on account of her.'" ¹⁰Abimelech said, "What is this you have done to us? One of the people might easily have lain with your wife, and you would have brought guilt upon us." ¹¹So Abimelech charged all the people, saying, "He who touches this man or his wife shall surely be put to death."

Isaac followed Abraham's footsteps. `Like Abraham, he obeyed the Lord by settling down in Gerar (Genesis 26:1–5). Like Abraham, he will interact with a king named Abimelech, in the land of the Philistines (Genesis 22:21–24). And now, like Abraham, he will lie about his beautiful wife being his sister out of fear of someone killing him to take her (Genesis 26:7). The king, Abimelech, saw Isaac caressing his wife, Rebekah. Abimelech called out Isaac, saying Rebekah is his wife. How can he say that she is his sister? Isaac admitted that he thought he might be killed because of her. Abimelech said someone else could have lain with her that his would have guilt upon his people. He then told his people that anyone touching Isaac or Rebekah will be put to death.

Interestingly, neither Abraham nor Isaac are condemned for their action in the text itself—in fact, God protects them both, along with their wives. This is challenging, since the lie seems especially unloving and weak. Worse, it comes immediately following God's promise in the previous verses to be with Isaac and to bless him. Was this strategy, handed down from father to son, a demonstration of a lack of faith in God? Despite Isaac's fear and faithlessness, God still provided protection.

¹²Now Isaac sowed in that land and reaped in the same year a hundredfold. And the LORD blessed him, ¹³and the man became rich, and continued to grow richer until he became very wealthy; ¹⁴*for he had possessions of flocks and herds and a great household, so that the Philistines envied him.* ¹⁵*Now all the wells which his father's servants had dug in the days of Abraham his father, the Philistines stopped up by filling them with earth.* ¹⁶*Then Abimelech said to Isaac, "Go away from us, for you are too powerful for us."* ¹⁷*And Isaac departed from there and camped in the valley of Gerar, and settled there.*

Isaac sowed in the land and reaped in the same year a hundredfold. God blessed him and he became very rich. He was blessed with possessions of flocks and herds and a great household. The Philistines envied him and started filling up the wells that his father had dug with earth. Abimelech, the king, told Isaac to leave the land of Philistines because his was too rich and powerful so Isaac and his family moved to the valley of Gerar.

¹⁸*Then Isaac dug again the wells of water which had been dug in the days of his father Abraham, for the Philistines had stopped them up after the death of Abraham; and he gave them the same names which his father had given them.* ¹⁹*But when Isaac's servants dug in the valley and found there a well of flowing water,* ²⁰*the herdsmen of Gerar quarreled with the herdsmen of Isaac, saying, "The water is ours!" So he named the well Esek, because they contended with him.* ²¹*Then they dug another well, and they quarreled over it too, so he named it Sitnah.* ²²*He moved away from there and dug another well, and they did not quarrel over it; so he named it Rehoboth, for he said, "At last the LORD has made room for us, and we will be fruitful in the land."*

Isaac needs to find water quickly to support his family and all his animals. The Philistines had stopped the previous wells dug there by Abraham. He gave these well the same name that his father had given them years ago. We must think how precious water was in south Israel and how treasured it was all people and animals living in the desert. When Isaac's servants found a well of flowing water, the herdsman of Gerar quarreled with the herdsman of Isaac. The headman's of Gerar claimed the water was theirs. Every well that Isaac's servants dug the Gerar herdmen quarreled about it. However, a third well was dug and the Gerar's herdsman did not quarrel with this one. Isaac named it Rehoboth because the Lord has made room for us and his people will be fruitful in the land. Isaac was not a man who did well with quarrels so he kept moving his people and animals until they found a well not contested by the Gerar herdsman.

23Then he went up from there to Beersheba. 24The LORD appeared to him the same night and said,
"I am the God of your father Abraham;
Do not fear, for I am with you.
I will bless you, and multiply your descendants,
For the sake of My servant Abraham."
25So he built an altar there and called upon the name of the LORD, and pitched his tent there; and there Isaac's servants dug a well.

It's not clear if just Isaac or others in his family went with him south to Beersheba. We also imagine that Isaac moved to Beersheba many years later. The Lord appeared to Isaac that same night and said that He is the God of Abraham. Never be afraid, for I am with you. God said this often to his people, e.g. Isaiah 41:10 and John 14:27. God through other writers remind us never to be afraid many times throughout the Bible. God promises Isaac His blessing and will multiply his descendants for the sake of His servant Abraham. Isaac built an altar in Beersheba, as well as an animal sacrifice and called upon the name of the Lord. His pitched his tent there and his servants dug a well. This was Isaac's new home with all his family and animals.

26Then Abimelech came to him from Gerar with his adviser Ahuzzath and Phicol the commander of his army. 27Isaac said to them, "Why have you come to me, since you hate me and have sent me away from you?" 28They said, "We see plainly that the LORD has been with you; so we said, 'Let there now be an oath between us, even between you and us, and let us make a covenant with you, 29that you will do us no harm, just as we have not touched you and have done to you nothing but good and have sent you away in peace. You are now the blessed of the LORD.'" 30Then he made them a feast, and they ate and drank. 31In the morning they arose early and exchanged oaths; then Isaac sent them away and they departed from him in peace. 32Now it came about on the same day, that Isaac's servants came in and told him about the well which they had dug, and said to him, "We have found water." 33So he called it Shibah; therefore the name of the city is Beersheba to this day.

Isaac, living in Beersheba in the region of Gerar, receives visitors King Abimelech and two of the leaders of Gerar: Ahuzzath, an advisor, and Phicol, the commander of the army. Previously, Abimelech had asked Isaac to move away from his people out of a combination of envy and fear

(Genesis 26:12–17). We mentioned before that likely Abimelech and Phicol are titles and not names. Isaac's response to seeing them was defensive and suspicious. Earlier in chapter 26, Isaac had become something of a threat to Abimelech simply because of his massive number of herds, flocks, servants, and need for water resources. Isaac left Gerar believing that Abimelech hates him (Genesis 26:27). However, now Abimelech wanted to establish peace and friendship with this man of God. Abimelech wanted to establish an oath and covenant with Isaac because he sees that Isaac's God is powerful and Isaac has been very blessed. Thus, Isaac made a feast and they all ate and drank. They took oaths not to do harm to one another. Abraham made a similar peace treaty with the king of Gerar in Genesis 21.

Isaac is having a good day. He has just sent King Abimelech back to Gerar, having made a covenant of peace with the Philistines (Genesis 26:23–31). Now his servants arrive with news that they've found water in the new well they have been digging, likely the one mentioned in verse 25. Because of the peace treaty, this discovery of much-needed water should not result in another nasty dispute over water rights (Genesis 26:18-22). God keeps His promises to Isaac. Isaac called the well Shibah that sounds like the Hebrew work for "oath". Shiba is the name of the city of Beersheba to this day.

[34]When Esau was forty years old he married Judith the daughter of Beeri the Hittite, and Basemath the daughter of Elon the Hittite; [35]and they brought grief to Isaac and Rebekah.

Verse 34 starts a very different story. The story jumps suddenly forward to Esau at the age of 40. It is possible that everything up to this point in the chapter, including all of Isaac's dealings with the Philistines in Gerar, took place before Jacob and Esau were born. Esau married two women at the age of 40. He doesn't appear to have married nearly as well, however. We're told that Esau marries two Canaanite women—Hittites, specifically. His marriages to Judith and Basemath are said to have made life bitter for his parents (Genesis 26:35). This angst is an issue of faith, not of race; the godless practices of the Canaanites will eventually earn them harsh judgment from God (Deuteronomy 7:1–4; 18:9–14). Esau's marriages to these two Hittite women are said to have made life bitter for both Isaac and Rebekah. They wanted more and better for Esau, apparently.

CHAPTER TWENTY-SEVEN

Jacob's Deception

Now it came about, when Isaac was old and his eyes were too dim to see, that he called his older son Esau and said to him, "My son." And he said to him, "Here I am." *²* Isaac said, "Behold now, I am old *and* I do not know the day of my death. *³* Now then, please take your gear, your quiver and your bow, and go out to the field and hunt game for me; *⁴* and prepare a savory dish for me such as I love, and bring it to me that I may eat, so that my soul may bless you before I die."

Isaac was old and his eyes were too dim to see. Isaac evidently thought he was near death (verse 2) and would not live much beyond his current 137 years, which was the age of Ishmael when he died (25:17). However, he did live another 43 years (Genesis 35:28). His twin sons were 77 years old. Isaac asked Esau to take his quiver and bow and hunt game for him. Isaac loved by the preparation Rebekah afterwards made. Not sure if Isaac meant to bless his wife or Esau. Ignoring the words of God to Rebekah (25:23), forgetting Esau's bartered birthright (25:33), and overlooking Esau's grievous marriages (26:35), Isaac was still intent on treating Esau as the eldest and granting him the blessing of birthright. The son thought, if I would bring him food he loved, while he was still feeling good, he would give me the best blessings he had.

⁵ Rebekah was listening while Isaac spoke to his son Esau. So when Esau went to the field to hunt for game to bring home, ⁶ Rebekah said to her son Jacob, "Behold, I heard your father speak to your brother Esau, saying, ⁷ 'Bring me some game and prepare a savory dish for me, that I may eat, and bless you in the presence of the Lord before my death.' ⁸ Now therefore, my son, listen to me as I command you. ⁹ Go now to the flock and bring me two choice young goats from there, that I may prepare them as a savory dish for your father, such as he loves. ¹⁰ Then you shall bring it to your father, that he may eat, so that he may bless you before his death." ¹¹ Jacob answered his mother Rebekah, "Behold, Esau my brother is a hairy man and I am a smooth man. ¹² Perhaps my father will feel me, then I will be as a deceiver in his sight, and I will bring upon myself a curse and not a blessing." ¹³ But his mother said to him, "Your curse be on me, my son; only obey my voice, and go, get them for me." ¹⁴ So he went and got them, and brought them to his mother; and his mother made savory food such as his father loved. ¹⁵ Then Rebekah took the best garments of Esau her elder son, which were with her in the house, and put them on Jacob her younger son. ¹⁶ And she put the skins of the young goats on his hands and on the smooth part of his neck. ¹⁷ She also gave the savory food and the bread, which she had made, to her son Jacob.

Desperation to secure patriarchal blessing for Jacob bred deception and trickery, with Rebekah believing her culinary skills could make goat's meat taste and smell like choice venison (verses 8-10), and make Jacob seem like Esau (verses 15-17). As his father directed and enjoined him; and thus, it was ordered by divine Providence, that there might be time and opportunity for Jacob to get the blessing before his brother. Rebekah told Jacob to bring me two choice young goats from there, that I may prepare them *as* a savory dish for your father. Then you shall bring *it* to your father, that he may eat, so that he may bless you before his death. Rebekah could fix that goat to taste like venison and trick Isaac into blessing Jacob. Jacob answered his mother Rebekah, "Behold, Esau my brother is a hairy man and I am a smooth man. Perhaps my father will feel me, then I will be as a deceiver in his sight, and I will bring upon myself a curse and not a blessing." But his mother said to him, "Your curse be on me, my son; only obey my voice, and go, get *them* for me. With his mother accepting full responsibility for the scheme and bearing the curse should it occur, Jacob reluctantly followed Rebekah's instructions. Esau, having been married for 37 years (Genesis. 26:35), would have had his own tents and his own wives to do for him; so how and why Rebekah came by some of his best clothes in her tent is unknown. Perhaps these garments were the official robes associated with the priestly functions of the head of the house, kept in her house until passed on to the oldest son. Perhaps Esau had, on occasion, worn them, thus their smell of the field (verse 27). Was Rebekah a deceiving woman, or was she remembering the thing God told her about her two sons before their birth? God told her that the older would serve the younger. You know, Esau really did not deserve the birthright. He sold it to Jacob for a bowl of soup. Did God give Rebekah this plan? Did she scheme this up herself, or did God give her this plan to save this blessing for Jacob? Jacob was God's choice from the beginning, but Hebrews gave the best blessing to their oldest son. It was the custom. Was this Rebekah's plan, or God's plan? God was not happy with Esau when he sold the birthright, and married two earthly women.

18 Then he came to his father and said, "My father." And he said, "Here I am. Who are you, my son?" 19 Jacob said to his father, "I am Esau your firstborn; I have done as you told me. Get up, please, sit and eat of my game, that you may bless me." 20 Isaac said to his son, "How is it that you have it so quickly, my son?" And he said, "Because the Lord your God caused it to happen to me." 21 Then Isaac said to Jacob, "Please come close, that I may feel you, my son, whether you are really my son Esau or not." 22 So Jacob came close to Isaac his father, and he felt him and said, "The voice is the voice of Jacob, but the hands are the hands of Esau." 23 He did not recognize him, because his hands were hairy like his brother Esau's hands; so he blessed him. 24 And he said, "Are you really my son Esau?" And he said, "I am." 25 So he said, "Bring it to me, and I will eat of my son's game, that I may bless you." And he brought it to him, and he ate; he also brought him wine and he drank. 26 Then his father Isaac said to him, "Please come close and kiss me, my son." 27 So he came close and kissed him; and when he smelled the smell of his garments, he blessed him and said, "See, the smell of my son
Is like the smell of a field which the Lord has blessed;
28 Now may God give you of the dew of heaven,
And of the fatness of the earth,
And an abundance of grain and new wine;
29 May peoples serve you,
And nations bow down to you;
Be master of your brothers,
And may your mother's sons bow down to you.
Cursed be those who curse you,
And blessed be those who bless you."

Jacob lied to Isaac. He lied about being Esau, he lied about killing venison, he lied about going into the field, he lied about coming back so quickly, and he lied about cooking the goats. He even lied about bring the Lord into this affair (Genesis 27:20). A lie had to sustain a lie, and a tangled web had begun to be woven (verses 21-24). Although Jacob received Isaac's blessing that day, the deceit caused severe consequences:

(1) He never saw his mother after that;
(2) Esau wanted him dead;
(3) Laban, his uncle, deceived him;
(4) His family life was full of conflict; and
(5) He was exiled for years from his family.

By the promise of God, he would have received the birthright (25:23). He didn't need to scheme this deception with his mother. "And said, the voice is Jacob's voice". Very like it, as if it was the same, as indeed it was. "But the hands are the hands of Esau". Are like them, being hairy as they; the feeling of the hands is as the feeling of the hands of Esau; they feel like them.

Blessings are associated with happiness and welfare. Isaac gave Jacob the patriarchal blessing. Goat, if it is fixed correctly, tastes like venison, so Isaac would not be able to tell the difference in taste. He was amazed how fast it was prepared, but his son, Jacob, had learned early from his father that it was ok to lie to save yourself. He also lied when he told his father he was Esau. His father could not understand, if he was Esau, why he had Jacob's voice. The hairy hands, and probably the odor from Esau's clothes, convinced the father that this was truly Esau. So, he blessed Jacob.

[30] Now it came about, as soon as Isaac had finished blessing Jacob, and Jacob had hardly gone out from the presence of Isaac his father, that Esau his brother came in from his hunting. [31] Then he also made savory food, and brought it to his father; and he said to his father, "Let my father arise and eat of his son's game, that you may bless me." [32] Isaac his father said to him, "Who are you?" And he said, "I am your son, your firstborn, Esau." [33] Then Isaac trembled violently, and said, "Who was he then that hunted game and brought it to me, so that I ate of all of it before you came, and blessed him? Yes, and he shall be blessed." [34] When Esau heard the words of his father, he cried out with an exceedingly great and bitter cry, and said to his father, "Bless me, even me also, O my father!" [35] And he said, "Your brother came deceitfully and has taken

away your blessing." ³⁶ *Then he said, "Is he not rightly named Jacob, for he has supplanted me these two times? He took away my birthright, and behold, now he has taken away my blessing." And he said, "Have you not reserved a blessing for me?"* ³⁷ *But Isaac replied to Esau, "Behold, I have made him your master, and all his relatives I have given to him as servants; and with grain and new wine I have sustained him. Now as for you then, what can I do, my son?"* ³⁸ *Esau said to his father, "Do you have only one blessing, my father? Bless me, even me also, O my father." So Esau lifted his voice and wept.*

In Genesis 27:30 after Isaac had finished blessing Jacob and Jacob left, that Esau came home from hunting. We don't know how long this was. When he asked Isaac to eat what Esau had brought home, Isaac asked who he was! When Isaac heard Esau telling the truth to him, he trembled violently and asked who what he who had just served him and Isaac blessed him. When Esau heard the words of his father, he cried out with an exceedingly great and bitter cry. He asked Isaac to bless him too. Yet Isaac replied that Jacob came deceitfully and taken your blessing away. Jacob took away your blessing twice---first your birthright and second his blessing. Esau protested, have you not reserved a blessing for me? But Isaac replied to Esau that Jacob was now is master, all Isaac's relatives were given to him as servants. As for you, Esau, what can I do? Esau asked if Isaac had only one blessing for himself, yet apparently Isaac did not. Esau just wept.

³⁹ *Then Isaac his father answered and said to him,*
"Behold, away from the fertility of the earth shall be your dwelling,
And away from the dew of heaven from above.
⁴⁰ *"By your sword you shall live,*
And your brother you shall serve.
But it shall come about when you become restless,
That you will break his yoke from your neck."

There was nothing left for Esau. He and family would need to live away from the fertility of the earth, in a land that is parched. He shall live by the sword and you will serve your brother Jacob. It will come about when you become restless that you will break his yoke from your neck. There will be continual strife between the two brothers. They would engage in a constant, internecine quarrel over fertility of the earth, and of the dew of heaven. Jacob would be dominant - until Esau would rebel in frustration and anger. Isaac predicts that they will frequently come to blows, and occasionally, Esau's descendants will enjoy the upper hand for a time.

⁴¹ So Esau bore a grudge against Jacob because of the blessing with which his father had blessed him; and Esau said to himself, "The days of mourning for my father are near; then I will kill my brother Jacob." ⁴² Now when the words of her elder son Esau were reported to Rebekah, she sent and called her younger son Jacob, and said to him, "Behold your brother Esau is consoling himself concerning you by planning to kill you. ⁴³ Now therefore, my son, obey my voice, and arise, flee to Haran, to my brother Laban! ⁴⁴ Stay with him a few days, until your brother's fury subsides, ⁴⁵ until your brother's anger against you subsides and he forgets what you did to him. Then I will send and get you from there. Why should I be bereaved of you both in one day?" ⁴⁶ Rebekah said to Isaac, "I am tired of living because of the daughters of Heth; if Jacob takes a wife from the daughters of Heth, like these, from the daughters of the land, what good will my life be to me?"

Esau, of course, bore a grudge again Jacob. Once his father was dead, Esau will plan to kill Jacob. Rebekah knew what Esau was thinking and told Jacob what eventually Esau was planning to do. She asked Jacob to flee and live near her brother, Laban. Let Esau's fury subside and he will forget what you did to him. Later she will bring him back home. She does not want to be bereaved of both of you in one day (Isaac and Jacob). Even today, Israelites generally think and behave much like their father Jacob, while Edomites (Esau's family) still retain the attitudes and drives of Esau. Rebekah does not tell Isaac her true fear that Esau would kill Jacob. Perhaps she doesn't think that would compel Isaac to act quickly enough. Perhaps she doesn't think Isaac would believe such a thing of his favorite son. Instead, Rebekah manipulates Isaac once again, this time by complaining about Esau's wives, the Hittite women who had made life bitter for both, according to Genesis 26:35. Now she says to Isaac colorfully that she hates her life because of those women. In fact, what good will her life even be if Jacob also marries one of the local women?

CHAPTER TWENTY-EIGHT

Jacob Is Sent Away

¹*So Isaac called Jacob and blessed him and charged him, and said to him, "You shall not take a wife from the daughters of Canaan.* ²*"Arise, go to Paddan-aram, to the house of Bethuel your mother's father; and from there take to yourself a wife from the daughters of Laban your mother's brother.* ³*"May God Almighty bless you and make you fruitful and multiply you, that you may become a company of peoples.* ⁴*"May He also give you the blessing of Abraham, to you and to your descendants with you, that you may possess the land of your sojournings, which God gave to Abraham."* ⁵*Then Isaac sent Jacob away, and he went to Paddan-aram to Laban, son of Bethuel the Aramean, the brother of Rebekah, the mother of Jacob and Esau.* ⁶*Now Esau saw that Isaac had blessed Jacob and sent him away to Paddan-aram to take to himself a wife from there, and that when he blessed him he charged him, saying, "You shall not take a wife from the daughters of Canaan,"* ⁷*and that Jacob had obeyed his father and his mother and had gone to Paddan-aram.* ⁸*So Esau saw that the daughters of Canaan displeased his father Isaac;* ⁹*and Esau went to Ishmael, and married, besides the wives that he had, Mahalath the daughter of Ishmael, Abraham's son, the sister of Nebaioth.*

Isaac called Jacob, blessed him, and told him not to take a wife from the daughters of Canaan. Isaac commands Jacob to go to Rebekah's brother's household in Paddan-aram in Mesopotamia to find a wife. Paddan-aram is in modern day Iraq, north of the Euphrates River. Under no circumstances should Jacob marry a local Canaanite woman (Genesis 28:1–2). Isaac also blesses Jacob again, this time giving to Jacob the full blessing of Abraham including a version of God's promises to Abraham

(Genesis 28:3–5). Jacob went to Paddam-aram where he met with Laban, the brother of Rebekah, mother of Jacob and Esau. He needed to go there to escape the potential evil of Esau and find his wife there. Esau knew his father was displeased that he married daughters of Canaan. Esau went to Ishmael, and married, besides the wives that he had, Mahalath the daughter of Ishmael, Abraham's son, the sister of Nebaioth.

[10] Then Jacob departed from Beersheba and went toward Haran. [11] He came to a certain place and spent the night there, because the sun had set; and he took one of the stones of the place and put it under his head, and lay down in that place. [12] He had a dream, and behold, a ladder was set on the earth with its top reaching to heaven; and behold, the angels of God were ascending and descending on it. [13] And behold, the LORD stood above it and said, "I am the LORD, the God of your father Abraham and the God of Isaac; the land on which you lie, I will give it to you and to your descendants. [14] "Your descendants will also be like the dust of the earth, and you will spread out to the west and to the east and to the north and to the south; and in you and in your descendants shall all the families of the earth be blessed. [15] "Behold, I am with you and will keep you wherever you go, and will bring you back to this land; for I will not leave you until I have done what I have promised you." [16] Then Jacob awoke from his sleep and said, "Surely the LORD is in this place, and I did not know it." [17] He was afraid and said, "How awesome is this place! This is none other than the house of God, and this is the gate of heaven."

Jacob left Beersheba, went toward Haran, and was weary by nightfall to bed down on the ground. The Lord appears to Jacob in a dream atop a ladder connecting earth to heaven with angels going up and down. The Lord stood at the top of the ladder in heaven and said that He is the Lord, the God of Abraham and Isaac, your grandfather and father. The land where you are, Jacob, I will give it to you and your descendants. All your descendant, whether they live in any direction, I will bless all your families. I will never leave you until I have done what I have promised. Jacob woke up from his dream and said, "the Lord is here and I did not know it". He even became afraid because he knew that God was awesome and where he was the gate to heaven.

[18] So Jacob rose early in the morning, and took the stone that he had put under his head and set it up as a pillar and poured oil on its top. [19] He called the name of that place Bethel; however, previously the name of the city had been Luz.

²⁰Then Jacob made a vow, saying, "If God will be with me and will keep me on this journey that I take, and will give me food to eat and garments to wear, ²¹and I return to my father's house in safety, then the LORD will be my God. ²²"This stone, which I have set up as a pillar, will be God's house, and of all that You give me I will surely give a tenth to You."

Jacob got up, used the stone that he had put under his head, and established a place that he called "Bethel" instead of its old name "Luz". Jacob then made a vow, asking God to always be with him, keep him on this journey and give him food to eat and garments to wear, as well as returning him to his father's house in safety, the Lord will be my God. This does seem like Jacob was repeating what God had already promised him. The stone he used to establish a pillar, a monument to God, will be His house, thus why he named this place "Bethel" (house of God). He also vowed that all that God gave to him, he will surely return a tenth to God. This was the first time that a vow of giving a tenth back to God was established.

CHAPTER TWENTY-NINE

Jacob Meets Rachel

¹Then Jacob went on his journey, and came to the land of the sons of the east. ²He looked, and saw a well in the field, and behold, three flocks of sheep were lying there beside it, for from that well they watered the flocks. Now the stone on the mouth of the well was large. ³When all the flocks were gathered there, they would then roll the stone from the mouth of the well and water the sheep, and put the stone back in its place on the mouth of the well.

Jacob went east on his journey, saw a well in the field and three flocks of sheep were lying beside this well. The well watered all the flocks as the stone on the mouth of the well was large. When all the flocks were gather there, shepherds would roll the stone from the mouth of the well and water the sheep, then put the stone back in its place on the mouth of the well.

⁴Jacob said to them, "My brothers, where are you from?" And they said, "We are from Haran." ⁵He said to them, "Do you know Laban the son of Nahor?" And they said, "We know him." ⁶And he said to them, "Is it well with him?" And they said, "It is well, and here is Rachel his daughter coming with the sheep." ⁷He said, "Behold, it is still high day; it is not time for the livestock to be gathered. Water the sheep, and go, pasture them." ⁸But they said, "We cannot, until all the flocks are gathered, and they roll the stone from the mouth of the well; then we water the sheep."

Jacob had travelled about 450 miles from Beersheba to Haran (Genesis 29:4). Notice the absence of prayer for divine guidance to the woman of God's choosing, which dominates the story of Abraham's servant's visit to the same area for the same purpose (choosing Rebekah). Also, Jacob arrived alone on foot whereas Abraham's servant came with a well-laden camel train. Jacob acted arrogantly when he said in verse 7 and 8, "Behold, it is still high day; it is not time for the livestock to be gathered. Water the sheep, and go, pasture them." But the men there said that they cannot until all the flocks are gathered, then they can roll the stone from the mouth of the cave of the well and water the sheep.

⁹While he was still speaking with them, Rachel came with her father's sheep, for she was a shepherdess. ¹⁰When Jacob saw Rachel the daughter of Laban his mother's brother, and the sheep of Laban his mother's brother, Jacob went up and rolled the stone from the mouth of the well and watered the flock of Laban his mother's brother. ¹¹Then Jacob kissed Rachel, and lifted his voice and wept. ¹²Jacob told Rachel that he was a relative of her father and that he was Rebekah's son, and she ran and told her father. ¹³So when Laban heard the news of Jacob his sister's son, he ran to meet him, and embraced him and kissed him and brought him to his house. Then he related to Laban all these things. ¹⁴Laban said to him, "Surely you are my bone and my flesh." And he stayed with him a month.

While Jacob was speaking to the men, Rachel came with her father's sheep, she was a shepherdess. When Jacob saw Rachel, the daughter of Laban, his mother's brother, and the sheep of Laban, Jacob rolled the stone from the mouth of the well and watered the flock of Laban. Then Jacob kissed Rachel and lifted his voice and wept. Jacob told Rachel that he was a relative of her father, his mother Rebekah was Laban sister, and she ran to tell her father. When Laban heard the news of Jacob being present, he ran to meet him, embraced him, kissed him and brought him to his house. Jacob stayed with Laban a month.

¹⁵Then Laban said to Jacob, "Because you are my relative, should you therefore serve me for nothing? Tell me, what shall your wages be?" ¹⁶Now Laban had two daughters; the name of the older was Leah, and the name of the younger was Rachel. ¹⁷And Leah's eyes were weak, but Rachel was beautiful of form and face. ¹⁸Now Jacob loved Rachel, so he said, "I will serve you seven years for your younger daughter Rachel." ¹⁹Laban said, "It is better that I give her to you than to give her to another man; stay with me." ²⁰So Jacob served seven years for Rachel and they seemed to him but a few days because of his love for her.

After Jacob has been with the family for a month and working for Laban, the uncle asks the nephew what wages he would ask to continue working for him. The implication is that Jacob is a good worker and very helpful to Laban. Jacob, who has come in part to find a wife, offers to work for seven years in exchange for marrying Laban's younger daughter Rachel, whom Jacob loves. His love for Rachel was so deep that the seven years working for Laban seemed like only a few days because of his love for her.

[21]Then Jacob said to Laban, "Give me my wife, for my time is completed, that I may go in to her." [22]Laban gathered all the men of the place and made a feast. [23]Now in the evening he took his daughter Leah, and brought her to him; and Jacob went in to her. [24]Laban also gave his maid Zilpah to his daughter Leah as a maid. [25]So it came about in the morning that, behold, it was Leah! And he said to Laban, "What is this you have done to me? Was it not for Rachel that I served with you? Why then have you deceived me?" [26]But Laban said, "It is not the practice in our place to marry off the younger before the firstborn. [27]"Complete the week of this one, and we will give you the other also for the service which you shall serve with me for another seven years." [28]Jacob did so and completed her week, and he gave him his daughter Rachel as his wife. [29]Laban also gave his maid Bilhah to his daughter Rachel as her maid. [30]So Jacob went in to Rachel also, and indeed he loved Rachel more than Leah, and he served with Laban for another seven years.

When seven years has passed, Laban throws a wedding feast. On the wedding night, however, Laban manages to switch out Rachel with her older, less attractive sister Leah. Jacob sleeps with Leah without realizing she is not Rachel; apparently in that time and place, this was enough to constitute a legal marriage. When Jacob realized what had happened, he demands to know why Laban has committed this outrageous deception. Laban calmly tells Jacob that their custom does not allow the younger daughter to marry first. Laban requests that Jacob complete the week with Leah and he will give Rachel but Jacob must work there another seven years. In spite of Laban's manipulation, Jacob agrees (Genesis 29:27–30). Of course, there was no law in marrying a younger woman (or man) over an older sibling. Laban was deceitful once again.

[31]Now the LORD saw that Leah was unloved, and He opened her womb, but Rachel was barren. [32]Leah conceived and bore a son and named him Reuben, for she said, "Because the LORD has seen my affliction; surely now my husband

will love me." ³³Then she conceived again and bore a son and said, "Because the LORD has heard that I am unloved, He has therefore given me this son also." So she named him Simeon. ³⁴She conceived again and bore a son and said, "Now this time my husband will become attached to me, because I have borne him three sons." Therefore, he was named Levi. ³⁵And she conceived again and bore a son and said, "This time I will praise the LORD." Therefore, she named him Judah. Then she stopped bearing.

Now married twice over, and with seven more years of unpaid work ahead of him, Jacob settles in. Leah, though, is deeply wounded by the fact that Jacob loves Rachel more than her. The Lord, who is always with Jacob, takes notice of Leah's heartbreak and allows her to begin having children while her younger, better-loved sister remains barren (Genesis 29:31). Leah bore four sons—Reuben, Simeon, Levi, and Judah. Judah means "praise" or "may God be praised". Yet Leah knows that Jacob will not love her as he does Rachel.

CHAPTER THIRTY

The Sons of Jacob

¹Now when Rachel saw that she bore Jacob no children, she became jealous of her sister; and she said to Jacob, "Give me children, or else I die." ²Then Jacob's anger burned against Rachel, and he said, "Am I in the place of God, who has withheld from you the fruit of the womb?" ³She said, "Here is my maid Bilhah, go in to her that she may bear on my knees, that through her I too may have children." ⁴So she gave him her maid Bilhah as a wife, and Jacob went in to her. ⁵Bilhah conceived and bore Jacob a son. ⁶Then Rachel said, "God has vindicated me, and has indeed heard my voice and has given me a son." Therefore she named him Dan. ⁷Rachel's maid Bilhah conceived again and bore Jacob a second son. ⁸So Rachel said, "With mighty wrestlings I have wrestled with my sister, and I have indeed prevailed." And she named him Naphtali.

Rachel saw that she bore Jacob no children; she became jealous of her sister, Leah. She asked Jacob to give her children or she would die. Jacob rightly replied that he is not God and only God can give children (Psalm 127:3-5). She asked Jacob to intercourse with Bilhah her maid. Bilhah had a son and name him Dan, then had another son and named him Naphtali. So now Jacob has six sons by two different women although Rachel considered Dan and Naphtali to be her sons.

⁹When Leah saw that she had stopped bearing, she took her maid Zilpah and gave her to Jacob as a wife. ¹⁰Leah's maid Zilpah bore Jacob a son. ¹¹Then Leah said, "How fortunate!" So she named him Gad. ¹²Leah's maid Zilpah bore Jacob a second son. ⁱ³Then Leah said, "Happy am I! For women will call me happy." So she named him Asher.

Leah took her maid, Zilpah and gave her to Jacob as another wife. Zilpah bore two more sons, Gad and Asher. Leah was very happy to have two sons through Zilpah. Jacob now had 8 sons.

¹⁴Now in the days of wheat harvest Reuben went and found mandrakes in the field, and brought them to his mother Leah. Then Rachel said to Leah, "Please give me some of your son's mandrakes." ¹⁵But she said to her, "Is it a small matter for you to take my husband? And would you take my son's mandrakes also?" So Rachel said, "Therefore he may lie with you tonight in return for your son's mandrakes." ¹⁶When Jacob came in from the field in the evening, then Leah went out to meet him and said, "You must come in to me, for I have surely hired you with my son's mandrakes." So he lay with her that night. ¹⁷God gave heed to Leah, and she conceived and bore Jacob a fifth son. ¹⁸Then Leah said, "God has given me my wages because I gave my maid to my husband." So she named him Issachar. ¹⁹Leah conceived again and bore a sixth son to Jacob. ²⁰Then Leah said, "God has endowed me with a good gift; now my husband will dwell with me, because I have borne him six sons." So she named him Zebulun. ²¹Afterward she bore a daughter and named her Dinah.

Jacob's oldest son, Reuben, found mandrakes (a Mediterranean plant of the nightshade family, with white or purple flowers and large yellow berries)

in the field and brought them home to his mother, Leah. Rachel then said to Leah that she's like some mandrakes. Leah rebelled and said, "you took my husband and now you want to take her son's mandrakes also?" Rachel then replied and said that Jacob could lie with you tonight in return for Reuben's mandrakes. When Jacob came home from the field that evening, Leah met him and said that she had hired Jacob to lie with her along with Reuben's mandrakes. Jacob lied with Leah and she conceived and bore Jacob a fifth son, named him Issachar. Leah conceived again and bore a six son, Zebulun. Then she bore again and she had a daughter, Dinah. Jacob now had ten sons and one daughter.

22Then God remembered Rachel, and God gave heed to her and opened her womb. 23So she conceived and bore a son and said, "God has taken away my reproach." 24She named him Joseph, saying, "May the LORD give me another son." 25Now it came about when Rachel had borne Joseph, that Jacob said to Laban, "Send me away, that I may go to my own place and to my own country.

26 "Give me my wives and my children for whom I have served you, and let me depart; for you yourself know my service which I have rendered you." 27 But Laban said to him, "If now it pleases you, stay with me; I have divined that the LORD has blessed me on your account." 28 He continued, "Name me your wages, and I will give it." 29 But he said to him, "You yourself know how I have served you and how your cattle have fared with me. 30 "For you had little before I came and it has increased to a multitude, and the LORD has blessed you wherever I turned. But now, when shall I provide for my own household also?"

God remembered Rachel and opened her womb. She conceived and bore a son, Joseph. After Joseph was born, Jacob said to Laban that he and family would like to go back to where they used to live. Laban knew the service that Jacob had rendered for many years. But Laban wanted them to stay because Laban divined that the Lord bless him on account of Jacob and his family. Name your wages and he will give it to Jacob. Yet Jacob came back and said how much he had served Laban and how his cattle had been risen with him. For Laban had little before Jacob can and it has increased to a multitude and the Lord has blessed you wherever Jacob turned. Now it's time that Jacob can provide for his own household.

31 So he said, "What shall I give you?" And Jacob said, "You shall not give me anything. If you will do this one thing for me, I will again pasture and keep your flock: 32 let me pass through your entire flock today, removing from there every speckled and spotted sheep and every black one among the lambs and the spotted and speckled among the goats; and such shall be my wages. 33 "So my honesty will answer for me later, when you come concerning my wages. Every one that is not speckled and spotted among the goats and black among the lambs, if found with me, will be considered stolen." 34 Laban said, "Good, let it be according to your word." 35 So he removed on that day the striped and spotted male goats and all the speckled and spotted female goats, every one with white in it, and all the black ones among the sheep, and gave them into the care of his sons. 36 And he put a distance of three days' journey between himself and Jacob, and Jacob fed the rest of Laban's flocks.

Laban asks again: What do you want from me? Jacob surprises him with a tricky answer of his own: Don't give me anything right now. Instead, Jacob will ask for a specific cut of the future profits in the following verses. Laban, predictably, will respond by trying to cheat Jacob. Jacob asks that any future black lambs or speckled and spotted sheep and goats be his payment. Apparently, most of the sheep in a flock were white all over, and most of the goats were entirely black. Jacob is asking for a seemingly small subset of the animals. As the following verses will reveal, Jacob believed he could produce a lot of these spotted and speckled animals with selective breeding (Genesis 30:37–39). Much later, Jacob will reveal his knowledge that God, not strange farming practices, is the real source of the animals' growth (Genesis 31:10–13).

> *[37] Then Jacob took fresh rods of poplar and almond and plane trees, and peeled white stripes in them, exposing the white which was in the rods. [38] He set the rods which he had peeled in front of the flocks in the gutters, even in the watering troughs, where the flocks came to drink; and they mated when they came to drink. [39] So the flocks mated by the rods, and the flocks brought forth striped, speckled, and spotted. [40] Jacob separated the lambs, and made the flocks face toward the striped and all the black in the flock of Laban; and he put his own herds apart, and did not put them with Laban's flock. [41] Moreover, whenever the stronger of the flock were mating, Jacob would place the rods in the sight of the flock in the gutters, so that they might mate by the rods; [42] but when the flock was feeble, he did not put them in; so the feebler were Laban's and the stronger Jacob's. [43] So the man became exceedingly prosperous, and had large flocks and female and male servants and camels and donkeys.*

Jacob takes sticks fresh from three specific kinds of trees and strips the bark to reveal the white underneath. This is, in part, a play on words: the Hebrew term for "white" is *laban*. With God's supernatural blessing, Jacob will use these sticks to influence how many striped, spotted, and speckled animals are born. It's important to realize Jacob has made this bargain for the off-color animals at the Lord's direction (Genesis 31:7–12). He has not dreamed this up on his own. The text does not appear to be suggesting that peeled sticks in or near a water source caused spotted or striped animals to be born. God is acting supernaturally to bless Jacob by causing a much higher than normal number of mixed-color offspring in response to Jacob's device of placing these sticks in front of the animals he wishes to influence. Using another method described in the following verse, the white sheep also produced black lambs. In other words, it is God, not the sticks, which are producing these results. Verse 40 describes his method for getting the white sheep to produce black lambs. This is a notoriously difficult verse to translate, and to interpret. It's possible that Jacob caused the white sheep to mate while facing the black and striped animals in the flock, causing them to produce black offspring.

As the off-color animals were born, Jacob separated them from the rest of the flock. In short, he separated his burgeoning flock from Laban's, allowing him to keep track of just how quickly his own wealth was growing. Still, the Lord blessed Jacob's strategy for getting solid-colored goats to give birth to mixed color goats and white sheep to give birth to black sheep. Jacob influenced the animals by what he placed in their line of sight during breeding. When the strong goats were mating, Jacob made sure they would see the sticks he had stripped and placed among them. As we will learn later, this is not because Jacob—or Scripture—believes that such techniques influence breeding. Rather, Jacob has already been told by God that this would happen, and the use of the sticks is simply Jacob's means of control over God's blessing (Genesis 31:7–12). Now we see that Jacob removes his sticks from sight when the weak or feeble animals are mating. In this way, he ensures that those animals give birth to solid white sheep and solid black goats. Over time, this selective breeding would result in Laban's sheep and goats becoming weaker, while Jacob's became stronger. Since God is on Jacob's side, Laban's tactics won't work. Instead, with God's intervention and Jacob's crafty strategy, the deal made Jacob a wealthy man in his own right. So many off-color sheep and goats were born into the flock that Jacob was apparently able to sell some of them to acquire male and female servants of his own, as well as camels and donkeys. The Lord promised great things to Jacob before he arrived in Laban's territory. Now God has demonstrated that His blessing continues to be on Jacob. Soon Jacob will be ready at last to return to the land of his own people.

CHAPTER THIRTY ONE

Jacob Leaves Secretly for Canaan

¹Now Jacob heard the words of Laban's sons, saying, "Jacob has taken away all that was our father's, and from what belonged to our father he has made all this wealth." ²Jacob saw the attitude of Laban, and behold, it was not friendly toward him as formerly. ³Then the LORD said to Jacob, "Return to the land of your fathers and to your relatives, and I will be with you." ⁴So Jacob sent and called Rachel and Leah to his flock in the field, ⁵and said to them, "I see your father's attitude, that it is not friendly toward me as formerly, but the God of my father has been with me. ⁶"You know that I have served your father with all my strength. ⁷"Yet your father has cheated me and changed my wages ten times; however, God did not allow him to hurt me. ⁸"If he spoke thus, 'The speckled shall be your wages,' then all the flock brought forth speckled; and if he spoke thus, 'The striped shall be your wages,' then all the flock brought forth striped. ⁹"Thus God has taken away your father's livestock and given them to me. ¹⁰"And it came about at the time when the flock were mating that I lifted up my eyes and saw in a dream, and behold, the male goats which were mating were striped, speckled, and mottled. ¹¹"Then the angel of God said to me in the dream, 'Jacob,' and I said, 'Here I am.' ¹²"He said, 'Lift up now your eyes and see that all the male goats which are mating are striped, speckled, and mottled; for I have seen all that Laban has been doing to you. ¹³'I am the God of Bethel, where you anointed a pillar, where you made a vow to Me; now arise, leave this land, and return to the land of your birth.'" ¹⁴Rachel and Leah said to him, "Do we still have any portion or inheritance in our father's house? ¹⁵"Are we not reckoned by him as foreigners? For he has sold us, and has also entirely consumed our purchase price. ¹⁶"Surely all the wealth which God

has taken away from our father belongs to us and our children; now then, do whatever God has said to you."

In chapter 31 of Genesis Jacob heard the words of Laban's sons, that Jacob had taken away all that was our father's and made Jacob very rich. Jacob also saw that the attitude of Laban was not as it was before, Laban was no longer friendly. The Lord said to Jacob to return to the land of your fathers and your relatives and I will be with you. Jacob called Rachel and Leah to his flock in the field, that their father's attitude toward him was no longer friendly, but God has been with me. You know that I have served your father with all my strength, yet your father has cheated me and changed my wages ten times and God will not allow him to hurt me. Jacob explained that he would be entitled to all the striped, specked and spotted goats and well as the black sheep. Yet Laban attempted multiple time to changed that agreement. The Lord intervened repeated to protect Jacob's interests, supernaturally causing only spotted or striped goats to be born to keep up with Laban's changing rules. God helped Jacob prosper at Laban's expense. Jacob said that God had taken away your father's livestock and given them to me.

Jacob said that when the flock were mating that he lifted up his eyes and saw in a dream that the male goats mating were striped, specked, and mottled. The angel of God said to Jacob in a dream, "Jacob" and I said "Here I am". Jacob replied to God "Here I am" like so many others did, e.g. Abraham in Genesis 22:1, Samuel in I Samuel 3:4, Isaiah in Isaiah 6:8, and other verses. God said, lift up your eyes now and see that all the male goats mating are striped, speckled, and mottled for I have seen all that Laban has been doing to you. God is the God of Bethel (house of God) where Jacob anointed a pillar, where he made a vow to God. Jacob finishes by telling Leah and Rachel that God spoke to Him, reminding Jacob of the sacred vow he had made at Bethel before meeting his Uncle Laban and his daughters. At Bethel, the Lord had appeared to Jacob in a dream and made great promises to him. Jacob had worshiped the Lord and built a pillar to Him. Now that same God, that good and faithful God, was commanding Jacob to return to the land of his people. He now must leave this land and return to the land of his birth (Canaan). Rachel and Leah said to him, "Do we still have any portion or inheritance in our father's house?" Are we not reckoned by him as foreigners? For he has sold us and has also entirely consume our purchased price. Surely all the wealth which God has taken away from our father belongs to us and our children; now, then do whatever God has said to you." Laban's greed is clear even to his own daughters.

[17] Then Jacob arose and put his children and his wives upon camels; [18] and he drove away all his livestock and all his property which he had gathered, his acquired livestock which he had gathered in Paddan-aram, to go to the land of Canaan to his father Isaac. [19] When Laban had gone to shear his flock, then Rachel stole the household idols that were her father's. [20] And Jacob deceived Laban the Aramean by not telling him that he was fleeing. [21] So he fled with all that he had; and he arose and crossed the Euphrates River, and set his face toward the hill country of Gilead.

Scripture does not explicitly indicate if Jacob packed up his family and left immediately after hearing that his wives would support him in the move away from Laban. We're not told how much time it took, but the implication is that they moved with some haste. Jacob wanted to get away without Laban knowing he was gone. Jacob had become wealthy. He had acquired camels, the preferred method of travel for women and children at the time. He apparently had enough camels to carry four wives and 11 sons. This caravan of Jacob's family and worldly goods would become very long. Jacob's family, all his personnel, livestock, and other property including livestock he had gathered at Paddam-aram to travel to Canaan again. While Laban has gone to shear his flock, Rachel stole the household idols that were his. As much as we'd like to think that Rachel had reasons stealing these items, they were simply an act of rebellion and revenge again her father. She never told him that he cared more about money than his own family. Jacob never told Laban that they were fleeing. They fled with all they had, crossed the Euphrates River, and aimed toward the hill country of Gilead. This is the first-time Gilead is mentioned in the bible. It is east of the Jordan River now part of Jordan.

[22] When it was told Laban on the third day that Jacob had fled, [23] then he took his kinsmen with him and pursued him a distance of seven days' journey, and he overtook him in the hill country of Gilead. [24] God came to Laban the Aramean in a dream of the night and said to him, "Be careful that you do not speak to Jacob either good or bad."

Laban was not told until the third day that Jacob had fled. It took him seven days until Laban found Jacob in the hill country. Even then God talked in a dream and said, "be careful that you do not speak to Jacob good or bad." Two question unanswerable here---Why did Laban listen to God and what would have happened it Laban spoke and acted badly to Jacob?

25Laban caught up with Jacob. Now Jacob had pitched his tent in the hill country, and Laban with his kinsmen camped in the hill country of Gilead. 26Then Laban said to Jacob, "What have you done by deceiving me and carrying away my daughters like captives of the sword? 27"Why did you flee secretly and deceive me, and did not tell me so that I might have sent you away with joy and with songs, with timbrel and with lyre; 28and did not allow me to kiss my sons and my daughters? Now you have done foolishly. 29"It is in my power to do you harm, but the God of your father spoke to me last night, saying, 'Be careful not to speak either good or bad to Jacob.' 30"Now you have indeed gone away because you longed greatly for your father's house; but why did you steal my gods?" 31Then Jacob replied to Laban, "Because I was afraid, for I thought that you would take your daughters from me by force. 32"The one with whom you find your gods shall not live; in the presence of our kinsmen point out what is yours among my belongings and take it for yourself." For Jacob did not know that Rachel had stolen them.

Laban caught up with Jacob. Jacob had pitched his tent in the hill country where Laban and his kinsmen also camped in the hill country. In spite of God's warning to Laban in a dream not to say anything to Jacob, good or bad, Laban has prepared a speech for his lying, fleeing son-in-law. Now he unleashes it. He begins, ironically, with the same words Jacob said to him on Jacob's wedding night some 13 years earlier: "What have you done?" Laban's first two accusations are that Jacob tricked him in this sudden departure and, worse, that Jacob had carried Laban's two daughters away as if they were captives or prisoners. Laban does not know, yet, that both Rachel and Leah expressed their full support for Jacob's plan to leave Laban and return to his homeland. Now Laban suggests that if Jacob had only told him ahead of time, Laban would have thrown a huge and happy goodbye party with music and laughter and celebration. This is almost certainly false; even if Laban convinced himself that he would have responded in such a way, Jacob would have known better. This comes across as the kind of manipulation Laban was known for. His prior actions certainly don't support a view of Laban as loving and supportive.

The objection from Laban in verse 27-28, however, is at least somewhat more believable. Jacob had left without giving Laban the chance to kiss his daughters and sons—a term including grandsons—farewell, something that would break any father's heart. Laban's daughters did not seem to mind leaving without saying goodbye to their father, but Laban's appeal here is not entirely amiss. Laban concludes by saying that Jacob has done foolishly. One thing that helps Genesis to resonate so deeply is stories like these, in which readers can see the validity of both points of view. Was Jacob wise to run without warning and give Laban no chance to try to manipulate him in some new way? Is Laban right that such action is dishonorable, no matter how dishonorable Laban himself had been?

Laban concludes in verse 29 by saying that it is in his power to do Jacob harm. Perhaps he means that he has the capability to physically harm Jacob and/or take by force from Jacob what he does not wish to release. Or Laban could mean that it would be within his legal rights to restrain Jacob or his wives, children, or belongings as escaped property that rightly belongs to him. Whatever he might mean, he tells Jacob he won't do it. Why? The God of Jacob's father warned him not to say anything good or bad to Jacob (verse 24). The point of that expression is that God does not want Laban to contradict Jacob. By this statement, from Laban, Jacob receives more evidence that God is with him, protecting him, even from his own father-in-law.

Before they part ways, however, Laban has one more accusation for Jacob: Why did you steal my gods (verse 30)? This is a reference to the idols stolen by Rachel (verse 19), an act no one—including Jacob—was aware of at the time. These idols were common in that era, and were probably intended to bring luck or protection to the family. This accusation, far more than the others, carries some legal heft. There is no question that stealing those objects, idols or not, was a theft of something of real value to Laban.

Coming at this point in the story of Genesis, Jacob's point resonates with the reader. We have seen Laban continually cheat, lie, manipulate, and threaten (Genesis 29:20–28; 30:31–36). Legally speaking, in that era, it's also possible that Laban had legal footing to claim that everything belonging to Jacob—who'd lived as an indentured servant for years—was actually Laban's property.

Why did Rachel steal Laban's gods? We're not told exactly. It may be that, in addition to worshiping Jacob's God, Rachel still felt the need to rely on the gods she grew up with for protection and provision. It may be that she felt possessing the idols would give her a stake in the family inheritance. In any case, Jacob is incensed by Laban's unexpected accusation about stealing the gods. The implication is that Jacob was in on the theft; to counter that assumption, Jacob rashly declares the death penalty upon anyone in his company who may be found with the stolen idols. He calls on the gathered relatives of Laban to serve as witnesses to a search by Laban for anything that belongs to him.

[33] So Laban went into Jacob's tent and into Leah's tent and into the tent of the two maids, but he did not find them. Then he went out of Leah's tent and entered Rachel's tent. [34] Now Rachel had taken the household idols and put them in the camel's saddle, and she sat on them. And Laban felt through all the tent but did not find them. [35] She said to her father, "Let not my lord be angry that I cannot rise before you, for the manner of women is upon me." So he searched but did not find the household idols. [36] Then Jacob became angry and contended with Laban; and Jacob said to Laban, "What is my transgression? What is my sin that you have hotly pursued me? [37] "Though you have felt through all my goods, what have you found of all your household goods? Set it here before my kinsmen and your kinsmen, that they may decide between us two. [38] "These twenty years I have been with you; your ewes and your female goats have not miscarried, nor have I eaten the rams of your flocks. [39] "That which was torn of beasts I did not bring to you; I bore the loss of it myself. You required it of my hand whether stolen by day or stolen by night. [40] "Thus I was: by day the heat consumed me and the frost by night, and my sleep fled from my eyes. [41] "These twenty years I have been in your house; I served you fourteen years for your two daughters and six years for your flock, and you changed my wages ten times. [42] "If the God of my father, the God of Abraham, and the fear of Isaac, had not been for me, surely now you would have sent me away empty-handed. God has seen my affliction and the toil of my hands, so He rendered judgment last night."

In verse 33 Jacob allows Laban to search the camp. Due to Rachel's quick thinking, and deception, Laban finds nothing. Rachel placed them in the camel's saddle and was sitting on the saddle. She could not rise because the manner of women is upon me. She is having her period and this would have agreed with the cultural views of her era. Her clothes, and anything she sat on, would have been considered "untouchable" at that time. Laban would not have dared touch her, or her saddle, or have asked her to stand, as a result. Feeling righteously indignant, Jacob finally expresses his fury to Laban, not just about the idol search, but also about twenty years of shabby treatment in spite of Jacob's faithful service. Only God's protection and blessing has kept Jacob from leaving empty-handed to return to his own people (Genesis 31:33–42).

[43] Then Laban replied to Jacob, "The daughters are my daughters, and the children are my children, and the flocks are my flocks, and all that you see is mine. But what can I do this day to these my daughters or to their children whom they have borne? [44] "So now come, let us make a covenant, you and I, and let it be a witness between you and me." [45] Then Jacob took a stone and set it up as a pillar. [46] Jacob said to his kinsmen, "Gather stones." So they took stones and made a heap, and they ate there by the heap. [47] Now Laban called it Jegar-sahadutha, but Jacob called it Galeed. [48] Laban said, "This heap is a witness between you and me this day." Therefore, it was named Galeed, [49] and Mizpah, for he said, "May the LORD watch between you and me when we are absent one from the other. [50] "If you mistreat my daughters, or if you take wives besides my daughters, although no man is with us, see, God is witness between you and me." [51] Laban said to Jacob, "Behold this heap and behold the pillar which I have set between you and me. [52] "This heap is a witness, and the pillar is a witness, that I will not pass by this heap to you for harm, and you will not pass by this heap and this pillar to me, for harm. [53] "The God of Abraham and the God of Nahor, the God of their father, judge between us." So Jacob swore by the fear of his father Isaac. [54] Then Jacob offered a sacrifice on the mountain, and called his kinsmen to the meal; and they ate the meal and spent the night on the mountain. [55] Early in the morning Laban arose, and kissed his sons and his daughters and blessed them. Then Laban departed and returned to his place.

Laban disagrees starting in verse 43. He still believes his daughters and their children and all that Jacob possesses belongs to him. Because Jacob's God has warned Laban, though, Laban won't fight for them. Instead, he offers an alternative both to protect himself in the future and to take control of the situation. He proposes a covenant that both men will swear never to harm the other (Genesis 31:43–50). Jacob agrees. The covenant is made and recognized with the building of a heap of stones, a sacrifice upon an altar, and the sharing of a meal. Finally, Laban rides off and Jacob turns to face his homeland as a free man.

CHAPTER THIRTY TWO

Jacob's Fear of Esau

¹*Now as Jacob went on his way, the angels of God met him. ²Jacob said when he saw them, "This is God's camp." So he named that place Mahanaim. ³Then Jacob sent messengers before him to his brother Esau in the land of Seir, the country of Edom. ⁴He also commanded them saying, "Thus you shall say to my lord Esau: 'Thus says your servant Jacob, "I have sojourned with Laban, and stayed until now; ⁵I have oxen and donkeys and flocks and male and female servants; and I have sent to tell my lord, that I may find favor in your sight."'"*

Angel of God met Jacob as he as walking. When Jacob saw them, he said "This is God camp". So he name that place Mahamaim, east of the Jordan River. We don't know exactly where that is, but it was also mentioned in Song of Solomon 6:13. Jacob sent messengers to his brother, Esau, in in the land of Seir, the country of Edom. He commanded his messages to say to Esau 'Thus says your servant Jacob, "I have sojourned with Laban, and stayed until now (over 20 years). I have oxen and donkeys *and* flocks and male and female servants; and I have sent to tell my lord, that I may find favor in your sight."'

⁶*The messengers returned to Jacob, saying, "We came to your brother Esau, and furthermore he is coming to meet you, and four hundred men are with him." ⁷Then Jacob was greatly afraid and distressed; and he divided the people who were with him, and the flocks and the herds and the camels, into two companies; ⁸for he said, "If Esau comes to the one company and attacks it, then the company which is left will escape."*

The messengers told Jacob when they saw him again and said that Esau is coming to meet him with four hundred men. Jacob was greatly afraid. He divided the people with him plus flocks, herds, and camels into two companies. Why? If Esau attacks with one company, then the other half of Jacob's companies will escape.

9Jacob said, "O God of my father Abraham and God of my father Isaac, O LORD, who said to me, 'Return to your country and to your relatives, and I will prosper you,' 10I am unworthy of all the lovingkindness and of all the faithfulness which You have shown to Your servant; for with my staff only I crossed this Jordan, and now I have become two companies. 11"Deliver me, I pray, from the hand of my brother, from the hand of Esau; for I fear him, that he will come and attack me and the mothers with the children. 12"For You said, 'I will surely prosper you and make your descendants as the sand of the sea, which is too great to be numbered.'"

With all his fear and distress Jacob prayed to God of his grandfather and father. He was reminded that God told him to return to your country and your relatives and God will prosper him so why should he be troubled by Esau and his men? Jacob prayed that he is unworthy of all the lovingkindness and of all the faithfulness God has shown to him. "Deliver me, I pray, from the hand of my brother, from the hand of Esau; for I fear him, that he will come and attack me *and* the mothers with the children. "For You said, 'I will surely prosper you and make your descendants as the sand of the sea, which is too great to be numbered.'" Jacob is both praying for God's protection and planning to give to Esau a huge amount of all his livestock. Jacob's actions are not entirely foolish—in fact, they are sensible—and his attitude is one of *fear*, but not *despair*. It would be fair to say Jacob is doing what he can to avoid a tragedy and relying on God to secure the results. Another possibility is that Jacob truly felt guilt for stealing the blessing from Esau 20 years earlier. That would make the sending of gifts a sincere attempt at making restitution with Esau.

13So he spent the night there. Then he selected from what he had with him a present for his brother Esau: 14two hundred female goats and twenty male goats, two hundred ewes and twenty rams, 15thirty milking camels and their colts, forty cows and ten bulls, twenty female donkeys and ten male donkeys. 16He delivered them into the hand of his servants, every drove by itself, and said to his servants, "Pass on before me, and put a space between droves." 17He commanded the one in front, saying, "When my brother Esau meets you and asks you, saying, 'To whom do you belong, and where are you going, and to whom do these animals in front of you belong?' [18]then you shall say, 'These belong to your servant Jacob; it is a present sent to my lord Esau. And behold, he also is behind us.'" [19]Then he commanded also the second and the third, and all those who followed the droves, saying, "After this manner you shall speak to Esau when you find him; [20]and you shall say, 'Behold, your servant Jacob also is behind us.'" For he said, "I will appease him with the present that goes before me. Then afterward I will see his face; perhaps he will accept me." [21]So the present passed on before him, while he himself spent that night in the camp.

Jacob has prepared to give Esau an enormous number of livestock: two hundred female goats and twenty male goats, two hundred ewes and twenty rams, thirty milking camels and their colts, forty cows and ten bulls, twenty female donkeys and ten male donkeys. He told his servants to pass before him and put a space between the droves of animals. This means that each type of animal--goats, sheep, camels, cows, and donkeys—would be given to Esau separately, impressing upon Esau how magnificent each type of livestock Jacob is given him. Jacob commanded the one in front that when Esau meets you and asks you three questions---To whom to you belong? Where are you going? Whom do these animals in front of you belong? You will say "These belong to your servant Jacob; it is a present sent to my lord Esau and, behold, he also is behind us". It was Jacob's hope that after all the droves of animals given to Esau, he will accept me. Jacob spent the night in the camp while his animals are presented to Esau. He could not sleep very long so he arose in the night and took his two wives and two maids and eleven children and crossed the ford of the Jabbok. Now he arose that same night and took his two wives and his two maids and his eleven children, and crossed the ford of the Jabbok, east of the Jordan River.

[24]Then Jacob was left alone, and a man wrestled with him until daybreak. [25]When he saw that he had not prevailed against him, he touched the socket of his thigh; so the socket of Jacob's thigh was dislocated while he wrestled with him. [26]Then he said, "Let me go, for the dawn is breaking." But he said, "I will not let you go unless you bless me." [27]So he said to him, "What is your name?" And he said, "Jacob." [28]He said, "Your name shall no longer be Jacob,

but Israel; for you have striven with God and with men and have prevailed." 29Then Jacob asked him and said, "Please tell me your name." But he said, "Why is it that you ask my name?" And he blessed him there. 30So Jacob named the place Peniel, for he said, "I have seen God face to face, yet my life has been preserved." 31Now the sun rose upon him just as he crossed over Penuel, and he was limping on his thigh. 32Therefore, to this day the sons of Israel do not eat the sinew of the hip which is on the socket of the thigh, because he touched the socket of Jacob's thigh in the sinew of the hip.

Genesis 32:24-32 describe Jacob wrestling with God. Can you imagine wrestling with God? Scholars debate whether Jacob with God Himself or an angel of God. Nevertheless, a mortal man wrestling with a representative from God, a supernatural being---bizarre image, isn't it?

Jacob wrestling with the Angel
https://commons.wikimedia.org/wiki/File:024.
Jacob_Wrestles_with_the_Angel.jpg

I've always thought that something is missing in this passage because there is no way mortal man can wrestle evenly with a supernatural, omnipotent angel. Obviously, God was not trying to defeat Jacob, but allowing Jacob to spar with Him as Jacob was struggling with many conflicts going on in his life. Even though Jacob had struggled with his relationship with his father-in-law, Laban, and was fearful about his impending struggle with his brother, Esau, Jacob's real struggle was with God. Jacob represents all of us who deal with all kinds of struggles and conflicts in our lives where we might think that these situations are between human beings when in fact they are opportunities for God to get our attention. Examine any conflict that you are struggling with right now---with a spouse, relative, boss, co-worker, neighbor, whoever---and realize that your real struggle is with God. On the surface, it may not be obvious, but be discerning and see what God is trying to do with and through you because of your conflict with another person.

At first read, it does appear that Jacob was wrestling evenly with God's representative. I do question the statement "…the man saw that he could not overpower him (Jacob)", but the man was not trying. Very interestingly, all the man had to do was touch Jacob's hip and the hip was wrenched. God was allowing Jacob to spar with him. Why? Jacob needed the experience of time and an all-night struggle with God to realize that he was not superior to God. All God had to do was to apply one iota of strength via a touch to dislocate his hip. Jacob needed to be exhausted from all his human strength to realize that his relationship with God was superficial and a change was needed. His hip was permanently damaged to remind him of his need for God, to rely on His strength, and to remain committed to God for the rest of his life. Physical defects always are a reminder of a person's need to rely on God's strength, not his/her own.

When God asked Jacob his name, he was testing Jacob's sincerely since the last time Jacob was asked his name (by his father) he answered falsely, "Esau" (Genesis 27:19). This time, after wrestling with God, Jacob was truthful. Thus, God changed Jacob's name to Israel. The name Jacob means "schemer" while the name Israel means "God prevails". The wrestling match with God made Jacob grapple with his faith and come to the point where God provoked Jacob to realize that a change in his life was needed to be a man of true faith, not superficial faith. He was no longer a schemer but a prince of God and through his name and heritage the entire nation of Israel was started. Proverbs 15:33 says that "before honor comes humility". Jacob's wrestling match with God humbled him to the point that he no longer needed to wrestle with God and subsequently God honored him.

Have you wrestled with God? No? What about your life's struggles? Have you not wrestled with God when you've experienced a tragedy, loss, sickness, or any other serious problem/conflict like Jacob was facing? These problems produce struggles with your faith and outlook on your life and consequently you wrestle with God. And what does the wrestling match produce? A renewed faith, a renewed purpose, a stronger sense of the power of God's presence in your life. When Jacob was struggling, God came to him. He has and will come to you too.

CHAPTER THIRTY THREE

Jacob Meets Esau

¹Then Jacob lifted his eyes and looked, and behold, Esau was coming, and four hundred men with him. So he divided the children among Leah and Rachel and the two maids. ²He put the maids and their children in front, and Leah and her children next, and Rachel and Joseph last. ³But he himself passed on ahead of them and bowed down to the ground seven times, until he came near to his brother. So he said, "The children whom God has graciously given your servant." ⁶Then the maids came near with their children, and they bowed down. ⁷Leah likewise came near with her children, and they bowed down; and afterward Joseph came near with Rachel, and they bowed down. ⁸And he said, "What do you mean by all this company which I have met?" And he said, "To find favor in the sight of my lord." ⁹But Esau said, "I have plenty, my brother; let what you have be your own." ¹⁰Jacob said, "No, please, if now I have found favor in your sight, then take my present from my hand, for I see your face as one sees the face of God, and you have received me favorably. ¹¹"Please take my gift which has been brought to you, because God has dealt graciously with me and because I have plenty." Thus he urged him and he took it.

Jacob awoke from his dream and behold he saw Esau coming plus the four hundred men with him. Perhaps bolded by his time with God he divided the children among Leah and Rachel and the two maids with Rachel and Joseph last. Esau passed on ahead of them and bowed to the ground seven times until he came near his brother. Then Esau ran to meet his brother and embraced him, fell on his neck and kissed him and they wept. Esau saw all the children and woman and asked "who are these with you?" Jacob replied that the children who God has graciously given to his servant. Then the maids came near the children and they all bowed down. Leah and her children did the same and then Jacob near Rachel and they bowed down. Esau asked, "What do you mean by all this company I have met?" Jacob's reply, "To find favor in the sight of my lord? But Esau then said, "I have plenty, my brother; let what you have be your own." Jacob replied, "No, please, if now I have found favor in your sight, take my present from my hand, for I see your face as one sees the face of God and you have received me favorably." Jacob again repeated that God has dealt graciously with him, he has plenty, and he wanted Esau to have the gifts of livestock.

12 Then Esau said, "Let us take our journey and go, and I will go before you." 13 But he said to him, "My lord knows that the children are frail and that the flocks and herds which are nursing are a care to me. And if they are driven hard one day, all the flocks will die. 14 "Please let my lord pass on before his servant, and I will proceed at my leisure, according to the pace of the cattle that are before me and according to the pace of the children, until I come to my lord at Seir. 15 Esau said, "Please let me leave with you some of the people who are with me." But he said, "What need is there? Let me find favor in the sight of my lord." 16 So Esau returned that day on his way to Seir. 17 Jacob journeyed to Succoth, and built for himself a house and made booths for his livestock; therefore, the place is named Succoth.

Esau offered to accompany Jacob and family on their way and would take the lead to offer protection. Yet Jacob replied that his children are frail and his livestock is nursing. If they are driving too hard they will die. Esau, please go ahead and we will proceed at our leisure until we meet you at Seir. Seir was a mountainous region stretching between the Dead Sea and the Gulf of Aqaba, between the southeastern border of Edom with Judah. Esau then offer some of his people to remain with Jacob. But Jacob said, "what need is there?" Let me find favor in the sight of my lord (referring to Esau). Esau and his men returned that day on his way to Seir. However, Jacob journey to Succoth and built a house there. Later he moved to Shechem, still east of the Jordan River. We do not know how many years this took. Apparently, Esau was not disappointed yet.

18 Now Jacob came safely to the city of Shechem, which is in the land of Canaan, when he came from Paddan-aram, and camped before the city. 19 He bought the piece of land where he had pitched his tent from the hand of the sons of

Hamor, Shechem's father, for one hundred pieces of money. ²⁰Then he erected there an altar and called it El-Elohe-Israel.

Jacob came safely to city of Shechem, in the land of Canaan. God fulfilled His promised to Jacob. Canaan is a city in the land God promised to Abraham and his sons. He bought land from Hamor, Shechem father, for one hundred pieces of money. This is the first ownership of land in Canaan since Abraham purchased the burial plot for Sarah. If we look ahead to John 4:5-12, Jesus stopped in Shechem and sat by a well. A Samaritan woman approached the well and Jesus asked her for water. The conversation turned to a spiritual chat and the woman asked Jesus if He was greater than our father, Jacob. He elected an altar there and called it El-Elohe-Israel, meaning God, the God of Israel, using his new name from Genesis 32:28.

CHAPTER THIRTY FOUR

The Treachery of Jacob's Sons

¹Now Dinah the daughter of Leah, whom she had borne to Jacob, went out to visit the daughters of the land. ²When Shechem the son of Hamor the Hivite, the prince of the land, saw her, he took her and lay with her by force. ³He was deeply attracted to Dinah the daughter of Jacob, and he loved the girl and spoke tenderly to her. ⁴So Shechem spoke to his father Hamor, saying, "Get me this young girl for a wife." ⁵Now Jacob heard that he had defiled Dinah his daughter; but his sons were with his livestock in the field, so Jacob kept silent until they came in. ⁶Then Hamor the father of Shechem went out to Jacob to speak with him. ⁷Now the sons of Jacob came in from the field when they heard it; and the men were grieved, and they were very angry because he had done a disgraceful thing in Israel by lying with Jacob's daughter, for such a thing ought not to be done.

Leah had one girl, Dinah, who went out to visit the daughters of the land. It is difficult to pin down Dinah's age at this point, but she was probably thirteen or fourteen years old. She was curious enough to leave the safety of the camp and to explore, so it is unlikely that she was still playing with dolls. She was certainly physically mature enough to draw attention from men. When Shechem, the son of Hamor the Hivite, the prince of the land, saw Dinah, he took her and lay with her by force. Suffice it to say that the text is clear: Dinah was raped. She may have sinned by leaving the camp. She may have lusted to see a pagan festival with all its pageantry. She may have even dressed or walked in an inappropriate manner. But the fact remains that she was taken against her will and violated. Shechem as deeply attracted to Dinah and he loved the girl and spoke tenderly to her.

He even wanted to marry her and spoke to his father Hamor about this. Yet, his initial rape of her was heard by her father, Jacob, but his sons were with his livestock in the field so Jacob did nothing. Hamor spoke to Jacob about this. The sons of Jacob came in from the field and heard of Dinah's rape. They were grieved and very angry because Shechem had done such a disgraceful thing. Forcible rape against Dinah ought not to be done.

8But Hamor spoke with them, saying, "The soul of my son Shechem longs for your daughter; please give her to him in marriage. 9"Intermarry with us; give your daughters to us and take our daughters for yourselves. 10"Thus you shall live with us, and the land shall be open before you; live and trade in it and acquire property in it." 11Shechem also said to her father and to her brothers, "If I find favor in your sight, then I will give whatever you say to me. 12"Ask me ever so much bridal payment and gift, and I will give according as you say to me; but give me the girl in marriage."

Hamor in verse 8 intercedes for Shechem, saying that Shechem longs for Dinah, please give Dinah to him in marriage. Hamor is a Canaanite and Canaanites cannot marry Jacob's family who have a covenant with God. Hamor proposed that Jacob's family and his family could exchange daughters in marriage. This would become far more than a marriage between a Canaanite man and Dinah. It would ruin the covenant family who previously made a covenant with God. Hamor and Shechem thought themselves to be generous, but they insulted Dinah's family even more.

13But Jacob's sons answered Shechem and his father Hamor with deceit, because he had defiled Dinah their sister. 14They said to them, "We cannot do this thing, to give our sister to one who is uncircumcised, for that would be a disgrace to us. 15"Only on this condition will we consent to you: if you will become like us, in that every male of you be circumcised, 16then we will give our daughters to you, and we will take your daughters for ourselves, and we will live with you and become one people. 17"But if you will not listen to us to be circumcised, then we will take our daughter and go."

Jacob's sons answered Shechem and Hamor deceitfully because he had defiled Dinah their sister. Jacob's deceitfulness was passed on to his children. It was a deception that would end up being murderous. If every male of you is circumcised, then we will give our daughters to you. Hamor and Shechem agreed to such an extreme demand because circumcision was not *only* practiced among the Israelites, but some other ancient peoples also circumcised their males. Shechem and Hamor knew of the practice from the rituals of other nations. If they refused, then the brothers would take our daughter and go somewhere. Of course, we knew that they would eventually destroy Shechem and Hamor.

[18] Now their words seemed reasonable to Hamor and Shechem, Hamor's son. [19] The young man did not delay to do the thing, because he was delighted with Jacob's daughter. Now he was more respected than all the household of his father. [20] So Hamor and his son Shechem came to the gate of their city and spoke to the men of their city, saying, [21] "These men are friendly with us; therefore, let them live in the land and trade in it, for behold, the land is large enough for them. Let us take their daughters in marriage, and give our daughters to them. [22] "Only on this condition will the men consent to us to live with us, to become one people: that every male among us be circumcised as they are circumcised. [23] "Will not their livestock and their property and all their animals be ours? Only let us consent to them, and they will live with us." [24] All who went out of the gate of his city listened to Hamor and to his son Shechem, and every male was circumcised, all who went out of the gate of his city.

Their words pleased Hamor and Shechem. Beyond the obviously deep attraction Shechem had for Dinah, they were also pleased to begin to marry into a family so large, wealthy, and influential. They were respected by their community so each male agreed to be circumcised. All Jacob's family possession would be theirs. Every male was circumcised. The men of Shechem agreed and all received the painful and potentially dangerous operation of circumcision.

[25] Now it came about on the third day, when they were in pain, that two of Jacob's sons, Simeon and Levi, Dinah's brothers, each took his sword and came upon the city unawares, and killed every male. [26] They killed Hamor and his son Shechem with the edge of the sword, and took Dinah from Shechem's house, and went forth. [27] Jacob's sons came upon the slain and looted the city, because they had defiled their sister. [28] They took their flocks and their herds and their donkeys, and that which was in the city and that which was in the field; [29] and they captured and looted all their wealth and all their little ones and their wives, even all that was in the houses. [30] Then Jacob said to Simeon and Levi, "You have brought trouble on me by making me odious among the inhabitants of the land, among the Canaanites and the Perizzites; and my

men being few in number, they will gather together against me and attack me and I will be destroyed, I and my household." ³¹*But they said, "Should he treat our sister as a harlot?"*

All males of Hamor and Shechem were circumcised and in pain. On the third day of their pain, Simeon and Levi, Dinah's brothers, took his sword, went to the city of the Canaanites and killed every male, including Hamor and Shechem. They brought Dinah home. Other sons came upon the slain and looted the city. What happened to all the women and children? In verse 29 they looted all their wealth and little one and their wives, even all that was in the houses. They were taken as slaves. They took all the flocks and herds and donkeys. Jacob was quite upset over all the trouble they have caused; they have made his family odious among the inhabitants of the land, including the Canaanites and Perizzites. He was not concerned with right and wrong, only that he and his family would be pursued by others. Jacob's men were few in number. They will be attacked and destroyed. Yet Jacob's sons replied, "They treated Dinah as a harlot". Jacob and his family would forever be forsaken by others for all their murders. God's covenant through Jacob and family would never be the same.

CHAPTER THIRTY FIVE

Jacob Moves to Bethel

¹Then God said to Jacob, "Arise, go up to Bethel and live there, and make an altar there to God, who appeared to you when you fled from your brother Esau." ²So Jacob said to his household and to all who were with him, "Put away the foreign gods which are among you, and purify yourselves and change your garments; ³and let us arise and go up to Bethel, and I will make an altar there to God, who answered me in the day of my distress and has been with me wherever I have gone." ⁴So they gave to Jacob all the foreign gods which they had and the rings which were in their ears, and Jacob hid them under the oak which was near Shechem.

Despite the horror of Jacob's sons, God told Jacob to move to Bethel and live there and make an alter there to God, who appeared to Jacob when he fled from brother Esau. Bethel was first mentioned in Genesis 12 and 13 as a place near where Abram stayed and built an altar on his way to Egypt and on his return. More famously it is mentioned again in Genesis 28 when Jacob, fleeing from the wrath of his brother Esau, falls asleep on a stone and dreams of a ladder stretching between Heaven and Earth and thronged with angels; God stands at the top of the ladder, and promises Jacob the land of Canaan; when Jacob awakes he anoints the stone with oil and names the place Bethel. Another account, here in Genesis 35:1 repeats the covenant with God and the naming of the place (as El-Bethel), and makes this the site of Jacob's own change of name to Israel. Jacob told his household and all who were with him, "Put away the foreign gods among you, purity yourselves and change your garments, let us arise and go up to Bethel. I will make an altar there to God who answered me in the day of my distress and has been with me wherever I have gone." They gave to Jacob all the foreign gods they had and the rings in their ears and Jacob hid them under the oak which was near Shechem. It had been thirty years since Jacob vowed to return to Bethel, including ten years after Jacob built a place in Succoth. Bethel was only thirty miles north of Shechem. Why was God silent for so many years? Jacob was not listening to God.

⁵As they journeyed, there was a great terror upon the cities which were around them, and they did not pursue the sons of Jacob. ⁶So Jacob came to Luz (that is, Bethel), which is in the land of Canaan, he and all the people who were with him. ⁷He built an altar there, and called the place El-bethel, because there God had revealed Himself to him when he fled from his brother. ⁸Now Deborah, Rebekah's nurse, died, and she was buried below Bethel under the oak; it was named Allon-bacuth.

As Jacob and family moved some 30 miles northward, there was great terror upon the cities around them. No one pursued the sons of Jacob. Why? Because God put great terror in others. People were convinced of the fierceness of Jacob's sons and God power behind them. In obedience to the command of God, Jacob finally returned to Bethel, and there he built an altar, calling the place El-Bethel, for the God of Bethel had revealed Himself there. It was here at Bethel that Deborah, Rebekah's maid, died. We are not told why or when she came to stay with Jacob. It is possible that she came bearing the news of Rebekah's death and then stayed on with Jacob. No doubt Deborah was one to whom Jacob felt very attached, especially if he knew that his mother had died.

⁹Then God appeared to Jacob again when he came from Paddan-aram, and He blessed him. ¹⁰God said to him,
"Your name is Jacob;
You shall no longer be called Jacob,
But Israel shall be your name."
Thus He called him Israel.
¹¹God also said to him,
"I am God Almighty;
Be fruitful and multiply;
A nation and a company of nations shall come from you,
And kings shall come forth from you.

*¹²"The land which I gave to Abraham and Isaac,
I will give it to you,
And I will give the land to your descendants after you."*

¹³Then God went up from him in the place where He had spoken with him. ¹⁴Jacob set up a pillar in the place where He had spoken with him, a pillar of stone, and he poured out a drink offering on it; he also poured oil on it. ¹⁵So Jacob named the place where God had spoken with him, Bethel.

Verse 9 is unusual in that it almost seems to overlook the time which lapsed between Jacob's departure from Paddan-aram (where Abraham and his father Terah settled after leaving Ur of the Chaldees, Abraham's brother Nahor settled in the area. Abraham sent his steward, back there to find a wife among his kinfolk for his son, Isaac. The steward found Rebecca and his going up to Bethel. Verse 9 brushes aside ten years as though they did not exist. Whenever the people of God choose to go their way, they must always return to the point where they departed from the revealed will of God. While it should have taken Jacob only days to get from Paddan-aram, it took ten years. No real growth or progress in Jacob's spiritual life could take place until he returned to Bethel. The blessings spoken by God are remarkably similar to those given to Abraham back in Genesis 17:4-7. Virtually nothing new was promised Jacob here, and the former promises given to him at Bethel 30 years before were simply reiterated. God visibly ascended before Jacob's eyes from the place where He had spoken (verse 13). Jacob set up a pillar there and poured oil and wine upon it (verse 14). Again, Jacob gave this place, which was presently known as Luz, the name Bethel (verse 6). Once the Israelites possessed this land, it would become known by the name which Jacob had given it. For Jacob, this event served as a rededication to the God Who had set His love on Him in eternity past and Who had sought him out thirty years before when he was fleeing from Esau. For the sons of Jacob and all those who were in his household, this may have been the first clear evidence and explanation of the faith which he possessed but so poorly practiced before them. Soon they must take up the torch of faith, and the purposes of God will be carried on through them. The faith of Jacob must become the faith of his children.

¹⁶Then they journeyed from Bethel; and when there was still some distance to go to Ephrath, Rachel began to give birth and she suffered severe labor. ¹⁷When she was in severe labor the midwife said to her, "Do not fear, for now you have another son." ¹⁸It came about as her soul was departing (for she died), that she named him Ben-oni; but his father called him Benjamin. ¹⁹So Rachel died and was buried on the way to Ephrath (that is, Bethlehem). ²⁰Jacob set up a pillar over her grave; that is the pillar of Rachel's grave to this day. ²¹Then Israel journeyed on and pitched his tent beyond the tower of Eder.

Rachel gave birth to another son, Benjamin. Yet she died as a result of the birth. She was buried on the way to Ephrath, today it is Bethlehem. Jacob set a pillar over her grave, still the pillar to this day. Israel journeyed on and pitched his tent beyond the tower of Eder.

²²It came about while Israel was dwelling in that land, that Reuben went and lay with Bilhah his father's concubine, and Israel heard of it.

Reuben was the oldest child of Jacob. Yet while they were dwelling in that land (near Bethlehem) Reuben went and lay with Bilhah his father's concubine and mother of Dan and Napthtali. Jacob heard of it. Eventually Jacob will take away the rights of the firstborn (Genesis 49:34). It appears that this act is not described in terms of lust or sexual desire, such as the incident with Shechem and Dinah. Bilhah was much older and no mention of her attractiveness. Why did Reuben react with Bilhah this way?

Now there were twelve sons of Jacob— ²³the sons of Leah: Reuben, Jacob's firstborn, then Simeon and Levi and Judah and Issachar and Zebulun; ²⁴the sons of Rachel: Joseph and Benjamin; ²⁵and the sons of Bilhah, Rachel's maid: Dan and Naphtali; ²⁶and the sons of Zilpah, Leah's maid: Gad and Asher. These are the sons of Jacob who were born to him in Paddan-aram. ²⁷Jacob came to his father Isaac at Mamre of Kiriath-arba (that is, Hebron), where Abraham and Isaac had sojourned. ²⁸Now the days of Isaac were one hundred and eighty years. ²⁹Isaac breathed his last and died and was gathered to his people, an old man of ripe age; and his sons Esau and Jacob buried him.

We know about Jacob's twelve sons plus a daughter. They are listed again in Genesis 35:23-26. All born in Paddan-aram in Mesopotamia. Then Jacob came to his father Isaac in Hebron with both Abraham and Isaac had sojourned. Perhaps the most difficult thing in the world for Jacob to do was to stand before his father, whom he had deceived in order to obtain the blessing. Jacob's reluctance to return to Bethel and to his father came from his sense of guilt and shame. But reconciliation with God and the renewal at Bethel necessitated the reconciliation described in verses 27-29. Had the tragedy of Dinah or the slaughter of the Shechemites not occurred, Jacob likely would have become a Canaanite. We need problems and challenges in our lives to help us overcome them. We can never resist what God eventually needs us to do.

CHAPTER THIRTY SIX

Esau Moves

¹*Now these are the records of the generations of Esau (that is, Edom). ²Esau took his wives from the daughters of Canaan: Adah the daughter of Elon the Hittite, and Oholibamah the daughter of Anah and the granddaughter of Zibeon the Hivite; ³also Basemath, Ishmael's daughter, the sister of Nebaioth. ⁴Adah bore Eliphaz to Esau, and Basemath bore Reuel, ⁵and Oholibamah bore Jeush and Jalam and Korah. These are the sons of Esau who were born to him in the land of Canaan.*

Chapter 36 of Genesis focuses on the family of Esau, Jacob's twin brother. His wives were from Canaan that caused much grief to Isaac and Rebekah (Genesis 26:24-35). He had three wives, Adah, daughter of Elon the Hittite (also called Basemath in Genesis 26:34), Oholibamah, daughter of Anah (Hivite family and called Judith in Genesis 26:34), and Basemath, daughter of Ishmael (also called Mahalath in Genesis 28:9). We are told about the sons of Esau. Adah bore Eliphaz to Esau, Basemath bore Reuel, and Oholibamah bore Jeush, Jalam and Korah. These were the five sons of Esau, who were born to him in Canaan. It is ironic that Esau's sons were born in the Promised Land, and except for Benjamin, Jacob's sons were born outside the Land. Also, one of Esau's wives, Basemath, was a daughter of Ishmael. Thus, a direct link between the Ishmaelites (the unfavored son of Abraham) and the Edomites (the unfavored son of Isaac) was formed.

⁶*Then Esau took his wives and his sons and his daughters and all his household, and his livestock and all his cattle and all his goods which he had acquired in*

the land of Canaan, and went to another land away from his brother Jacob. ⁷For their property had become too great for them to live together, and the land where they sojourned could not sustain them because of their livestock. ⁸So Esau lived in the hill country of Seir; Esau is Edom.

Esau took his blessing that he had received from Isaac (27:39-40), his wives and sons and an untold number of daughters and all the members of his household, as well as his livestock and all his other animals and all the goods he had acquired in Canaan, and moved to a land some distance from his brother Jacob (36:6). He moved southward into the mountainous regions southwest of the Dead Sea. Their possessions were too great for them to remain together; the land where they were staying could not support them both because of their livestock (36:7). This is the same issue that separated Abraham and Lot (13:6). There was obviously plenty of land in Canaan, but the problem was that Canaan was comprised of city states. Each city state held a large amount of land around it, so actual neutral space open for grazing was very small. Esau, who became Edom, settled in the hill country of Seir (36:8). Although Esau is outside the covenant promise of God, he is blessed by his children (36:4 5) and his prosperity (36:6-7).

⁹These then are the records of the generations of Esau the father of the Edomites in the hill country of Seir. ¹⁰These are the names of Esau's sons: Eliphaz the son of Esau's wife Adah, Reuel the son of Esau's wife Basemath. ¹¹The sons of Eliphaz were Teman, Omar, Zepho and Gatam and Kenaz. ¹²Timna was a concubine of Esau's son Eliphaz and she bore Amalek to Eliphaz. These are the sons of Esau's wife Adah. ¹³These are the sons of Reuel: Nahath and Zerah, Shammah and Mizzah. These were the sons of Esau's wife Basemath. ¹⁴These were the sons of Esau's wife Oholibamah, the daughter of Anah and the granddaughter of Zibeon: she bore to Esau, Jeush and Jalam and Korah.

Verses 9-14 of Genesis give an overview of Esau's sons. Verses 15-19 tell of the chiefs of the sons of Esau. Verses 20-30 provide the genealogy of the sons of Seir, verses 31-39 describe the kings of Edom and verses 40-43 give the chiefs of Esau. In verse 12 Timna was a concubine of Esau's son Eliphaz and she bore Amalek to Eliphaz. Later Amalek became the father of the Amalekites who were recurrent enemies of the Israelites. They lived in the Negev along the fringes of the southern Canaan. They are mentioned as

Israel's enemy in Exodus 17:8-16 where Moses need to keep in hands lifted for the Israelites to keep winning.

15 These are the chiefs of the sons of Esau. The sons of Eliphaz, the firstborn of Esau, are chief Teman, chief Omar, chief Zepho, chief Kenaz, 16 chief Korah, chief Gatam, chief Amalek. These are the chiefs descended from Eliphaz in the land of Edom; these are the sons of Adah. 17 These are the sons of Reuel, Esau's son: chief Nahath, chief Zerah, chief Shammah, chief Mizzah. These are the chiefs descended from Reuel in the land of Edom; these are the sons of Esau's wife Basemath. 18 These are the sons of Esau's wife Oholibamah: chief Jeush, chief Jalam, chief Korah. These are the chiefs descended from Esau's wife Oholibamah, the daughter of Anah. 19 These are the sons of Esau (that is, Edom), and these are their chiefs.

Chiefs (verses 15-19) were "leader of a thousand" or "the leader of a large group." What we see here are the prominent descendants of Esau. The people of their tribes would be called after their name. This first list contains those who descend from Esau's firstborn son Eliphaz by his wife Adah. This second list is given to show the link of Esau's son Reuel by his wife Basemath. And this third list is given for the chiefs who came from Esau's wife Aholibamah. Interestingly, God had these names recorded and preserved not through Esau and his descendants, but through the people of Israel. In other words, God felt the list was so important that He had it kept by His chosen and specially loved people.

20 These are the sons of Seir the Horite, the inhabitants of the land: Lotan and Shobal and Zibeon and Anah, 21 and Dishon and Ezer and Dishan. These are the chiefs descended from the Horites, the sons of Seir in the land of Edom. 22 The sons of Lotan were Hori and Hemam; and Lotan's sister was Timna. 23 These are the sons of Shobal: Alvan and Manahath and Ebal, Shepho and Onam. 24 These are the sons of Zibeon: Aiah and Anah—he is the Anah who found the hot springs in the wilderness when he was pasturing the donkeys of his father Zibeon.25 These are the children of Anah: Dishon, and Oholibamah, the daughter of Anah.26 These are the sons of Dishon: Hemdan and Eshban and Ithran and Cheran.27 These are the sons of Ezer: Bilhan and Zaavan and Akan. 28 These are the sons of Dishan: Uz and Aran. 29 These are the chiefs descended from the Horites: chief Lotan, chief Shobal, chief Zibeon, chief Anah, 30 chief Dishon, chief Ezer, chief Dishan. These are the chiefs descended from the Horites, according to their various chiefs in the land of Seir. ³¹ Now these are the kings who reigned in the land of Edom before any king reigned over the sons of Israel. ³² Bela the son of Beor reigned in Edom, and the name of his city was Dinhabah. ³³ Then Bela died, and Jobab the son of Zerah of Bozrah became king in his place. ³⁴ Then Jobab died, and Husham of the land of the Temanites became king in his place. ³⁵ Then Husham died, and Hadad the son of Bedad, who defeated Midian in the field of Moab, became king in his place; and the name of his city was Avith. ³⁶ Then Hadad died, and Samlah of Masrekah became king in his place. ³⁷ Then Samlah died, and Shaul of Rehoboth on the Euphrates River became king in his place. ³⁸ Then Shaul died, and Baal-hanan the son of Achbor became king in his place. ³⁹ Then Baal-hanan the son of Achbor died, and Hadar became king in his place; and the name of his city was Pau; and his wife's name was Mehetabel, the daughter of Matred, daughter of Mezahab. ⁴⁰ Now these are the names of the chiefs descended from Esau, according to their families and their localities, by their names: chief Timna, chief Alvah, chief Jetheth, ⁴¹ chief Oholibamah, chief Elah, chief Pinon, ⁴² chief Kenaz, chief Teman, chief Mibzar, ⁴³ chief Magdiel, chief Iram. These are the chiefs of Edom (that is, Esau, the father of the Edomites), according to their habitations in the land of their possession.

Verses 20-43 relate to the sons of Seir. This group of people, the sons of Seir, is surely being introduced for three reasons. The first is to show who the land belonged to prior to Esau taking it over, and thus where the name came from. Secondly, it's used to show the merging of the Edomites with these people. They intermarried to some extent and eventually, the Edomites dispossessed and destroyed the Horite people. And finally, they are detailed to show us the state of man and his circumstances in a world where we have a conscience about God. The man named Seir is said to be a Horite. The Horite was first introduced in chapter 14 at the times that the kings of the east came and attacked the land of Canaan. The name "Horite" means a troglodyte; a cave dweller. There in the land of awareness, they lived in caves. Throughout the Bible, caves are places where people go to hide away or to secret something away. Lot was afraid of living in Zoar and so he and his daughters moved to a cave. God cares about all these Edomite people, sons of Seir. If you sometimes feel as if God is unconcerned about you, all you need to do is come to a long and meticulous list like Genesis 36 to see that He cares for you and He willing to go to extraordinary steps to call you His own. One lesson that we can take home from all of this is that although the line of promise, from Adam, through Abraham, Isaac, and Jacob is highlighted, God has still watched over the other people of the world in the process. None are lost to Him. Every son of Adam, pictured by the people of Edom, is named and remembered. The details of their lives are known to God. These lists are written and recorded to show that the promises that were made to Esau were fulfilled exactly as they were given.

CHAPTER THIRTY SEVEN

Joseph's Dream

¹Now Jacob lived in the land where his father had sojourned, in the land of Canaan. ²These are the records of the generations of Jacob. Joseph, when seventeen years of age, was pasturing the flock with his brothers while he was still a youth, along with the sons of Bilhah and the sons of Zilpah, his father's wives. And Joseph brought back a bad report about them to their father. ³Now Israel loved Joseph more than all his sons, because he was the son of his old age; and he made him a varicolored tunic. ⁴His brothers saw that their father loved him more than all his brothers; and so they hated him and could not speak to him on friendly terms.

The story of Joseph began in Genesis 37. Jacob lived in the land of Canaan where his father had sojourned. The following are the records of the generations of Jacob. Joseph was seventeen and was pasturing the flock with his brothers as a youth, along with the sons of Bilhah and the sons of Zilpah, his father's wives. Joseph brought bad a bad report about them to his father. What was the bad report? Perhaps how they were dealing with the flock. Jacob loved Joseph more than all his sons because he was the son of his old age. He made Joseph a varicolored (ornate or striped) tunic. His brothers saw that their father loved him more than any other son They hated him and could not speak to him on friendly terms. Another biblical example where no parent should love one child over any other children.

⁵Then Joseph had a dream, and when he told it to his brothers, they hated him even more. ⁶He said to them, "Please listen to this dream which I have had; ⁷for behold, we were binding sheaves in the field, and lo, my sheaf rose up and also stood erect; and behold, your sheaves gathered around and bowed down to my sheaf." ⁸*Then his brothers said to him, "Are you actually going to reign over us? Or are you really going to rule over us?" So they hated him even more for his dreams and for his words.*

Joseph had a dream and then told his brothers (he should not have done this). They hated him even more. He told them about his dream. They were all binding sheaves in the field. His sheaf arose and stood erect while his brothers sheaves gathered around and bowed to Joseph's sheaf. Their response was direct, "are you actually going to reign over us? Are you going to rule over us"? They hated him even more for his dreams and his words.

⁹*Now he had still another dream, and related it to his brothers, and said, "Lo, I have had still another dream; and behold, the sun and the moon and eleven stars were bowing down to me."* ¹⁰*He related it to his father and to his brothers; and his father rebuked him and said to him, "What is this dream that you have had? Shall I and your mother and your brothers actually come to bow ourselves down before you to the ground?"* ¹¹*His brothers were jealous of him, but his father kept the saying in mind.*

Joseph did not stop with one dream. He had a second dream and again told his brothers. "Lo, I have had another dream and behold, the sun and moon and eleven stars were bowing down to him". The eleven stars were his eleven brothers. He related his dream to Jacob and his brothers and his father rebuked him. Jacob did not like his dreaming and how it implicated his father and his brothers. Jacob said that they would not bow themselves before him to the ground. His brothers were jealous of him, but his father kept that saying in mind. Jacob did not understand the dream, but did not forget about it.

¹²*Then his brothers went to pasture their father's flock in Shechem.* ¹³*Israel said to Joseph, "Are not your brothers pasturing the flock in Shechem? Come, and I will send you to them." And he said to him, "I will go."* ¹⁴*Then he said to him, "Go now and see about the welfare of your brothers and the welfare of the flock, and bring word back to me." So he sent him from the valley of Hebron, and he came to Shechem.*

The Book of Genesis

The brothers went out to pasture their father's flock in Shechem. Israel (Jacob) ask Joseph why he was not pasturing the flock with them? Israel asked him to go out with them. Joseph said that he would go. Israel asked Joseph to see about the welfare of the brothers and the welfare of the flock and report back to Israel. Did not father or son see the danger that was coming? Joseph had to walk about sixty miles from Hebron to Shechem.

¹⁵A man found him, and behold, he was wandering in the field; and the man asked him, "What are you looking for?" ¹⁶He said, "I am looking for my brothers; please tell me where they are pasturing the flock." ¹⁷Then the man said, "They have moved from here; for I heard them say, 'Let us go to Dothan.'" So Joseph went after his brothers and found them at Dothan.

A man found him wandering in the field; Joseph was lost. The man asked who he was looking for. Joseph replied that he was looking for his brothers, where are they? The man replied that they had moved from here for he heard them say, "Let us go to Dotham". Dotham was over sixty miles from Shechem. So Joseph walked another sixty miles to find them.

¹⁸When they saw him from a distance and before he came close to them, they plotted against him to put him to death. ¹⁹They said to one another, "Here comes this dreamer! ²⁰"Now then, come and let us kill him and throw him into one of the pits; and we will say, 'A wild beast devoured him.' Then let us see what will become of his dreams!" ²¹But Reuben heard this and rescued him out of their hands and said, "Let us not take his life." ²²Reuben further said to them, "Shed no blood. Throw him into this pit that is in the wilderness, but do not lay hands on him"—that he might rescue him out of their hands, to restore him to his father. ²³So it came about, when Joseph reached his brothers, that they stripped Joseph of his tunic, the varicolored tunic that was on him; ²⁴and they took him and threw him into the pit. Now the pit was empty, without any water in it.

When his brothers saw him walking from a distance they plotted how to kill him. They called Joseph "this dreamer". They decided to kill him and throw him into one of the pits. They will tell their father that a wild beast devoured him. So long to his dreams. But the oldest son, Reuben, did not want them to kill Joseph even though he was angry with Joseph as the other brothers. Reuben said "let us not take his life, shed no blood. Throw him into a pit in the wilderness, but do not lay hands on him". It is viewed that Reuben intended later to rescue Joseph and restore him to Jacob. When Joseph reached his brothers, they grabbed him, took off his varicolored tunic that was on him and threw him into the pit. The pit was empty including no water. They intended to starve/dehydrate him to death. Think how awful Joseph felt about all this.

[25] Then they sat down to eat a meal. And as they raised their eyes and looked, behold, a caravan of Ishmaelites was coming from Gilead, with their camels bearing aromatic gum and balm and myrrh, on their way to bring them down to Egypt. [26] Judah said to his brothers, "What profit is it for us to kill our brother and cover up his blood? [27] "Come and let us sell him to the Ishmaelites and not lay our hands on him, for he is our brother, our own flesh." And his brothers listened to him. [28] Then some Midianite traders passed by, so they pulled him up and lifted Joseph out of the pit, and sold him to the Ishmaelites for twenty shekels of silver. Thus they brought Joseph into Egypt.

While Joseph was in a pit, likely to die there, his brothers sat down to eat a meal. Very cruel and heartless. But as they were eating they saw a caravan of Ishmaelites coming from Gilead. Remember that the Ishmaelites were from the great uncle of these sons. Judah said to his brothers "why kill our brother and cover up his blood (even if he starved). Let's sell Joseph to the Ismaelites and make some money from him." Again, how heartless are they? They pulled up him from the pit and sold him to the Ismaelities for twenty shekels of silver. They chose to give him up for slavery for the rest of his life……or so they thought.

[29] Now Reuben returned to the pit, and behold, Joseph was not in the pit; so he tore his garments. [30] He returned to his brothers and said, "The boy is not there; as for me, where am I to go?" [31] So they took Joseph's tunic, and slaughtered a male goat and dipped the tunic in the blood; [32] and they sent the varicolored tunic and brought it to their father and said, "We found this; please examine it to see whether it is your son's tunic or not." [33] Then he examined it and said, "It is my son's tunic. A wild beast has devoured him; Joseph has surely been torn to pieces!" [34] So Jacob tore his clothes, and put sackcloth on his loins and mourned for his son many days. [35] Then all his sons and all his daughters arose to comfort him, but he refused to be comforted. And he said, "Surely I will go down to Sheol in mourning for my son." So his father wept for him. [36] Meanwhile, the Midianites sold him in Egypt to Potiphar, Pharaoh's officer, the captain of the bodyguard.

Apparently, Reuben was not around when they sold Joseph and was horrified when he found out. Most scholars believe that he returned to rescue Joseph from the pit. He tore his garments, a show of public and powerful expression of grief in ancient times. He returned to his brothers and asked "where am I to go?" Where can he go to find Joseph? He does not know what he can do. The brothers took Joseph's tunic and slaughtered a male goat. The blood on the coat would make it appear that wild animals ravaged and devoured Joseph. Jacob replied that it was Joseph's tunic and a wild best had devoured him. Jacob, like Reuben before, tore his clothes and put sackcloth on his loins and mourned Joseph for many days. Again, how cruel of these sons to slave Joseph and to lie about it. How cruel to see their family anguish over Joseph and none come forth and explain to Jacob. All is sons and daughters arose to comfort him, but he refused to be comforted. Jacob said that he would enter Sheol (permanent place of the dead) mourning for his son. He wept a long time. Meanwhile, the Midianites sold Joseph to Potiphar, Pharaoh officer, the captain of the bodyguard. Egypt was a large and thriving kingdom for over 1000 years before Joseph came. They were wealthy and had massive resources. God did not leave Joseph or Jacob although it took a while for them to notice this.

CHAPTER THIRTY EIGHT

Judah and Tamar

¹And it came about at that time, that Judah departed from his brothers and visited a certain Adullamite, whose name was Hirah. ²Judah saw there a daughter of a certain Canaanite whose name was Shua; and he took her and went in to her. ³So she conceived and bore a son and he named him Er. ⁴Then she conceived again and bore a son and named him Onan. ⁵She bore still another son and named him Shelah; and it was at Chezib that she bore him.

We turn to the fourth son of Jacob, Judah, in Genesis 38. It is Judah who was in the lineage to Jesus Christ. Judah visited a Adullamite (Canaan), a man whose name was Hirah. He then saw a daughter of a Canaanite whose name as Shua and he had sex with her (we don't know the mother of this woman). His first son was Er, then she also bore Onan and Shelah, born in a place called Chezib.

⁶Now Judah took a wife for Er his firstborn, and her name was Tamar. ⁷But Er, Judah's firstborn, was evil in the sight of the LORD, so the LORD took his life. ⁸Then Judah said to Onan, "Go in to your brother's wife, and perform your duty as a brother-in-law to her, and raise up offspring for your brother." ⁹Onan knew that the offspring would not be his; so when he went in to his brother's wife, he wasted his seed on the ground in order not to give offspring to his brother. ¹⁰But what he did was displeasing in the sight of the LORD; so He took his life also. ¹¹Then Judah said to his daughter-in-law Tamar, "Remain a widow in your father's house until my son Shelah grows up"; for he thought, "I am afraid that he too may die like his brothers." So Tamar went and lived in her father's house.

Then Judah took a wife for Er his firstborn and her name was Tamar. Er was so evil in the sight of the Lord that the Lord took his life. His sins were not mentioned, but he must have done something quite heinous to the Lord. Judah said to Oran, "go into your brother's wife and perform your duty as a brother-in-law to her and raise the offspring for your brother". In those days if a brother died, the younger brother was to marry his widow and carry on as the husband. Yet Onan masturbated rather than having sex with Er's wife. This was displeasing in the sight of the Lord and his life was taken too. Again, we do not know how he passed away. Then Judah said to Tamar, the daughter-in-law of Er, remain a widow in your father's house until the third son, Shelah, grew up. Judah was afraid that Shelah might also die like his brothers. Tamar then lived in her father's house.

¹²Now after a considerable time Shua's daughter, the wife of Judah, died; and when the time of mourning was ended, Judah went up to his sheepshearers at Timnah, he and his friend Hirah the Adullamite. ¹³It was told to Tamar, "Behold, your father-in-law is going up to Timnah to shear his sheep." ¹⁴So she removed her widow's garments and covered herself with a veil, and wrapped herself, and sat in the gateway of Enaim, which is on the road to Timnah; for she saw that Shelah had grown up, and she had not been given to him as a wife. ¹⁵When Judah saw her, he thought she was a harlot, for she had covered her face. ¹⁶So he turned aside to her by the road, and said, "Here now, let me come in to you"; for he did not know that she was his daughter-in-law. And she said, "What will you give me, that you may come in to me?" ¹⁷He said, therefore, "I will send you a young goat from the flock." She said, moreover, "Will you give a pledge until you send it?" ¹⁸He said, "What pledge shall I give you?" And she said, "Your seal and your cord, and your staff that is in your hand." So he gave them to her and went in to her, and she conceived by him. ¹⁹Then she arose and departed, and removed her veil and put on her widow's garments.

Shua's daughter, the wife of Judah, died. When the time of mourning ended, Judah when to his sheepshearers at Timnah (a Philistine city in Canaan), both he and his friend Hirah the Adullamite. Tamar was told that her father-in-law was going to Timnah to shear his sheep. Tamar removed her widow's garments and covered herself with a veil, wrapped herself and sat at the gateway of Enaim, on the road to Timnah. She saw that Shelah has grown up and she has not been given to him as a wife.

Tamar dressed herself as a prostitute since she had not been given to any other man. Her main purpose was to reproach her father-in-law with fraud by which he has deceived her. She committed an atrocious crime with Judah. Judah thought that she was a harlot for she had covered her face. So he turned to her by the road and expressed that he wished to have sex with her. He did not know that she was Tamar at the time. She asked what will he give to here to have sex with her? He replied, "I will send you a young goat from the flock". She asked, "will you give me a pledge until you send it?" He replied, "what pledge shall I give you". She replied, "your seal and your cord and the staff that is in your hand. He did this, had sex, and she became pregnant by Judah, her father-in-law. She arose and departed and then removed her veil and put on her widow's garments.

[20]When Judah sent the young goat by his friend the Adullamite, to receive the pledge from the woman's hand, he did not find her. [21]He asked the men of her place, saying, "Where is the temple prostitute who was by the road at Enaim?" But they said, "There has been no temple prostitute here." [22]So he returned to Judah, and said, "I did not find her; and furthermore, the men of the place said, 'There has been no temple prostitute here.'" [23]Then Judah said, "Let her keep them, otherwise we will become a laughingstock. After all, I sent this young goat, but you did not find her."

Genesis 38:20-23 basically says that Judah's friend the Adullamite could not find Tamar. No one had seen Tamar as a prostitute; they did not know her. The Adullamite returned to Judah and reported that no one has seem this prostitute. Then Judah said, "Let them keep the goat and his belongings or else we would become a laughingstock. Judah young goat was not procured by Tamar.

[24]Now it was about three months later that Judah was informed, "Your daughter-in-law Tamar has played the harlot, and behold, she is also with child by harlotry." Then Judah said, "Bring her out and let her be burned!" [25]It was while she was being brought out that she sent to her father-in-law, saying, "I am with child by the man to whom these things belong." And she said, "Please examine and see, whose signet ring and cords and staff are these?" [26]Judah recognized them, and said, "She is more righteous than I, inasmuch as I did not give her to my son Shelah." And he did not have relations with her again.

Judah was informed three months later that his daughter-in-law Tamar had played harlot and she was pregnant by harlotry. Judah said that she should be brought out and let her be burned. Tamar had behaved immorally. Someone who knew her well had informed Judah. Her sin had to be dealt with and Judah decided that she had to be burned. Later it was described in Leviticus 21:9, "Also the daughter of any priest, if she profanes herself by harlotry, she profanes her father; she shall be burned with fire." Judah was very harsh about her, potential wife of his third son, Shelah, that she had to be burned. Yet Tamar said "I am with child by the man to whom these things belong, then she showed the signet ring and cords and staff of Judah". Judah recognized these things as his. Judah replied, "She is more righteous than I since he took her for himself rather than give her to his son Shelah". He did not have relations with her again.

[27]It came about at the time she was giving birth, that behold, there were twins in her womb. [28]Moreover, it took place while she was giving birth, one put out a hand, and the midwife took and tied a scarlet thread on his hand, saying, "This one came out first." [29]But it came about as he drew back his hand, that behold, his brother came out. Then she said, "What a breach you have made for yourself!" So he was named Perez. [30]Afterward his brother came out who had the scarlet thread on his hand; and he was named Zerah.

When Tamar was about to give birth, there were twins in her womb. Her twins were named Perez and Zerah. Perez was listed in Ruth as part of the lineage of King David and, eventually, Jesus Christ (Matthew 1:3). It is incredible that Judah and Tamar, despite their sins, are listed as directed descendants of David and Jesus.

CHAPTER THIRTY NINE

Joseph's Success in Egypt

¹*Now Joseph had been taken down to Egypt; and Potiphar, an Egyptian officer of Pharaoh, the captain of the bodyguard, bought him from the Ishmaelites, who had taken him down there.* ²*The LORD was with Joseph, so he became a successful man. And he was in the house of his master, the Egyptian.* ³*Now his master saw that the LORD was with him and how the LORD caused all that he did to prosper in his hand.* ⁴*So Joseph found favor in his sight and became his personal servant; and he made him overseer over his house, and all that he owned he put in his charge.* ⁵*It came about that from the time he made him overseer in his house and over all that he owned, the LORD blessed the Egyptian's house on account of Joseph; thus the LORD'S blessing was upon all that he owned, in the house and in the field.* ⁶*So he left everything he owned in Joseph's charge; and with him there he did not concern himself with anything except the food which he ate.*

Started in Genesis 39, the rest of Genesis (chapters 39-50) focus on the life of Joseph. Joseph lived the rest of his life like Jesus did. The Lord was with Joseph, so he became a successful man. And he was in the house of his master, the Egyptian. Now his master saw that the Lord was with him and *how* the Lord caused all that he did to prosper in his hand. Joseph found favor in his sight and became his personal servant; and he made him overseer over his house, and all that he owned he put in his charge. It came about that from the time he made him overseer in his house and over all that he owned, the Lord blessed the Egyptian's house on account of Joseph; thus the Lord's blessing was upon all that he owned, in the house and in the field. So he left everything he owned in Joseph's charge;

and with him *there* he did not concern himself with anything except the food which he ate.

Now Joseph was handsome in form and appearance. ⁷It came about after these events that his master's wife looked with desire at Joseph, and she said, "Lie with me." ⁸But he refused and said to his master's wife, "Behold, with me *here,* my master does not concern himself with anything in the house, and he has put all that he owns in my charge. ⁹"There is no one greater in this house than I, and he has withheld nothing from me except you, because you are his wife. How then could I do this great evil and sin against God?" ¹⁰As she spoke to Joseph day after day, he did not listen to her to lie beside her *or* be with her. ¹¹Now it happened one day that he went into the house to do his work, and none of the men of the household was there inside. ¹²She caught him by his garment, saying, "Lie with me!" And he left his garment in her hand and fled, and went outside. ¹³When she saw that he had left his garment in her hand and had fled outside, ¹⁴she called to the men of her household and said to them, "See, he has brought in a Hebrew to us to make sport of us; he came in to me to lie with me, and I screamed. ¹⁵"When he heard that I raised my voice and screamed, he left his garment beside me and fled and went outside." ¹⁶So she left his garment beside her until his master came home. ¹⁷Then she spoke to him with these words, "The Hebrew slave, whom you brought to us, came in to me to make sport of me; ¹⁸and as I raised my voice and screamed, he left his garment beside me and fled outside."

Potiphar wife looked with desire at Joseph because of his good loos and she even said, "lie with me". But Joseph refused and said to his master's wife, "Behold, with me *here,* my master does not concern himself with anything in the house, and he has put all that he owns in my charge. In Genesis 39:9 Joseph said, "There is no one greater in this house than I, and he has withheld nothing from me except you, because you are his wife. "How then could I do such a wicked thing and sin against God?" This is Joseph's response to the queen of Egypt who wanted Joseph to have sex with her. Have you ever been in a similar situation where someone asked you to do something that you knew was against a law of God, be it sexual temptation or any other kind of temptation? Did you respond as Joseph did or did you give in to the temptation? Temptations like these can be very, very powerful. Note Oscar Wilde's quote: "The only way to get rid of temptation is to yield to it". That is <u>not</u> good Christian advice.

Sexual temptation is especially powerful. And it is everywhere. You cannot pick up a celebrity-based magazine or, for that matter, any magazine displayed by the supermarket checkout and not be bombarded with sexual messages? I'm uncertain that I agree with this, but I read somewhere where the primary driving force behind the development of the internet, VCRs, DVDs and other media technologies was/is pornography. It is true that pornography is very addictive, especially to men. Here are some facts/statistics[6]

- Revenue from pornography is greater than all combined revenues of all professional sports teams and all revenues of ABC, CBS, and NBC.
- 68 million pornographic search engine requests every day (25% of all search engine requests).
- 47% of all Christians admitted that pornography is a major problem in the home (This is very difficult to believe).
- 20% of all adults admitting to pornography addictions.
- 1 of 3 visitors to adult web sites are women.
- More people view porn websites on Sunday than any other day of the week.
- And there are far worse facts related to child pornography and crime.

Sexual additions have been around since Adam and Eve with so many biblical stories describing people succumbing to moral failures (and how many famous people have been in the headlines for the same reason?). The one exception is this story of Joseph. He was a rare person who refused to submit to moral failure just as today it is rare for anyone to run away from sexual temptation, exactly what you are to do (I Corinthians 6:18).

Why was Joseph a moral man when everyone else around him was not and so many today immoral? His secret was that he allowed God to be

---

[6] http://www.familysafemedia.com/pornography_statistics.html; many other website statistics available

the center of his life and to control all his thoughts and actions. You read throughout Genesis 39 that the Lord was with him. The battle against sexual temptation is won spiritually, not physically. You must "flee immorality" because it is recognized biblically that sexual temptation is too powerful to overcome it physically. You must fight it spiritually, first by allowing the Lord to control your thoughts and actions, second by doing all you can to keep yourself away from all sources of sexual temptation and third, make a covenant with your eyes as succumbing to sexual temptation starts with the eyes (Job 31:1, Proverbs 4:25, Matthew 6:22). However, like Joseph, it's impossible to be totally isolated from sexual temptation so when it confronts you, you must do as Joseph did---flee it.

Joseph realized that to yield to sexual temptation was a sin against his master (the Pharaoh), a sin against himself, and a sin against God. With these three components of such sin, as he says, how could he possibly do such a wicked thing? Is this how you think? Is this how you act? How close are you to the Lord such that His influence in you will enable you to say and do what Joseph said and did when tempted? And if you have failed in your past, the Lord will forgive you if you sincerely ask Him and if you resolve to repent of such sin. The Lord always gives you hope for changing your ways (Jeremiah 29:11). However, you must have the personal desire and rely on the personal power of the Lord to enable you to overcome and resist the temptation(s) in your life.

Potiphar's wife spoke to Joseph day after day, but he would not lie with her. One day he went into the house to do his work and none of the men were inside. She grabbed his garment and again said "lie with me". He fled, but left his garment with her. She called the men of the household and said, "see, my husband brought a Hebrew to make sport of us; when he came to lie with me I screamed. He fled but left his garment beside me. She repeated these words in Genesis 39:16-18 to her master and husband when he came home.

[19] Now when his master heard the words of his wife, which she spoke to him, saying, "This is what your slave did to me," his anger burned. [20] So Joseph's master took him and put him into the jail, the place where the king's prisoners were confined; and he was there in the jail. [21] But the LORD was with Joseph and extended kindness to him, and gave him favor in the sight of the chief jailer. [22] The chief jailer committed to Joseph's charge all the prisoners who were

in the jail; so that whatever was done there, he was responsible for it. ²³*The chief jailer did not supervise anything under Joseph's charge because the LORD was with him; and whatever he did, the LORD made to prosper.*

When the master heard the words of his wife, his anger burned. Joseph was put in jail. Potiphar would have killed him, but he didn't truly believe his wife and wanted to spare Joseph. We also see the injustice in what Potiphar did because Joseph suffered for someone else's sin. But he had the Lord on his side. How terrible it was for Joseph to be moved from a life of luxury to a life in prison for something he did not do. Yet God was with Joseph. He was given favorable sight in the eyes of the chief jailer. The chief jailer committed to Joseph's charge all the prisoners who were in the jail; so that whatever was done there, he was responsible *for it.* The chief jailer did not supervise anything under Joseph's charge because the LORD was with him; and whatever he did, the LORD made to prosper. God always blesses his children who trust Him the most.

CHAPTER FORTY

Joseph Interprets a Dream

¹Then it came about after these things, the cupbearer and the baker for the king of Egypt offended their lord, the king of Egypt. ²Pharaoh was furious with his two officials, the chief cupbearer and the chief baker. ³So he put them in confinement in the house of the captain of the bodyguard, in the jail, the same place where Joseph was imprisoned. ⁴The captain of the bodyguard put Joseph in charge of them, and he took care of them; and they were in confinement for some time. ⁵Then the cupbearer and the baker for the king of Egypt, who were confined in jail, both had a dream the same night, each man with his own dream and each dream with its own interpretation. ⁶When Joseph came to them in the morning and observed them, behold, they were dejected. ⁷He asked Pharaoh's officials who were with him in confinement in his master's house, "Why are your faces so sad today?" ⁸Then they said to him, "We have had a dream and there is no one to interpret it." Then Joseph said to them, "Do not interpretations belong to God? Tell it to me, please."

The cupbearer and the baker for the king of Egypt offended their Lord, the king of Egypt. A cupbearer was an officer with high rank in Egypt, as well as other leaders in Persia, Assyria, and Jewish monarchs. It was his duty to fill the kings cup and present it to him personally. We don't know why these two officers made the king furious. They were put in confinement in the house of the captain of the bodyguard, in jail, where Joseph was imprisoned. The captain put Joseph in charge of them, Joseph took care of them, and they were confirmed for a long time (we don't know how long). One night both the cupbearer and the baker had a dream, each with its own interpretation. The next morning Joseph noticed how rejected they were and asked Pharaoh's officials why their faces were so sad. Their response was that no one could interpret their dreams. Joseph's answer was that God produces the dreams and Joseph could interpret the dreams for them if they would tell him.

⁹So the chief cupbearer told his dream to Joseph, and said to him, "In my dream, behold, there was a vine in front of me; ¹⁰and on the vine were three branches. And as it was budding, its blossoms came out, and its clusters produced ripe grapes. ¹¹"Now Pharaoh's cup was in my hand; so I took the grapes and squeezed them into Pharaoh's cup, and I put the cup into Pharaoh's hand." ¹²Then Joseph said to him, "This is the interpretation of it: the three branches are three days; ¹³within three more days Pharaoh will lift up your head and restore you to your office; and you will put Pharaoh's cup into his hand according to your former custom when you were his cupbearer. ¹⁴"Only keep me in mind when it goes well with you, and please do me a kindness by mentioning me to Pharaoh and get me out of this house. ¹⁵"For I was in fact kidnapped from the land of the Hebrews, and even here I have done nothing that they should have put me into the dungeon."

The chief cupbearer told his dream to Joseph. In his dream, behold, there was a vine in front of me and on the vine were were three branches. As the vine was budding its blossoms came out and its clusters produced ripe grapes. Now Pharaoh's cup was in my hand, I took the grapes and squeezed them into the Pharaoh's and put the cup into Pharaoh's hand. Joseph replied that the three branches are three days; within three more days Pharaoh will lift your head and restore you to your office. You will put Pharaoh's cup into his hand according to your former custom when you were his cupbearer. Joseph then added that that he was the interpreter and can get him out of this house.

¹⁶When the chief baker saw that he had interpreted favorably, he said to Joseph, "I also saw in my dream, and behold, there were three baskets of white bread on my head; ¹⁷and in the top basket there were some of all sorts of baked food for Pharaoh, and the birds were eating them out of the basket on my head." ¹⁸Then Joseph answered and said, "This is its interpretation: the three baskets are three days; ¹⁹within three more days Pharaoh will lift up your head from you and will hang you on a tree, and the birds will eat your flesh off you."

When the chief baker saw Joseph had interpreted favorably the cupbearer's dream, he shared his dream with Joseph. In his dream, there were three baskets of white bread on my head. The top basket contained sorts of baked food for Pharaoh and the birds were eating them out of that basket on my head. Joseph replied that the three baskets are three days. Within three more days Pharaoh will lift your head from you and hang you on a tree and the birds will eat your flesh off you. Joseph's interpretation was graphic and perhaps cruel to the baker, but Joseph cannot lie as we have already seen throughout his life. He told the baker that he had three days to prepare for his death.

[20]Thus it came about on the third day, which was Pharaoh's birthday, that he made a feast for all his servants; and he lifted up the head of the chief cupbearer and the head of the chief baker among his servants. [21]He restored the chief cupbearer to his office, and he put the cup into Pharaoh's hand; [22]but he hanged the chief baker, just as Joseph had interpreted to them. [23]Yet the chief cupbearer did not remember Joseph, but forgot him.

At the third day, which was Pharaoh's birthday, he made a feast for all his servants. He lifted up the head of the chief cupbearer and the head of the chief baker among his servants. What this means is that Pharaoh arraigned and tried the two prisoners. The cupbearer was restored to his office just as Joseph predicted, but the chief baker was hanged as Joseph predicted. Yet once free the chief cupbearer did not remember Joseph. He forgot all about Joseph. This is our human nature; we forget and neglect in prosperity about this being neglected. Joseph realized that he would be delivered by God in another way.

CHAPTER FORTY ONE

Pharaoh's Dream

¹Now it happened at the end of two full years that Pharaoh had a dream, and behold, he was standing by the Nile. ²And lo, from the Nile there came up seven cows, sleek and fat; and they grazed in the marsh grass. ³Then behold, seven other cows came up after them from the Nile, ugly and gaunt, and they stood by the other cows on the bank of the Nile. ⁴The ugly and gaunt cows ate up the seven sleek and fat cows. Then Pharaoh awoke. ⁵He fell asleep and dreamed a second time; and behold, seven ears of grain came up on a single stalk, plump and good. ⁶Then behold, seven ears, thin and scorched by the east wind, sprouted up after them. ⁷The thin ears swallowed up the seven plump and full ears. Then Pharaoh awoke, and behold, it was a dream. ⁸Now in the morning his spirit was troubled, so he sent and called for all the magicians of Egypt, and all its wise men. And Pharaoh told them his dreams, but there was no one who could interpret them to Pharaoh.

Joseph remained in prison another two years. Then Pharaoh had a dream and behold he was standing by the Nile. From the Nile came up seven cows, sleek and fat, and they grazed in the marsh grass. Then behold, seven other cows came after them from the Nile, ugly and gaunt and stood by the other healthy cows on the bank of the Nile. Yet the ugly and gaunt cows ate up the seven sleek and fat cows. Pharaoh awoke and remembered the dream but had no idea what it meant. The next time he fell asleep, he dreamed about seven ears of grain came up on a single stalk, plump and good. Then behold, seven ears, thin and scorched by the east wind, spouted up and then the thin and scorched ears of grain swallowed up the seven plumb and full ears. Pharaoh awake and his spirit was troubled. He called all the magicians of Egypt, all its wise men, explained his dream, but no one was able to interpret the dream.

⁹Then the chief cupbearer spoke to Pharaoh, saying, "I would make mention today of my own offenses. ¹⁰"Pharaoh was furious with his servants, and he put me in confinement in the house of the captain of the bodyguard, both me and the chief baker. ¹¹"We had a dream on the same night, he and I; each of us dreamed according to the interpretation of his own dream. ¹²"Now a Hebrew youth was with us there, a servant of the captain of the bodyguard, and we related them to him, and he interpreted our dreams for us. To each one he interpreted according to his own dream. ¹³"And just as he interpreted for us, so it happened; he restored me in my office, but he hanged him."

The chief cupbearer spoke to Pharaoh and was reminded two years ago that a Hebrew youth was with him and the chief baker in prison and he interpreted our dreams. The chief cupbearer was restored to his office while chief baker was hanged.

¹⁴Then Pharaoh sent and called for Joseph, and they hurriedly brought him out of the dungeon; and when he had shaved himself and changed his clothes, he came to Pharaoh. ¹⁵Pharaoh said to Joseph, "I have had a dream, but no one can interpret it; and I have heard it said about you, that when you hear a dream you can interpret it." ¹⁶Joseph then answered Pharaoh, saying, "It is not in me; God will give Pharaoh a favorable answer." ¹⁷So Pharaoh spoke to Joseph, "In my dream, behold, I was standing on the bank of the Nile; ¹⁸and behold, seven cows, fat and sleek came up out of the Nile, and they grazed in the marsh grass. ¹⁹"Lo, seven other cows came up after them, poor and very ugly and gaunt, such as I had never seen for ugliness in all the land of Egypt; ²⁰and the lean and ugly cows ate up the first seven fat cows. ²¹"Yet when they had devoured them, it could not be detected that they had devoured them, for they were just as ugly as before. Then I awoke. ²²"I saw also in my dream, and behold, seven ears, full and good, came up on a single stalk; ²³and lo, seven ears, withered, thin, and scorched by the east wind, sprouted up after them; ²⁴and the thin ears swallowed the seven good ears. Then I told it to the magicians, but there was no one who could explain it to me."

Joseph was hurriedly brought out of Potiphar's dungeon, but he did not face Pharaoh until he had shaved and changed his clothes. This was not just "cleaning up," which surely was needed; it was a cultural concession.

To the Hebrews, a beard was a mark of dignity, but for the Egyptian it was an offensive thing. When Joseph came before Pharaoh, the distressing dreams of the previous night were immediately brought up. Pharaoh had heard that Joseph could interpret them. Pharaoh repeated his dream to Joseph (Genesis 41:26-27).

²⁵Now Joseph said to Pharaoh, "Pharaoh's dreams are one and the same; God has told to Pharaoh what He is about to do. ²⁶"The seven good cows are seven years; and the seven good ears are seven years; the dreams are one and the same. ²⁷"The seven lean and ugly cows that came up after them are seven years, and the seven thin ears scorched by the east wind will be seven years of famine. ²⁸"It is as I have spoken to Pharaoh: God has shown to Pharaoh what He is about to do. ²⁹"Behold, seven years of great abundance are coming in all the land of Egypt; ³⁰and after them seven years of famine will come, and all the abundance will be forgotten in the land of Egypt, and the famine will ravage the land. ³¹"So the abundance will be unknown in the land because of that subsequent famine; for it will be very severe. ³²"Now as for the repeating of the dream to Pharaoh twice, it means that the matter is determined by God, and God will quickly bring it about. ³³"Now let Pharaoh look for a man discerning and wise, and set him over the land of Egypt. ³⁴"Let Pharaoh take action to appoint overseers in charge of the land, and let him exact a fifth of the produce of the land of Egypt in the seven years of abundance. ³⁵"Then let them gather all the food of these good years that are coming, and store up the grain for food in the cities under Pharaoh's authority, and let them guard it. ³⁶"Let the food become as a reserve for the land for the seven years of famine which will occur in the land of Egypt, so that the land will not perish during the famine." ³⁷Now the proposal seemed good to Pharaoh and to all his servants.

Joseph replied that "it is not me, but God will give Pharaoh a favorable answer." The seven good cows are seven years; and the seven good ears are seven years; the dreams are one and the same. And the seven lean and ugly cows that came up after them are seven years, and the seven thin ears scorched by the east wind shall be seven years of famine. Let Pharaoh take action to appoint overseers in charge of the land, and let him exact a fifth of the produce of the land of Egypt in the seven years of abundance. Then let them gather all the food of these good years that are coming, and store up the grain for food in the cities under Pharaoh's authority, and let them guard it. And let the food become as a reserve for the land for the seven years of famine which will occur in the land of Egypt, so that the land may not perish during the famine. Joseph skillfully interpreted the two dreams. His interpretation closely followed the two dreams a fact which could hardly have been unnoticed by Pharaoh and which added credibility to Joseph's explanation. The two dreams, while different in some details, were one in their meaning (verse 25).

38 Then Pharaoh said to his servants, "Can we find a man like this, in whom is a divine spirit?" 39 So Pharaoh said to Joseph, "Since God has informed you of all this, there is no one so discerning and wise as you are. 40 "You shall be over my house, and according to your command all my people shall do homage; only in the throne I will be greater than you." 41 Pharaoh said to Joseph, "See, I have set you over all the land of Egypt." 42 Then Pharaoh took off his signet ring from his hand and put it on Joseph's hand, and clothed him in garments of fine linen and put the gold necklace around his neck. 43 He had him ride in his second chariot; and they proclaimed before him, "Bow the knee!" And he set him over all the land of Egypt. 44 Moreover, Pharaoh said to Joseph, "Though I am Pharaoh, yet without your permission no one shall raise his hand or foot in all the land of Egypt." 45 Then Pharaoh named Joseph Zaphenath-paneah; and he gave him Asenath, the daughter of Potiphera priest of On, as his wife. And Joseph went forth over the land of Egypt.

The best that Joseph could have dared to hope for was a release from his imprisonment. How far beyond this was his elevation to a position of power and prestige! Tokens of his new authority were the signet ring, fine garments, a gold necklace, and the royal chariot, preceded by those who proclaimed the fame and position of Joseph (verses 42, 43). Just as Joseph was second only to Potiphar, now he was to answer only to Pharaoh (verses 40, 44). Pharaoh took two other highly symbolic actions which helped to cement Joseph's new position with the people of the land. First, Joseph was given an Egyptian name. An Egyptian name, whatever it meant, signified that in Pharaoh's mind Joseph was not a "mere Hebrew" (which were despised by the people of Egypt (43:32, 46:34), but an Egyptian. Among the American Indians the counterpart to this would have been to make Joseph a blood-brother of the tribe. This is further confirmed by the gift of an Egyptian wife, Asenath (verse 45). Many Christians are troubled by the fact that Joseph took a wife from among the Egyptians. Yet were could Joseph have gone to find a wife? Let me ask you a very practical question. Had you been Joseph, where would you have gone to find a godly wife? Not to Judah, who was willing to sleep with a Canaanite cult prostitute? Not his brothers who tried to kill him. Not to Laban? The only woman he could not marry was a Canaanite woman, forbidden by God. Only marriage to a Canaanite woman was forbidden by God (Genesis 24:3, Genesis 28:1). Later (Deuteronomy 20:17-18) Israel was to destroy the Hittite, the Amorite, the Canaanite, the Perizzite, the Hivite, and the Jebusite as God commanded them to do.

[46]Now Joseph was thirty years old when he stood before Pharaoh, king of Egypt. And Joseph went out from the presence of Pharaoh and went through all the land of Egypt. [47]During the seven years of plenty the land brought forth abundantly. [48]So he gathered all the food of these seven years which occurred in the land of Egypt and placed the food in the cities; he placed in every city the food from its own surrounding fields. [49]Thus Joseph stored up grain in great abundance like the sand of the sea, until he stopped measuring it, for it was beyond measure.

Joseph was thirty years old when he stood before Pharaoh, king of Egypt. Joseph was accurate in his interpretation and what happened. He went out from the present of Pharaoh throughout the land and prepared for the famine to come. Egypt became very prepared for the famine to come because of Joseph's predication. He always acknowledged God for the interpretive skills God gave him and for bearing with him during his years of imprisonment (somewhere between two and thirteen years).

[50]Now before the year of famine came, two sons were born to Joseph, whom Asenath, the daughter of Potiphera priest of On, bore to him. [51]Joseph named the firstborn Manasseh, "For," he said, "God has made me forget all my trouble and all my father's household." [52]He named the second Ephraim, "For," he said, "God has made me fruitful in the land of my affliction."

The year before the famine came, two sons were born to Joseph and Asenatha, the daughter of Potiphera priest of On in ancient Egypt. Some theories believe that Potiphera was the same as Potiphar. The first son was named Manasseh that means that "God has made me forget all my trouble and all my father's household." Joseph by now had forgiven and forgotten his troubles with his former family and how that had sold him. He named the second Ephraim, "For God has made me fruitful in the land of my affliction." Through God's providence, Joseph was now fruitful in the land that initially brought him affliction.

⁵³When the seven years of plenty which had been in the land of Egypt came to an end, ⁵⁴and the seven years of famine began to come, just as Joseph had said, then there was famine in all the lands, but in all the land of Egypt there was bread. ⁵⁵So when all the land of Egypt was famished, the people cried out to Pharaoh for bread; and Pharaoh said to all the Egyptians, "Go to Joseph; whatever he says to you, you shall do." ⁵⁶When the famine was spread over all the face of the earth, then Joseph opened all the storehouses, and sold to the Egyptians; and the famine was severe in the land of Egypt. ⁵⁷The people of all the earth came to Egypt to buy grain from Joseph, because the famine was severe in all the earth.

When seven years of plenty in Egypt came to an end and several years of famine began, just as God through Joseph had said, there was a famine in all the land. Yet in Egypt there was bread. Pharaoh had Egyptians go to Joseph and do whatever he says to do. Pharaoh did this to other lands on the face of the earth, all who were experiencing famine, Joseph opened the storehouses and sold to Egyptians to sell to others. The people of all the earth came to Egypt to buy from grain Joseph because of famine in all the earth. Please note that Joseph was not a priest or minister or had some spiritual gift. His gift was skill and knowledge and it did not matter to Pharaoh who his god was. When we need special care, we will go to the person who is best, regardless of his faith. While I believe that God elevated Joseph because he trusted in God and obeyed, I am just as confident that Pharaoh elevated him because he was diligent and skillful in what he did. Piety without proficiency is folly. We praise God in our work as well as in our words. One without the other is useless. Joseph's life is a commentary on the principle that: "He who is faithful in a very little thing is faithful also in much; and he who is unrighteous in a very little thing is unrighteous also in much" (Luke 16:10). The biblical principle which we must practice is rather this: "Commit your works to the Lord, and your plans will be established" (Proverbs 16:3).

CHAPTER FORTY TWO

Joseph's Brothers Sent to Egypt

¹Now Jacob saw that there was grain in Egypt, and Jacob said to his sons, "Why are you staring at one another?" ²He said, "Behold, I have heard that there is grain in Egypt; go down there and buy some for us from that place, so that we may live and not die." ³Then ten brothers of Joseph went down to buy grain from Egypt. ⁴But Jacob did not send Joseph's brother Benjamin with his brothers, for he said, "I am afraid that harm may befall him." ⁵So the sons of Israel came to buy grain among those who were coming, for the famine was in the land of Canaan also.

Jacob somehow heard that there was grain in Egypt. During a drought like the Middle East was experiencing, what else could people do when they could not plant or reap? He viciously asked his sons why are they staring at one another? His sons probably had never experienced hunger and need like this and they were willing to do anything. He then said for his sons to travel to Egypt to buy some grain so that they will live and not die. Ten of Joseph brothers sent to buy grain in Egypt. The youngest, Benjamin, stayed home with Jacob for Jacob was fearful for his life. Perhaps Jacob also wanted one of his sons to be with him and help him. Many people besides Jacob's sons went to Egypt for grain because the famine was widespread including all of Canaan. A map is included here to indicate the routes that Jacob and his sons took from Canaan to Egypt and back. To walk either way during these times that the brothers and finally Jacob walked from Canaan to Egypt was somewhere around 380-400 miles. That might take them around 10-11 days of walking!

The Book of Genesis

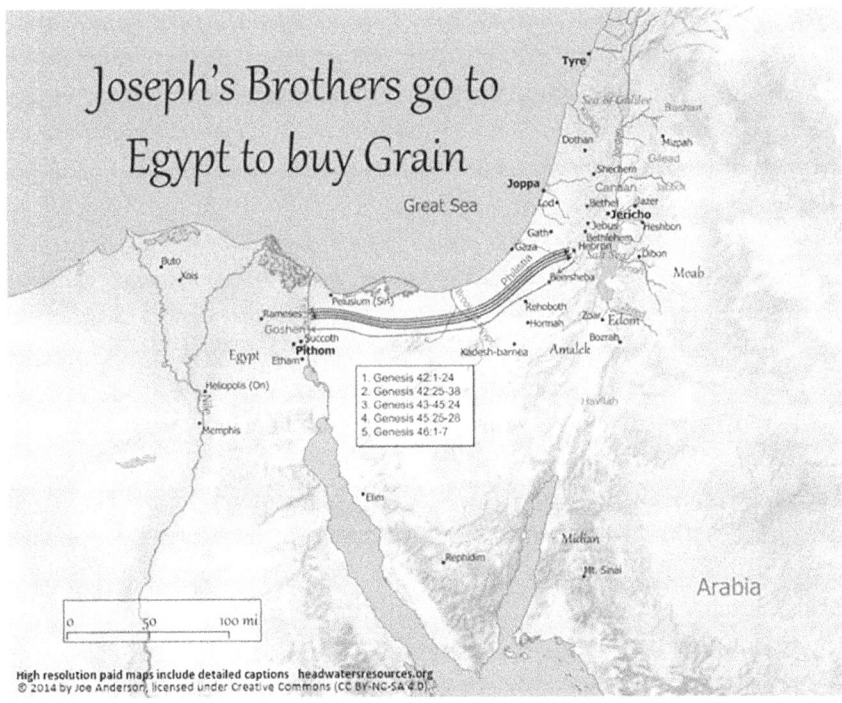

Created by Joe Anderson, licensed under Creative Commons

⁶*Now Joseph was the ruler over the land; he was the one who sold to all the people of the land. And Joseph's brothers came and bowed down to him with their faces to the ground. ⁷When Joseph saw his brothers he recognized them, but he disguised himself to them and spoke to them harshly. And he said to them, "Where have you come from?" And they said, "From the land of Canaan, to buy food."*

Joseph was ruler over all the land. He sold to people the grain they needed. Joseph's brothers came from Israel and they bowed to him with their faces to the ground. Joseph recognized them, but disguised himself to them and spoke to them harshly. His harshness was to prevent them from recognize who Joseph really was. He had not seen them in over 20 years. When he spoke to them he asked where they came from and they said from the land of Canaan, here to buy food.

⁸*But Joseph had recognized his brothers, although they did not recognize him. ⁹Joseph remembered the dreams which he had about them, and said to them,*

"You are spies; you have come to look at the undefended parts of our land." ¹⁰Then they said to him, "No, my lord, but your servants have come to buy food. ¹¹"We are all sons of one man; we are honest men, your servants are not spies." ¹²Yet he said to them, "No, but you have come to look at the undefended parts of our land!" ¹³But they said, "Your servants are twelve brothers in all, the sons of one man in the land of Canaan; and behold, the youngest is with our father today, and one is no longer alive." ¹⁴Joseph said to them, "It is as I said to you, you are spies; ¹⁵by this you will be tested: by the life of Pharaoh, you shall not go from this place unless your youngest brother comes here! ¹⁶"Send one of you that he may get your brother, while you remain confined, that your words may be tested, whether there is truth in you. But if not, by the life of Pharaoh, surely you are spies." ¹⁷So he put them all together in prison for three days.*

Far more is meant by verse 9 than that Joseph merely remembered his dreams about his brothers and recognized their fulfillment in their bowing down to him. All this would have done would have been to puff up his pride. Joseph not only realized the fulfillment of his dreams but also the reason for them. He saw that God had a purpose for placing him in his position of power, and this purpose was for him to function as the family head, protecting and preserving his family. He had great power and prestige, but God had given these to him for a purpose much greater than merely to seek revenge. Joseph's severity was feigned, not real. He needed to learn more information without his brothers realizing who he was or what he was attempting to accomplish. His harshness was intended to produce fear, for at this point in the lives of his brothers' fear produced more facts than faith. All brothers would be detained except one, who could be dispatched to bring back the proof of their honesty. How cleverly Joseph handled this situation to bring about his desired ends without his brothers seeing his purpose in it all.

¹⁸Now Joseph said to them on the third day, "Do this and live, for I fear God: ¹⁹if you are honest men, let one of your brothers be confined in your prison; but as for the rest of you, go, carry grain for the famine of your households, ²⁰and bring your youngest brother to me, so your words may be verified, and you will not die." And they did so. ²¹Then they said to one another, "Truly we are guilty concerning our brother, because we saw the distress of his soul when he pleaded with us, yet we would not listen; therefore this distress has come upon us." ²²Reuben answered them, saying, "Did I not tell you, 'Do not sin against the boy'; and you would not listen? Now comes the reckoning for his blood." ²³They did not know, however, that Joseph understood, for there was an interpreter between them. ²⁴He turned away from them and wept. But when he returned to them and spoke to them, he took Simeon from them and bound him before their eyes. ²⁵Then Joseph gave orders to fill their bags with grain and to restore every man's money in his sack, and to give them provisions for the journey. And thus it was done for them.

Those three days must have been miserable. They must have been filled with fear and foreboding. Would they ever return to their father? Would they ever regain their freedom? And, most delicate, who would be the one who was released to return to Canaan while the others remained captive? For them, Joseph's experience, which took years, was condensed to days. Joseph's words to them were like the sunrise dispelling the darkness. His words are filled with hope and encouragement, not fear and judgment. "Do this and live," Joseph urged them (verse 18). Life, not death, joy, not misery, was what Joseph desired for his brothers. But certain changes had to occur before this could be their experience. The self-interest and cruelty which had caused them to sell him into slavery must be dealt with. That would not come easily or quickly, but it would come.

The heart of Joseph is openly revealed in verse 24. Having overheard the spiritual soul-searching that went on among his brothers, Joseph could contain his emotions no longer. He had to leave their presence, lest by his tears they should discover his identity. Joseph's actions were not those of a man who did not care for his brothers, but of one who cared so much that he resisted the urge to identify himself to promote their spiritual well-being.

²⁶So they loaded their donkeys with their grain and departed from there. ²⁷As one of them opened his sack to give his donkey fodder at the lodging place, he saw his money; and behold, it was in the mouth of his sack. ²⁸Then he said to his brothers, "My money has been returned, and behold, it is even in my sack." And their hearts sank, and they turned trembling to one another, saying, "What is this that God has done to us?"

The brothers loaded their donkeys with their grain and left Egypt. Later as one of them opened his sack to give to his donkey, he saw his money in the mouth of his sack. His money has returned and everyone's heart sank.

What has God done to us? They were distraught, for they saw that this was the hand of God, not fate, and that this might be discovered back in Pharaoh palace where their brother Simeon was being held prisoner. If this missing money was made known to Joseph, things might not go so well for them on their next visit.

²⁹When they came to their father Jacob in the land of Canaan, they told him all that had happened to them, saying, ³⁰"The man, the lord of the land, spoke harshly with us, and took us for spies of the country. ³¹"But we said to him, 'We are honest men; we are not spies. ³²'We are twelve brothers, sons of our father; one is no longer alive, and the youngest is with our father today in the land of Canaan.' ³³"The man, the lord of the land, said to us, 'By this I will know that you are honest men: leave one of your brothers with me and take grain for the famine of your households, and go. ³⁴'But bring your youngest brother to me that I may know that you are not spies, but honest men. I will give your brother to you, and you may trade in the land.'" ³⁵Now it came about as they were emptying their sacks, that behold, every man's bundle of money was in his sack; and when they and their father saw their bundles of money, they were dismayed. ³⁶Their father Jacob said to them, "You have bereaved me of my children: Joseph is no more, and Simeon is no more, and you would take Benjamin; all these things are against me." ³⁷Then Reuben spoke to his father, saying, "You may put my two sons to death if I do not bring him back to you; put him in my care, and I will return him to you." ³⁸But Jacob said, "My son shall not go down with you; for his brother is dead, and he alone is left. If harm should befall him on the journey you are taking, then you will bring my gray hair down to Sheol in sorrow."

When the brother returned to Canaan and saw Jacob, they told him all that had happened. The man in Egypt, still didn't know that he was their brother, spoke harshly to them and treated them as spies. They admitted that they were twelve brothers although one no longer alive (they thought that this was Joseph) and the youngest (Benjamin) was with their father in Canaan. Older brother, Simeon, was left in Egypt. The lord of the land (Joseph) told them that he will realize that they are honest men if they leave one of your brothers with him. Take grain for the famine of your household and go. But come back and bring your youngest brother to Joseph that he may know that you are not spies, but honest men.

When the brothers were emptying their sacks, they found every man's bundle of money in each sack. Again, they were dismayed as was their father! Jacob said to them, "You have bereaved me of my children. Joseph was dead (he thought) and Simeon is a prisoner in Eygpt and you need to take Benjamin back there, all against me". Jacob's response is "poor me". Jacob was victimized by his sons for trying to kill Joseph. His life was miserable although God was always gracious to Jacob. For Joseph brothers, God was punishing them for their acts against Joseph. For Joseph, his suffering was ultimately from the hand of a loving heavenly Father, Who was near in his affliction. Reuben spoke to his father, saying that Jacob could kill Reuben's sons if he does not bring Benjamin back to you. Jacob, however, said that his son would not go with you and he alone is left. If harm should befall him on this journey, my gray hair will be destroyed in Sheol. Jacob was more partial to Benjamin than any of his other sons. Just shows how selfish Jacob was and his sons, except for Joseph, followed him.

CHAPTER FORTY-THREE

The Return to Egypt

¹Now the famine was severe in the land. ²So it came about when they had finished eating the grain which they had brought from Egypt, that their father said to them, "Go back, buy us a little food." ³Judah spoke to him, however, saying, "The man solemnly warned us, 'You shall not see my face unless your brother is with you.' ⁴"If you send our brother with us, we will go down and buy you food. ⁵"But if you do not send him, we will not go down; for the man said to us, 'You will not see my face unless your brother is with you.'" ⁶Then Israel said, "Why did you treat me so badly by telling the man whether you still had another brother?" ⁷But they said, "The man questioned particularly about us and our relatives, saying, 'Is your father still alive? Have you another brother?' So we answered his questions. Could we possibly know that he would say, 'Bring your brother down'?" ⁸Judah said to his father Israel, "Send the lad with me and we will arise and go, that we may live and not die, we as well as you and our little ones. ⁹"I myself will be surety for him; you may hold me responsible for him. If I do not bring him back to you and set him before you, then let me bear the blame before you forever. ¹⁰"For if we had not delayed, surely by now we could have returned twice."

Famine still severe in the land. They had nearly eaten the grain they returned from the first visit; thus, their father told them to return to Egypt for more grain. Judah spoke to Jacob saying that the man in Egypt warned them that they will not see his face unless Benjamin is with them. Israel (meaning governed by God) then complained to his sons why they treated him so poorly by telling the man (Joseph) that they had another brother. Of course, none except for Joseph knew that a younger brother had not been sent the first time. Judah said to Jacob, sent Benjamin with me and we will arise and go. None of us will be hurt or killed. I will be a surety for him, meaning that Judah will take responsibility for Benjamin, you may hold me responsible for him. If I do not bring him back to you and you see him, let me bear the blame before you forever. We could have been there and already returned if Benjamin's life was not Jacob's main concern.

11 Then their father Israel said to them, "If it must be so, then do this: take some of the best products of the land in your bags, and carry down to the man as a present, a little balm and a little honey, aromatic gum and myrrh, pistachio nuts and almonds. 12 "Take double the money in your hand, and take back in your hand the money that was returned in the mouth of your sacks; perhaps it was a mistake. 13 "Take your brother also, and arise, return to the man; 14 and may God Almighty grant you compassion in the sight of the man, so that he will release to you your other brother and Benjamin. And as for me, if I am bereaved of my children, I am bereaved." 15 So the men took this present, and they took double the money in their hand, and Benjamin; then they arose and went down to Egypt and stood before Joseph.

Jacob finally agree to let the brothers take Benjamin to Egypt. However, Jacob, always being shrewd, had the best products of his land in their bags, including balm, honey, aromatic gum, myrrh, pistachio nuts and almonds. This, hopefully, would appease Joseph and cause him to think well of them. Also, take double the money in your hand, and take back in your hand the money that was returned in the mouth of your sacks; perhaps it was a mistake. Jacob prayed may God Almighty grant you compassion in the sight of the man, so that he will release to you your other brother and Benjamin. And as for me, if I am bereaved of my children, I am bereaved. Jacob was not afraid to admit that he was bereaved if anything happened to his sons. He gave up his own will and assume that God was in control. He gave over to God.

16 When Joseph saw Benjamin with them, he said to his house steward, "Bring the men into the house, and slay an animal and make ready; for the men are to dine with me at noon." 17 So the man did as Joseph said, and brought the men to Joseph's house. 18 Now the men were afraid, because they were brought to Joseph's house; and they said, "It is because of the money that was returned in our sacks the first time that we are being brought in, that he may seek occasion against us and fall upon us, and take us for slaves with our donkeys."

[19]So they came near to Joseph's house steward, and spoke to him at the entrance of the house, [20]and said, "Oh, my lord, we indeed came down the first time to buy food, [21]and it came about when we came to the lodging place, that we opened our sacks, and behold, each man's money was in the mouth of his sack, our money in full. So we have brought it back in our hand. [22]"We have also brought down other money in our hand to buy food; we do not know who put our money in our sacks." [23]He said, "Be at ease, do not be afraid. Your God and the God of your father has given you treasure in your sacks; I had your money." Then he brought Simeon out to them. [24]Then the man brought the men into Joseph's house and gave them water, and they washed their feet; and he gave their donkeys fodder. [25]So they prepared the present for Joseph's coming at noon; for they had heard that they were to eat a meal there.

Joseph saw that Benjamin was with them. It does surprise me that Joseph could even recognize his little brother. He ordered his house steward to prepare an animal for their noon meal. The men were afraid because they were brought to Joseph's house and believed that the money that was returned in their sacks that they were brought in, the Joseph could use the occasion against them and fall on them and take them for slaves. They came near to Josephs house steward and spoke to him. They said, "Oh, my lord, we indeed came down the first time to buy food and each man's sack was full of money of his sack, money in full." We have brought back the money plus other money in our hand to buy food. We do not know who put the money in our sacks. The house steward said, "Be at ease, do not be afraid. Your God and the God of your father, Jacob, has given you treasure in your sacks. I had your money." Then he brought out Simeon to them. The house steward brought the men into Joseph's house and gave them water and they washed their feed and he gave their donkey's fodder. They prepared the present for Joseph's coming at noon, for they heard that they were to eat a meal there.

[26]When Joseph came home, they brought into the house to him the present which was in their hand and bowed to the ground before him. [27]Then he asked them about their welfare, and said, "Is your old father well, of whom you spoke? Is he still alive?" [28]They said, "Your servant our father is well; he is still alive." They bowed down in homage. [29]As he lifted his eyes and saw his brother Benjamin, his mother's son, he said, "Is this your youngest brother, of whom you spoke to me?" And he said, "May God be gracious to you, my son."

³⁰Joseph hurried out for he was deeply stirred over his brother, and he sought a place to weep; and he entered his chamber and wept there. ³¹Then he washed his face and came out; and he controlled himself and said, "Serve the meal." ³²So they served him by himself, and them by themselves, and the Egyptians who ate with him by themselves, because the Egyptians could not eat bread with the Hebrews, for that is loathsome to the Egyptians. ³³Now they were seated before him, the firstborn according to his birthright and the youngest according to his youth, and the men looked at one another in astonishment. ³⁴He took portions to them from his own table, but Benjamin's portion was five times as much as any of theirs. So they feasted and drank freely with him.

When Joseph arrived, the brothers gave him the present in their hands and bowed the ground before him. He asked them about their welfare, included if their father was alive and well. The brothers bowed in homage, then Joseph saw his younger brother, Benjamin. Joseph asked if this man was Benjamin and this was confirmed. Joseph then left the room for he was stirred deeply over his younger brother and he sought a place to weep. Emotions were just ripping Joseph up. He thought he'd never see him again and here he is. Oh, he yearns so much to just take hold of him and grab him and all. And he just started weeping and so he turned and ran out of the room into his own private chamber. And he just wept for the joy and the excitement of the reunion. Joseph washed his face and returned to the room. Joseph ate by himself, the Jews by themselves and the Egyptians by themselves. There were three tables. Joseph because of his position had his own table by himself. The Egyptians that were eating there had their separate table and his brothers had their separate table because the Egyptians did not want to sit with them. He set them in order around the table from the oldest right around to the youngest. And they noticed that he had set them in the order of their birth. Joseph make sure that Benjamin had five times a much food as the others. They all feasted and drank with Joseph.

CHAPTER FORTY-FOUR

The Brothers Are Brought Back

Then he commanded his house steward, saying, "Fill the men's sacks with food, as much as they can carry, and put each man's money in the mouth of his sack. ² Put my cup, the silver cup, in the mouth of the sack of the youngest, and his money for the grain." And he did as Joseph had told him. ³ As soon as it was light, the men were sent away, they with their donkeys. ⁴ They had just gone out of the city, and were not far off, when Joseph said to his house steward, "Up, follow the men; and when you overtake them, say to them, 'Why have you repaid evil for good? ⁵ Is not this the one from which my lord drinks and which he indeed uses for divination? You have done wrong in doing this.'"

Joseph commanded his house steward, "Fill the men's sacks with food as much as they can carry, and put each man's money in the mouth of his sack. Put my cup, the silver cup, in the mouth of the sacks of the youngest, Benjamin, and his money for the grain". The steward did as Joseph told him. At daylight, the men were sent away with their donkeys. They were not far off when Joseph told his house steward, "Up, follow the men and when you overtake them, ask "why have you repaid evil for good. Is not this silver cup the one that our lord, Joseph, drinks and which he uses for divination (the practice that seeks to foretell future events)? You have done wrong to take this silver cup". The discovery of the cup in Benjamin's possession would bring him into greater trouble and danger.

⁶So he overtook them and spoke these words to them. ⁷They said to him, "Why does my lord speak such words as these? Far be it from your servants to do such a thing. ⁸ "Behold, the money which we found in the mouth of our sacks we have brought back to you from the land of Canaan. How then could we steal silver or gold from your lord's house? ⁹"With whomever of your servants it is found, let him die, and we also will be my lord's slaves." ¹⁰So he said, "Now let it also be according to your words; he with whom it is found shall be my slave, and the rest of you shall be innocent." ¹¹Then they hurried, each man lowered his sack to the ground, and each man opened his sack. ¹²He searched, beginning with the oldest and ending with the youngest, and the cup was found in Benjamin's sack. ¹³Then they tore their clothes, and when each man loaded his donkey, they returned to the city.*

Joseph's house steward overtook them and told them about the stolen silver cup. The brothers said, "Why does my lord speak words like this? Far be it from your servants to do such a thing. Behold the money that we found in the mouth of our sacks we brought back to you from Canaan. How could be steal silver or gold from your lord's house? If any of us did this, let him die and the others will be your slaves." The steward's words must have come upon them like a thunderbolt, and one of their most predominant feelings must have been the humiliating and galling sense of being made so often objects of suspicion. The house steward agreed with them in that whoever was found to have the silver cup will be Joseph's slave while the rest of you are innocent. Each man hurried to lower his sack to the ground and opened it. The house steward began with the oldest and finished with the youngest brother. The cup was found in Benjamin's sack. The brothers tore their clothes and then returned to Joseph, feeling so humiliated.

¹⁴When Judah and his brothers came to Joseph's house, he was still there, and they fell to the ground before him. ¹⁵Joseph said to them, "What is this deed that you have done? Do you not know that such a man as I can indeed practice divination?" ¹⁶So Judah said, "What can we say to my lord? What can we speak? And how can we justify ourselves? God has found out the iniquity of your servants; behold, we are my lord's slaves, both we and the one in whose possession the cup has been found." ¹⁷But he said, "Far be it from me to do this. The man in whose possession the cup has been found, he shall be my slave; but as for you, go up in peace to your father."

Judah and his brothers arrived at Joseph's house; they fell to the ground before him. Joseph asked "What deed have you done? The silver cup was used by Joseph to practice divination." Again, Divination was communication with a deity for the purpose of determining the deity's knowledge, resulting in clarification of a decision or discernment of the future. Judah replied, "What can we say to you, the lord. How can we justify this? God has found out the iniquity of your servants. We are now your slaves, all of us."

[18] Then Judah approached him, and said, "Oh my lord, may your servant please speak a word in my lord's ears, and do not be angry with your servant; for you are equal to Pharaoh. [19] "My lord asked his servants, saying, 'Have you a father or a brother?' [20] "We said to my lord, 'We have an old father and a little child of his old age. Now his brother is dead, so he alone is left of his mother, and his father loves him.' [21] "Then you said to your servants, 'Bring him down to me that I may set my eyes on him.' [22] "But we said to my lord, 'The lad cannot leave his father, for if he should leave his father, his father would die.' [23] "You said to your servants, however, 'Unless your youngest brother comes down with you, you will not see my face again.' [24] "Thus it came about when we went up to your servant my father, we told him the words of my lord. [25] "Our father said, 'Go back, buy us a little food.' [26] "But we said, 'We cannot go down. If our youngest brother is with us, then we will go down; for we cannot see the man's face unless our youngest brother is with us.' [27] "Your servant my father said to us, 'You know that my wife bore me two sons; [28] and the one went out from me, and I said, "Surely he is torn in pieces," and I have not seen him since. [29] 'If you take this one also from me, and harm befalls him, you will bring my gray hair down to Sheol in sorrow.' [30] "Now, therefore, when I come to your servant my father, and the lad is not with us, since his life is bound up in the lad's life, [31] when he sees that the lad is not with us, he will die. Thus your servants will bring the gray hair of your servant our father down to Sheol in sorrow. [32] "For your servant became surety for the lad to my father, saying, 'If I do not bring him back to you, then let me bear the blame before my father forever.' [33] "Now, therefore, please let your servant remain instead of the lad a slave to my lord, and let the lad go up with his brothers. [34] "For how shall I go up to my father if the lad is not with me—for fear that I see the evil that would overtake my father?"

Judah approached Joseph, indicating that Joseph was equal to Pharaoh. The brothers shared with Joseph that they have a father and their smallest brother, Benjamin. One brother was dead (they thought Joseph) so Benjamin alone was left of their mother and father. You request that we bring Benjamin to Egypt so Joseph could see him. Jacob protested that

Benjamin cannot leave or else his father would die. Yet Joseph told his servants that unless Benjamin comes back with you, you will not see Joseph again. The brother then shared this with their father, Jacob. Jacob said, "Go back and buy some food." But we said that we cannot go down there unless Benjamin is with us because Joseph will not see us without Benjamin. Jacob replied that his wife (Rachel) bore me two sons. One is dead (they thought was Joseph), torn to pieces by wild animals, and the other, Benjamin, if harmed, will bring my gray hair down to Sheol in sorrow. Indeed, if the brother return to Canaan without Benjamin, Jacob will die. His brothers, servants of Joseph, will being the gray hair of their father down to Sheol in sorrow. Judah then asked that he remain in Egypt instead of the lad as a slave to Joseph and let the lad go home with the rest of the brothers. How shall Judah return to Jacob if Benjamin is not with me. He fears that he will see the evil that would overtake his father. Judah was asking to be the substitute for the boy. Judah told Joseph that it would be easier to be a servant the rest of his life than to live with the knowledge that he had brought grief on his father to kill him. This plea had to touch Joseph's heart; Joseph would forgive them all, just as Christ forgave all of us.

CHAPTER FORTY-FIVE

Joseph Deals Kindly with His Brothers

¹Then Joseph could not control himself before all those who stood by him, and he cried, "Have everyone go out from me." So there was no man with him when Joseph made himself known to his brothers. ²He wept so loudly that the Egyptians heard it, and the household of Pharaoh heard of it. ³Then Joseph said to his brothers, "I am Joseph! Is my father still alive?" But his brothers could not answer him, for they were dismayed at his presence.

They had thought before that they might lose their lives, but now they knew that they deserved to die. What would they do? We need to look at the next few lines and see a type of Jesus. We deserved to die the cruel death of the cross but Jesus, the beloved Son of the Father, took our place to give us eternal life. His brothers had thought before that they might lose their lives, but now they knew that they deserved to die. What would they do? We need to look at the next few lines and see a type of Jesus. We deserved to die the cruel death of the cross but Jesus, the beloved Son of the Father, took our place to give us eternal life. Joseph the beloved son of Jacob made a way for his family to live. Joseph then asked everyone to leave except for his family. Then Joseph told his brothers that he was the brother they thought had been killed years ago. Stunned by the revelation of who it really was with whom they dealt, the brothers then heard expressed a masterpiece of recognition of and submission to the sovereignty of God, i.e., His providential rule over the affairs of life, both good and bad. Joseph could not refrain himself any longer. "And there stood no man with him, while Joseph made himself known unto his brethren." Not that Joseph was ashamed of them, and of owning before them the relation he was with them. Joseph could stand this no more. He broke down and began to cry in front of everyone. The Egyptians, who were with Joseph, were asked to leave the room. Joseph told his brothers who he was.

⁴And he said, "I am your brother Joseph, whom you sold into Egypt. ⁵"Now do not be grieved or angry with yourselves, because you sold me here, for God sent me before you to preserve life. ⁶"For the famine has been in the land these two years, and there are still five years in which there will be neither plowing nor harvesting. ⁷"God sent me before you to preserve for you a remnant in the earth, and to keep you alive by a great deliverance. ⁸"Now, therefore, it was not you who sent me here, but God; and He has made me a father to Pharaoh and lord of all his household and ruler over all the land of Egypt. ⁹"Hurry and go up to my father, and say to him, 'Thus says your son Joseph, "God has made me lord of all Egypt; come down to me, do not delay. ¹⁰"You shall live in the land of Goshen, and you shall be near me, you and your children and your children's children and your flocks and your herds and all that you have. ¹¹"There I will also provide for you, for there are still five years of famine to come, and you and your household and all that you have would be impoverished."' ¹²"Behold, your eyes see, and the eyes of my brother Benjamin see, that it is my mouth which is speaking to you. ¹³"Now you must tell my father of all my splendor in Egypt, and all that you have seen; and you must hurry and bring my father down here." ¹⁴Then he fell on his brother Benjamin's neck and wept, and Benjamin wept on his neck. ¹⁵He kissed all his brothers and wept on them, and afterward his brothers talked with him.

Joseph said for his brothers to come closer to him. Then he said that "I am your brother Joseph who you sold to Egypt. Do not grieved or angry with yourselves so selling me here." God used him to ensure that God used him before you to preserve life. Joseph asked his brothers not to grieve or be angry with yourselves. God gave Joseph the ability to interpret dreams and that's why Pharaoh made him the second in command in all of Egypt. He reminded them that only two years have passed and there are still five years of no plowing or harvesting because of the famine. God send me before you to preserve for you a remnant in the earth and to keep you alive by great deliverance. It was not you who sent me here, but God and He has made me a father to Pharaoh and lord of all his household and ruler over all the land of Egypt. He was trying to make them understand that he was sent ahead to prepare a place, where his family can be saved.

Joseph was not holding a grudge. He realized that his time here was part of a great plan that God had, to get the children of Israel into Egypt. God told Abraham they would spend 400 years in Egypt. This was fulfillment of that prophecy.

Hurry to their father, Jacob, and tell him that God has make me lord of all of Egypt. Please come down quickly. You will live in the land of Goshen, you shall me near me, you and your children and your grandchildren plus your flocks and herds and all that you have. The "Land of Goshen" was an Egyptian region (47:6 – 27), in the eastern delta area (47:11), not far from the court at Memphis. It was highly suitable for cattle (47:4-6), but hated by the Egyptians (46:34). Thus, it provided good seclusion. This isolation would provide for Israel's distinctive cultural preservation under conditions favorable to their growth and unity. I will provide for you since there are still five years of famine to come. Behold, your eyes see, the eyes of my brother Benjamin see that it is my mouth speaking to you. Tell my father my splendor in Egypt and you must hurry and bring my father here. Then Joseph fell on his brother's neck and wept and Benjamin did the same. Joseph kissed all his brother and wept on them and afterward all his brothers spoked to him. It had been 22 years since Joseph was sold into slavery.

[16]Now when the news was heard in Pharaoh's house that Joseph's brothers had come, it pleased Pharaoh and his servants. [17]Then Pharaoh said to Joseph, "Say to your brothers, 'Do this: load your beasts and go to the land of Canaan, [18]and take your father and your households and come to me, and I will give you the best of the land of Egypt and you will eat the fat of the land.' [19]"Now you are ordered, 'Do this: take wagons from the land of Egypt for your little ones and for your wives, and bring your father and come. [20]'Do not concern yourselves with your goods, for the best of all the land of Egypt is yours.'"

Pharaoh and his servants were very pleased to hear the news about Joseph's brother had come. Pharaoh told Joseph, "Say to your brothers, load your beast and go to land of Canaan, then take your father and your households and come to me and I will give you the best in the land of Egypt and they will eat the fat of the land". Pharaoh ordered to take wagons from the land of Egypt for your little ones and your wives and bring your father to Egypt. Do not concern yourselves with your goods, for the best of all the land of Egypt is yours. Pharaoh was delighted because Joseph's brothers had come, and it had made Joseph so happy. All this time, Joseph was highly respected by the Pharaoh and his servants. All Egypt was grateful to Joseph for his plan to keep them alive. Whatever it takes to made Joseph happy made everyone happy.

[21] Then the sons of Israel did so; and Joseph gave them wagons according to the command of Pharaoh, and gave them provisions for the journey. [22] To each of them he gave changes of garments, but to Benjamin he gave three hundred pieces of silver and five changes of garments. [23] To his father he sent as follows: ten donkeys loaded with the best things of Egypt, and ten female donkeys loaded with grain and bread and sustenance for his father on the journey. [24] So he sent his brothers away, and as they departed, he said to them, "Do not quarrel on the journey." [25] Then they went up from Egypt, and came to the land of Canaan to their father Jacob. [26] They told him, saying, "Joseph is still alive, and indeed he is ruler over all the land of Egypt." But he was stunned, for he did not believe them. [27] When they told him all the words of Joseph that he had spoken to them, and when he saw the wagons that Joseph had sent to carry him, the spirit of their father Jacob revived. [28] Then Israel said, "It is enough; my son Joseph is still alive. I will go and see him before I die."

Joseph gave his brothers wagons according to Pharaoh and other provisions for their journey back to Canaan. He gave them changes of garments and to Benjamin he gave three hundred pieces of silver and five changes of garments. To Joseph's father he sent ten donkeys loaded with the best things of Egypt and ten donkeys loaded with grain and bread and sustenance for Jacob for the journey. Joseph asked the brothers not to quarrel on their way back to Canaan. They then told Jacob that Joseph was alive. Jacob did not believe them until he saw all the wagons filled with so much from Egypt. Then his spirit was revived. We do not know if Jacob ever asked his sons why he was still alive, what did they do to him, and why did he end up in Egypt. Israel (Jacob who prevailed against God and men) then said that he must go to Egypt and see his long-lost son. For Jacob to learn that his son was still alive was like Jesus disciples learning that Jesus had been raised from the dead.

CHAPTER FORTY-SIX

Jacob Moves to Egypt

¹So Israel set out with all that he had, and came to Beersheba, and offered sacrifices to the God of his father Isaac. ²God spoke to Israel in visions of the night and said, "Jacob, Jacob." And he said, "Here I am." ³He said, "I am God, the God of your father; do not be afraid to go down to Egypt, for I will make you a great nation there. ⁴"I will go down with you to Egypt, and I will also surely bring you up again; and Joseph will close your eyes."

Israel set out with all he had and came to Beersheba. Israel offered sacrifices to God of his father Isaac at Beersheba. God spoke to Israel in visions of the night and said "Jacob, Jacob". Jacob replied "Here I am". God then replied "I am God, God of your father; do not be afraid to go to Egypt, for I will make you a great nation there. I will go with you to Egypt and will bring you up again, and Joseph will close your eyes." Jacob will die in Egypt filled with peace with his son, Joseph, closing his eyes and he will return and be buried in Canaan.

⁵Then Jacob arose from Beersheba; and the sons of Israel carried their father Jacob and their little ones and their wives in the wagons which Pharaoh had sent to carry him. ⁶They took their livestock and their property, which they had acquired in the land of Canaan, and came to Egypt, Jacob and all his descendants with him: ⁷his sons and his grandsons with him, his daughters and his granddaughters, and all his descendants he brought with him to Egypt.

Jacob arose from Beersheba and his sons carried their father and their little ones and their wives in the wagons that Pharaoh arranged to carry them. They took their livestock and property, acquired in Canaan and came to Egypt. Jacob brought all his descendants with him, his sons, grandsons, daughters, granddaughter, everyone he brought to Egypt. All Jacob's descendants are listed stated in Genesis 46:8-27.

⁸Now these are the names of the sons of Israel, Jacob and his sons, who went to Egypt: Reuben, Jacob's firstborn. ⁹The sons of Reuben: Hanoch and Pallu and Hezron and Carmi. ¹⁰The sons of Simeon: Jemuel and Jamin and Ohad and Jachin and Zohar and Shaul the son of a Canaanite woman. ¹¹The sons of Levi: Gershon, Kohath, and Merari. ¹²The sons of Judah: Er and Onan and Shelah and Perez and Zerah (but Er and Onan died in the land of Canaan). And the sons of Perez were Hezron and Hamul. ¹³The sons of Issachar: Tola and Puvvah and Iob and Shimron. ¹⁴The sons of Zebulun: Sered and Elon and Jahleel. ¹⁵These are the sons of Leah, whom she bore to Jacob in Paddan-aram, with his daughter Dinah; all his sons and his daughters numbered thirty-three. ¹⁶The sons of Gad: Ziphion and Haggi, Shuni and Ezbon, Eri and Arodi and Areli. ¹⁷The sons of Asher: Imnah and Ishvah and Ishvi and Beriah and their sister Serah. And the sons of Beriah: Heber and Malchiel. ¹⁸These are the sons of Zilpah, whom Laban gave to his daughter Leah; and she bore to Jacob these sixteen persons. ¹⁹The sons of Jacob's wife Rachel: Joseph and Benjamin. ²⁰Now to Joseph in the land of Egypt were born Manasseh and Ephraim, whom Asenath, the daughter of Potiphera, priest of On, bore to him. ²¹The sons of Benjamin: Bela and Becher and Ashbel, Gera and Naaman, Ehi and Rosh, Muppim and Huppim and Ard. ²²These are the sons of Rachel, who were born to Jacob; there were fourteen persons in all. ²³The sons of Dan: Hushim. ²⁴The sons of Naphtali: Jahzeel and Guni and Jezer and Shillem. ²⁵These are the sons of Bilhah, whom Laban gave to his daughter Rachel, and she bore these to Jacob; there were seven persons in all. ²⁶All the persons belonging to Jacob, who came to Egypt, his direct descendants, not including the wives of Jacob's sons, were sixty-six persons in all, ²⁷and the sons of Joseph, who were born to him in Egypt were two; all the persons of the house of Jacob, who came to Egypt, were seventy.

Strictly speaking, there were only sixty-six went to Egypt; but to these add Joseph and his two sons, and Jacob the head of the clan, and the whole number amounts to seventy. All the souls that went with Jacob into Egypt, "that came out of his loins (Exodus 1:5)," were eleven sons, one daughter, fifty grandchildren, and four great-grandsons; in all, sixty-six.

Jacob, Joseph and his two sons, are four; and thus, all the souls belonging to the family of Jacob which went into Egypt were seventy.

²⁸Now he sent Judah before him to Joseph, to point out the way before him to Goshen; and they came into the land of Goshen. ²⁹Joseph prepared his chariot and went up to Goshen to meet his father Israel; as soon as he appeared before him, he fell on his neck and wept on his neck a long time. ³⁰Then Israel said to Joseph, "Now let me die, since I have seen your face, that you are still alive." ³¹Joseph said to his brothers and to his father's household, "I will go up and tell Pharaoh, and will say to him, 'My brothers and my father's household, who were in the land of Canaan, have come to me; ³²and the men are shepherds, for they have been keepers of livestock; and they have brought their flocks and their herds and all that they have.' ³³ "When Pharaoh calls you and says, 'What is your occupation?' ³⁴you shall say, 'Your servants have been keepers of livestock from our youth even until now, both we and our fathers,' that you may live in the land of Goshen; for every shepherd is loathsome to the Egyptians."

Jacob sent Judah ahead of them, to point the way before him to Goshen. Joseph prepared his chariot and went up to Goshen to meet his father Israel. When they finally met, Joseph fell on the neck of Jacob and wept a long time. Then Israel said to Joseph, "Now let me die, since I have seen your face and you are still alive." Joseph then said to his brothers and to the entire household, "I will go up and tell Pharaoh that his brothers and all his father's household, who were in the land of Canaan, have come to me and the men are shepherds, have been keepers of livestock and they have brought their flocks and herds and all they have." When Pharaoh calls you and asks what is your occupation, you shall say your servants have been keepers of livestock from our youth to now, both we and our fathers, that you may live in the land of Goshen. Every shepherd is loathsome to the Egyptians. Indeed, Egyptians were not friends to shepherds so Jacob and family settled in Goshen.

The Book of Genesis

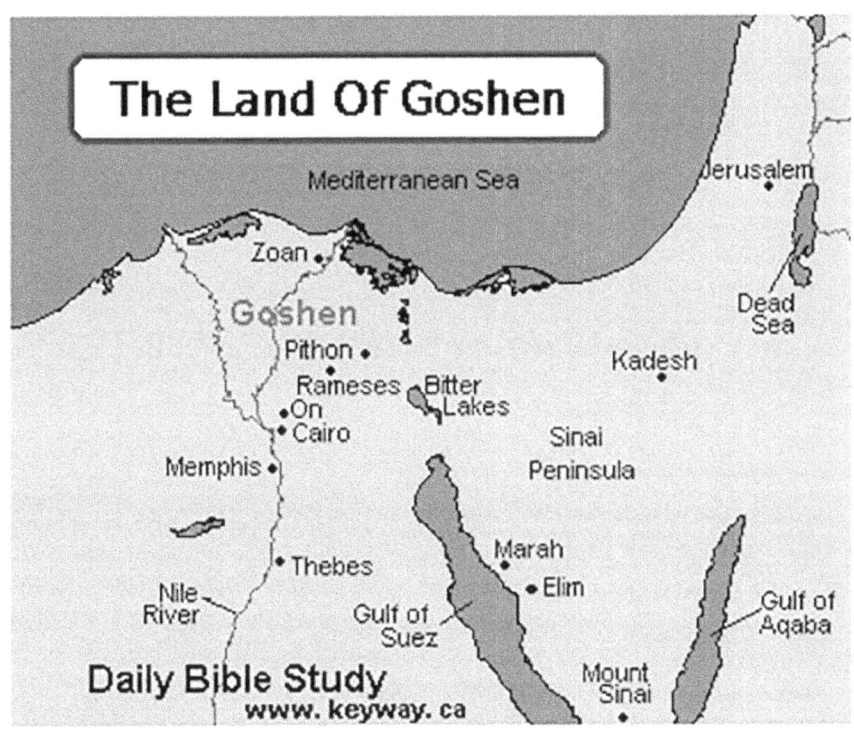

Created by Wayne Bland,
HYPERLINK "http://www.keyway.ca" www.keyway.ca,
Daily Bible Study,

We learn from Joseph how to be (1) He cared for aged father, (2) He continued to work (see Genesis 47:13-16), and (3) He maintained his faith even Living in a pagan environment (Genesis 50:15-26)

CHAPTER FORTY-SEVEN

Jacob's Family Settle in Goshen

¹Then Joseph went in and told Pharaoh, and said, "My father and my brothers and their flocks and their herds and all that they have, have come out of the land of Canaan; and behold, they are in the land of Goshen." ²He took five men from among his brothers and presented them to Pharaoh. ³Then Pharaoh said to his brothers, "What is your occupation?" So they said to Pharaoh, "Your servants are shepherds, both we and our fathers." ⁴They said to Pharaoh, "We have come to sojourn in the land, for there is no pasture for your servants' flocks, for the famine is severe in the land of Canaan. Now, therefore, please let your servants live in the land of Goshen." ⁵Then Pharaoh said to Joseph, "Your father and your brothers have come to you. ⁶"The land of Egypt is at your disposal; settle your father and your brothers in the best of the land, let them live in the land of Goshen; and if you know any capable men among them, then put them in charge of my livestock."

Joseph told Pharaoh that his father, his brothers, and all their livestock have exited Canaan to come to the land of Goshen. Joseph picked five brothers (five represents "grace") and presented them to Pharaoh. Pharaoh asked them "What is your occupation?" They replied, "We are shepherds, both our father and us". They asked Pharaoh because of the famine is severe in the land of Canaan that could they live in the land of Goshen in Egypt. Pharaoh said to Joseph, "Your father and brothers have come to you. The land of Egypt is at your disposal. Settle your father and brothers in the best of the land including Goshen. If you have any capable men among them, put them in charge of my livestock."

⁷Then Joseph brought his father Jacob and presented him to Pharaoh; and Jacob blessed Pharaoh. ⁸Pharaoh said to Jacob, "How many years have you lived?" ⁹So Jacob said to Pharaoh, "The years of my sojourning are one hundred and thirty; few and unpleasant have been the years of my life, nor have they attained the years that my fathers lived during the days of their sojourning." ¹⁰And Jacob blessed Pharaoh, and went out from his presence. ¹¹So Joseph settled his father and his brothers and gave them a possession in the land of Egypt, in the best of the land, in the land of Rameses, as Pharaoh had ordered. ¹²Joseph provided his father and his brothers and all his father's household with food, according to their little ones.

Joseph brought his father to present to Pharaoh; Jacob blessed Pharaoh. Pharaoh asked Jacob how many years have you lived? Jacob responded that the years of his sojourning (staying temporarily; not possessing the land of Canaan) are one hundred and thirty; few and unpleasant (many crises and sorrows) have been the years of my life, nor have they attained the years that my fathers lived during their days of their sojourning. Jacob blessed Pharaoh again and went out from his presence. Joseph settled his father and brothers and gave them land in the land of Egypt, the best of the land, in the land of Rameses, as Pharaoh had ordered. Joseph provided his father and brothers and his father's household with food for their little ones.

¹³Now there was no food in all the land, because the famine was very severe, so that the land of Egypt and the land of Canaan languished because of the famine. ¹⁴Joseph gathered all the money that was found in the land of Egypt and in the land of Canaan for the grain which they bought, and Joseph brought the money into Pharaoh's house. ¹⁵When the money was all spent in the land of Egypt and in the land of Canaan, all the Egyptians came to Joseph and said, "Give us food, for why should we die in your presence? For our money is gone." ¹⁶Then Joseph said, "Give up your livestock, and I will give you food for your livestock, since your money is gone." ¹⁷So they brought their livestock to Joseph, and Joseph gave them food in exchange for the horses and the flocks and the herds and the donkeys; and he fed them with food in exchange for all their livestock that year. ¹⁸When that year was ended, they came to him the next year and said to him, "We will not hide from my lord that our money is all spent, and the cattle are my lord's. There is nothing left for my lord except our bodies and our lands. ¹⁹"Why should we die before your eyes, both we and our land? Buy us and our land for food, and we and our land will be slaves to Pharaoh. So give us seed, that we may live and not die, and that the land may not be desolate."

Both the lands of Canaan and the land of Egypt languished because of severe famine. Joseph gathered all the money he could find in the land of Egypt and the land of Canaan for the grain they had bought and brought the money into Pharaoh's house. People came to Joseph and said, "Give us food for why should be die in your presence for lack of food. We have no money." Joseph replied, "Give up your livestock and I will give you food." The Egyptians brought their livestock to Joseph and Joseph gave them food in exchange for horses and flocks and herds and donkeys. A year later they came to Joseph and said that they have no money and all their livestock is his. They have nothing left for their lord except our bodies and our lands. Why should we die before your eyes? Buy us and our land for food; and we and our land will be slaves to Pharaoh. Pharaoh would be the master, not Joseph. Give us seed, that we may live and not die and this land may not be desolate.

[20]*So Joseph bought all the land of Egypt for Pharaoh, for every Egyptian sold his field, because the famine was severe upon them. Thus the land became Pharaoh's.* [21]*As for the people, he removed them to the cities from one end of Egypt's border to the other.* [22]*Only the land of the priests he did not buy, for the priests had an allotment from Pharaoh, and they lived off the allotment which Pharaoh gave them. Therefore, they did not sell their land.* [23]*Then Joseph said to the people, "Behold, I have today bought you and your land for Pharaoh; now, here is seed for you, and you may sow the land.* [24]*"At the harvest you shall give a fifth to Pharaoh, and four-fifths shall be your own for seed of the field and for your food and for those of your households and as food for your little ones."* [25]*So they said, "You have saved our lives! Let us find favor in the sight of my lord, and we will be Pharaoh's slaves."* [26]*Joseph made it a statute concerning the land of Egypt valid to this day, that Pharaoh should have the fifth; only the land of the priests did not become Pharaoh's.*

Joseph bought all the land of Egypt for Pharaoh as every Egyptian sold his field because the famine was so severe. Why did not the Egyptians save for the famine to come if Joseph had predicted this? Perhaps humankind has not changed in that people still don't wish to save much. Joseph accumulated one fifth of the crops of the land during the abundant years.

That left four-fifths of a bumper crop for the Egyptians. Should they not have been storing up grain for the famine as well as Joseph? Why not spend some of this excess profit? Once people sold their land, Joseph removed them to one end of Egypt's border to the other. Joseph did not buy the priest's land and lived off what Pharaoh had given them. Once Joseph bought their land for Pharaoh, he gave them seed to sow the land.

²⁷Now Israel lived in the land of Egypt, in Goshen, and they acquired property in it and were fruitful and became very numerous. ²⁸Jacob lived in the land of Egypt seventeen years; so the length of Jacob's life was one hundred and forty-seven years. ²⁹When the time for Israel to die drew near, he called his son Joseph and said to him, "Please, if I have found favor in your sight, place now your hand under my thigh and deal with me in kindness and faithfulness. Please do not bury me in Egypt, ³⁰but when I lie down with my fathers, you shall carry me out of Egypt and bury me in their burial place." And he said, "I will do as you have said." ³¹He said, "Swear to me." So he swore to him. Then Israel bowed in worship at the head of the bed.

Israel lived in the land of Egypt, in Goshen and they acquired property in it and were fruitful and became very numerous. Jacob lived in the land of Egypt seventeen years, putting him at one hundred and forty-seven years. Knowing that the day of his departure drew near, Jacob purposed to make his death a testimony to his faith and a stimulus to the faith and obedience of his descendants. Jacob urged Joseph, his most trusted son, to swear a solemn oath promising that he would not bury his father in Egypt, but in Canaan in the cave of Machpelah with his forefathers. This would serve as a reminder to his descendants that Egypt was not home, but only a place to sojourn until God brought them back "home" to Canaan, the land of promise. The faith of Jacob, as he was dying, was his blessing each of the sons of Joseph, as he worshipped by leaning on top of his staff: By faith Jacob, as he was dying, blessed each of the sons of Joseph, and worshipped, leaning on the top of his staff (Hebrews 11:21). Little wonder, for this is surely the high point of Jacob's spiritual life. For the first time, Jacob has ceased striving to do something for God and simply stopped to worship and adore Him.

CHAPTER FORTY-EIGHT

Israel's Last Days

¹Now it came about after these things that Joseph was told, "Behold, your father is sick." So he took his two sons Manasseh and Ephraim with him. ²When it was told to Jacob, "Behold, your son Joseph has come to you," Israel collected his strength and sat up in the bed. ³Then Jacob said to Joseph, "God Almighty appeared to me at Luz in the land of Canaan and blessed me, ⁴and He said to me, 'Behold, I will make you fruitful and numerous, and I will make you a company of peoples, and will give this land to your descendants after you for an everlasting possession.' ⁵"Now your two sons, who were born to you in the land of Egypt before I came to you in Egypt, are mine; Ephraim and Manasseh shall be mine, as Reuben and Simeon are. ⁶"But your offspring that have been born after them shall be yours; they shall be called by the names of their brothers in their inheritance. ⁷"Now as for me, when I came from Paddan, Rachel died, to my sorrow, in the land of Canaan on the journey, when there was still some distance to go to Ephrath; and I buried her there on the way to Ephrath (that is, Bethlehem)."

Joseph was told at Genesis 48:1 that his father was sick. We don't know when this was but perhaps close to Jacob's last year. Joseph took his two sons, Manasseh and Ephraim with him to see Jacob and Jacob knew that he was coming. Jacob sat up in bed, then said to Joseph, "God Almighty appeared to me at Luz in the land of Canaan and blessed me." God then said to Jacob, "I will make you fruitful and numerous and I will make you a company of peoples and will give this land to your descendant after you for an everlasting possession." Jacob is speaking now, "Now your two sons, who were born to you in the land of Egypt before I came to you in Egypt, are mine; Ephraim and Manasseh shall be mine, as Reuben and Simeon are. "But your offspring that have been born after them shall be yours; they shall be called by the names of their brothers in their inheritance. "Now as for me, when I came from Paddan, Rachel died, to my sorrow, in the land of Canaan on the journey, when there was still some distance to go to Ephrath; and I buried her there on the way to Ephrath (that is, Bethlehem)."

⁸When Israel saw Joseph's sons, he said, "Who are these?" ⁹Joseph said to his father, "They are my sons, whom God has given me here." So he said, "Bring them to me, please, that I may bless them." ¹⁰Now the eyes of Israel were so dim from age that he could not see. Then Joseph brought them close to him, and he kissed them and embraced them. ¹¹Israel said to Joseph, "I never expected to see your face, and behold, God has let me see your children as well." ¹²Then Joseph took them from his knees, and bowed with his face to the ground. ¹³Joseph took them both, Ephraim with his right hand toward Israel's left, and Manasseh with his left hand toward Israel's right, and brought them close to him. ¹⁴But Israel stretched out his right hand and laid it on the head of Ephraim, who was the younger, and his left hand on Manasseh's head, crossing his hands, although Manasseh was the firstborn. ¹⁵He blessed Joseph, and said,
"The God before whom my fathers Abraham and Isaac walked,
The God who has been my shepherd all my life to this day,
¹⁶The angel who has redeemed me from all evil,
Bless the lads;
And may my name live on in them,
And the names of my fathers Abraham and Isaac;
And may they grow into a multitude in the midst of the earth."

Jacob saw Joseph's sons and asks, "Who are these?" Jacob gets up when he hears that Joseph is coming. He is weak and almost blind but his mind is clear and sharp. Jacob asked that he bless Manasseh and Ephraim; Joseph brought them close to him that he could kiss them and embrace them. Israel said to Joseph, "I never expected to see your face and behold, God has let me see you and your children as well." Joseph bowed his face to the ground with Ephraim with his right hand toward Israel's left and Manasseh with his left hand on Israel's right. Israel then stretched out his right hand on the Ephraim head who was younger and his left hand on Manasseh's head, replicating what Isaac did honoring the younger, Jacob, over the older, Esau. When Jacob stretches out his hands he crosses his arms so that his right hand touches Ephraim's head and his left Manasseh. Joseph's approach had been deliberate and well thought through.

[17] When Joseph saw that his father laid his right hand on Ephraim's head, it displeased him; and he grasped his father's hand to remove it from Ephraim's head to Manasseh's head. [18] Joseph said to his father, "Not so, my father, for this one is the firstborn. Place your right hand on his head." [19] But his father refused and said, "I know, my son, I know; he also will become a people and he also will be great. However, his younger brother shall be greater than he, and his descendants shall become a multitude of nations." [20] He blessed them that day, saying, "By you Israel will pronounce blessing, saying, 'May God make you like Ephraim and Manasseh!'" Thus he put Ephraim before Manasseh. [21] Then Israel said to Joseph, "Behold, I am about to die, but God will be with you, and bring you back to the land of your fathers. [22] "I give you one portion more than your brothers, which I took from the hand of the Amorite with my sword and my bow."

[17] When Joseph saw that his father laid his right hand on Ephraim's head, it displeased him; and he grasped his father's hand to remove it from Ephraim's head to Manasseh's head. [18] Joseph said to his father, "Not so, my father, for this one is the firstborn. Place your right hand on his head." [19] But his father refused and said, "I know, my son, I know; he also will become a people and he also will be great. However, his younger brother shall be greater than he, and his descendants shall become a multitude of nations." Jacob asked God to make Ephraim ahead of Manasseh despite Joseph's protests. Then Jacob (Israel) said that he is about to die, but God will be with you and bring you back to the land of your fathers.

In Genesis 48:22 Israel said, "And to you, as one who is over your brothers, I give the ridge of land I took from the Amorites with my sword and my bow." There is no account of an exploits by Jacob that would have conquered that part of the land. Back in Genesis 33:19 Jacob purchased from Hamor, the father of Shechem, a plot of ground when he pitched his tent. We read in John 4:12 that Jesus visited a Samaritan women who asked Jesus "Are you greater than our father Jacob who gave us this well and drank from it himself as did his sons and flocks and herds?" This must be the piece of land that Jacob took from the Amorite although no his conquest with sword and bow is not recorded. Ephraim and Manasseh, descendants of Jacob and Joseph, receive their inheritance.

CHAPTER FORTY-NINE

Israel's Prophecy Concerning His Sons

Taken from https://whatheisteachingme.wordpress.com/2010/05/19/genesis-49-the-blessing-of-jacobs-sons/

¹Then Jacob summoned his sons and said, "Assemble yourselves that I may tell you what will befall you in the days to come. ² "Gather together and hear, O sons of Jacob; and listen to Israel your father.

In Genesis 49, Jacob calls together his twelve sons and blesses them before his death. He calls each son by name and speaks of their pasts as well as their futures. He then speaks about each of his twelve sons.

³ "Reuben, you are my firstborn;
  My might and the beginning of my strength,
  Preeminent in dignity and preeminent in power.
⁴ "Uncontrolled as water, you shall not have preeminence,
  Because you went up to your father's bed;
  Then you defiled it—he went up to my couch.

Reuben was Jacob's firstborn son, born to his wife Leah. Leah had been forced on Jacob by her father, Laban. In Genesis 29:31, it specifically states that she was not loved by him. Because of this, God showed mercy to her by giving her a son, whom she named Reuben and said "It is because the LORD has seen my misery. Surely my husband will love me now." (Genesis 29:32). In Genesis 35, Reuben slept with Jacob's concubine, Bilhah. Jacob learned of this and Reuben lost all his inheritance. Later, in 1 Chronicles

5:1-2, it states that even though Reuben was the firstborn, because of his sin the firstborn rights were given to Joseph. Reuben could no longer even be listed first in the genealogical order. God sees sin no matter what it is. It's not just some simple act of indiscretion that can be overlooked whenever we sin – because of His righteousness and holiness, justice must be served when we sin. Unfortunately for Reuben, the concept of grace was still foreign, and he had to live with the consequence.

⁵ *"Simeon and Levi are brothers;*
 Their swords are implements of violence.
⁶ *"Let my soul not enter into their council;*
 Let not my glory be united with their assembly;
 Because in their anger they slew men,
 And in their self-will they lamed oxen.
⁷ *"Cursed be their anger, for it is fierce;*
 And their wrath, for it is cruel.
 I will disperse them in Jacob,
 And scatter them in Israel.

Simeon and Levi are Reuben's younger brothers, born to Leah. When Levi was born Leah said "Now at last my husband will become attached to me, because I have borne him three sons." Unfortunately for Leah, none of these 3 sons brought Jacob any closer to becoming attached to her, and Jacob didn't particularly become attached to any of these sons either. Reuben, of course, was because he defiled his father's marriage bed, but for Simeon and Levi, it was because of the revenge they enacted on the Shechemites when their ruler raped Dinah, Jacob's daughter. Simeon and Levi, with the help of the rest of their brothers, attacked the Shechemites and killed all males (Genesis 34) and hamstrung their oxen. Because of this, Jacob said "You have brought trouble on me by making me a stench to the Canaanites and Perizzites the people living in this land. We are few in number, and if they join forces against me and attack me, I and my household will be destroyed." (Genesis 34:30). Cursed be their anger, so fierce, and their fury, so cruel! I will scatter them in Jacob and disperse them in Israel." Jacob only curses his sons for their anger, not for their actions. It is interesting that later descendants of Levi will serve as priests for Israel. Moses was also from the tribe of Levi. Levi had three sons---Gershon, Kohath, and Merari, and Kohath through his wife Jochebed had three children—Miriam, Moses (Exodus 2:1), and Aaron.

⁸"Judah, your brothers shall praise you;
  Your hand shall be on the neck of your enemies;
  Your father's sons shall bow down to you.
⁹"Judah is a lion's whelp;
  From the prey, my son, you have gone up.
  He couches, he lies down as a lion,
  And as a lion, who dares rouse him up?
¹⁰"The scepter shall not depart from Judah,
  Nor the ruler's staff from between his feet,
  Until Shiloh comes,
  And to him shall be the obedience of the peoples.
¹¹"He ties his foal to the vine,
  And his donkey's colt to the choice vine;
  He washes his garments in wine,
  And his robes in the blood of grapes.
¹²"His eyes are dull from wine,
  And his teeth white from milk.

When Judah was born to Leah she said "This time I will praise the LORD." Judah's blessing is one of the longest, but Judah's descendants also play the largest role in the history of the nation of Israel. It is Judah's descendants who become the rulers of all the tribes of Israel, foretold in the blessing – "Judah, your brothers will praise you; your hand will be on the neck of your enemies; your father's sons will bow down to you…the scepter will not depart from Judah, nor the ruler's staff from between his feet, until he comes to whom it belongs and the obedience of the nations is his" (Genesis 49:8,10). Jacob also foretells of the coming of one of Jacob's descendants who will be greater than all others. Jacob also says that Judah will "tether his donkey to a vine, his colt to the choicest branch". Christ calls himself "the true vine" in John 15:1, and later Jacob calls Joseph "a fruitful vine" (Genesis 49:22). Joseph is seen by many as a figure who foreshadows the being of Christ.

¹³"Zebulun will dwell at the seashore;
  And he shall be a haven for ships,
  And his flank shall be toward Sidon.

¹⁴ *"Issachar is a strong donkey,*
   Lying down between the sheepfolds.
¹⁵ *"When he saw that a resting place was good*
   And that the land was pleasant,
   He bowed his shoulder to bear burdens,
   And became a slave at forced labor.
¹⁶ *"Dan shall judge his people,*
   As one of the tribes of Israel.
¹⁷ *"Dan shall be a serpent in the way,*
   A horned snake in the path,
   That bites the horse's heels,
   So that his rider falls backward.
¹⁸ *"For Your salvation I wait, O LORD.*
¹⁹ *"As for Gad, raiders shall raid him,*
   But he will raid at their heels.
²⁰ *"As for Asher, his food shall be rich,*
   And he will yield royal dainties.
²¹ *"Naphtali is a doe let loose,*
   He gives beautiful words.

Jacob describes sons 5 through 10 in quick order. Zebulun is told he will leave by the sea and become a haven for ships. The family of Zebulun after Joshua captured Israel received the region of Galilee along the shore of Lake Tiberias, reaching to the Mediterranean Sea. Upon returning from Egypt after the death King Herod, Joseph and Mary, with their child Jesus, took refuge in Galilee, the land allotted to Zebulun. Issachar is told that he will enjoy his new land, perhaps to the point that he would live as a slave to stay there, rather than fight for it. Dan is told that his tribe will provide justice for the people of Israel. The name Dan means "judge" or "he who vindicates," but there is no history linking the person of Dan to this prophecy. Samson, the future judge of Israel, does come from this tribe the tribe of Dan (Judges 13). Gad is told that he "will be attacked by a band of raiders, but he will attack them at their heels." (Genesis 49:19). It's interesting to note that "Gad was one of the tribes who chose to stay on the east side of the Jordan in Gilead (along with the Reubenites, see <u>Numbers 32</u>), rather than cross the Jordan and be with the other tribes within the promised land. Because of this, they were isolated from the other tribes, and thus, were subject to attacks by border raiders" (see Judges 10:8, Judges

11:4, 1 Chronicles 5:18, and Jeremiah 49:1). Asher is told that his "food will be rich; he will provide delicacies fit for a king." (Genesis 49:20). The tribe of Asher is later allotted an area that was prosperous and known for its wheat, olive oil, milk, and butter (all delicacies at that time). Naphtali is called "a doe set free that bears beautiful fawns." Some believe that this is a prophecy of the fact that a later prophetess and judge – Deborah – came from the tribe of Naphtali (Judges 4). Jacob's blessing that Naphtali gives beautiful words is thought to be a prophecy of the song of Deborah in Judges 5.

²²"Joseph is a fruitful bough,
  A fruitful bough by a spring;
  Its branches run over a wall.
²³"The archers bitterly attacked him,
  And shot at him and harassed him;
²⁴But his bow remained firm,
  And his arms were agile,
  From the hands of the Mighty One of Jacob
  (From there is the Shepherd, the Stone of Israel),
²⁵From the God of your father who helps you,
  And by the Almighty who blesses you
  With blessings of heaven above,
  Blessings of the deep that lies beneath,
  Blessings of the breasts and of the womb.
²⁶"The blessings of your father
  Have surpassed the blessings of my ancestors
  Up to the utmost bound of the everlasting hills;
  May they be on the head of Joseph,
  And on the crown of the head of the one distinguished among his brothers.

Jacob has already blessed Joseph and his two sons at an earlier time (see Genesis 48), so in this blessing Jacob refers mainly to Joseph's past of perseverance and staying strong through adversity. Joseph was a blessing to all those around him – to the Egyptians and to all those around Egypt – "Joseph is a fruitful vine, a fruitful vine near a spring, whose branches climb over a wall." Joseph was imprisoned and persecuted, but he stayed strong – "with bitterness archers attacked him; they shot at him with hostility. But his bow remained steady, his strong arms stayed limber."

It was because of God that Joseph was able to succeed – "…because of the hand of the Mighty One of Jacob, because of the Shepherd, the Rock of Israel, because of your father's God, who helps you, because of the Almighty, who blesses you…"

²⁷"Benjamin is a ravenous wolf;
In the morning he devours the prey,
And in the evening he divides the spoil."

Benjamin is told that he "is a ravenous wolf; in the morning he devours the prey, in the evening he divides the plunder." It is thought that this prophetically refers to the tribe of Benjamin's fierceness and courage. Historically, this is very accurate. For fierceness, note that Ehud, a judge of Israel mentioned in Judges 3 was a Benjamite. Under the guise of paying tribute, he got close to the king of Moab and plunged a sword into his fat belly. "Even the handle sank in after the blade, which came out his back. Ehud did not pull the sword out, and the fat closed in over it." (Judges 3:22). Also, the apostle Paul was a Benjamite, and he is remembered for how he fiercely persecuted the church before his conversion (see Acts 9). For courage, note that Mordecai and Esther were Benjamites, and few stories in the Bible tell of more courage than that of these two characters.

²⁸All these are the twelve tribes of Israel, and this is what their father said to them when he blessed them. He blessed them, every one with the blessing appropriate to him. ²⁹Then he charged them and said to them, "I am about to be gathered to my people; bury me with my fathers in the cave that is in the field of Ephron the Hittite, ³⁰in the cave that is in the field of Machpelah, which is before Mamre, in the land of Canaan, which Abraham bought along with the field from Ephron the Hittite for a burial site. ³¹"There they buried Abraham and his wife Sarah, there they buried Isaac and his wife Rebekah, and there I buried Leah— ³²the field and the cave that is in it, purchased from the sons of Heth." ³³When Jacob finished charging his sons, he drew his feet into the bed and breathed his last, and was gathered to his people.

Jacob, the father, blessed his twelve sons, each blessing specific for each of his twelve sons. He knew that he was about to die and asked his sons to take his body back to be buried with his fathers in a cave that is in the field of Ephron the Hittite, in the cave that is in the field of Machpelah, before Mamre, in the land of Canaan that Abraham bought along with the field from Ephron the Hittite for a burial site (Genesis 23). There they buried Abraham, his wife Sarah, Abraham's son Isaac and his wife Rebekah, and where Jacob buried Leah, purchased from the sons of Heth (Genesis 10, 23, 25). After Jacob charging his sons, he drew his feet into his bed, and breathed his last.

CHAPTER FIFTY

The Death of Israel

¹*Then Joseph fell on his father's face, and wept over him and kissed him.* ²*Joseph commanded his servants the physicians to embalm his father. So the physicians embalmed Israel.* ³*Now forty days were required for it, for such is the period required for embalming. And the Egyptians wept for him seventy days.* ⁴*When the days of mourning for him were past, Joseph spoke to the household of Pharaoh, saying, "If now I have found favor in your sight, please speak to Pharaoh, saying,* ⁵*'My father made me swear, saying, "Behold, I am about to die; in my grave which I dug for myself in the land of Canaan, there you shall bury me." Now therefore, please let me go up and bury my father; then I will return.'"* ⁶*Pharaoh said, "Go up and bury your father, as he made you swear."* ⁷*So Joseph went up to bury his father, and with him went up all the servants of Pharaoh, the elders of his household and all the elders of the land of Egypt,* ⁸*and all the household of Joseph and his brothers and his father's household; they left only their little ones and their flocks and their herds in the land of Goshen.* ⁹*There also went up with him both chariots and horsemen; and it was a very great company.* ¹⁰*When they came to the threshing floor of Atad, which is beyond the Jordan, they lamented there with a very great and sorrowful lamentation; and he observed seven days mourning for his father.* ¹¹*Now when the inhabitants of the land, the Canaanites, saw the mourning at the threshing floor of Atad, they said, "This is a grievous mourning for the Egyptians." Therefore it was named Abel-mizraim, which is beyond the Jordan.*

After Jacob's death, Joseph fell on his father's face, wept and kissed him. Joseph commanded his servants the physicians to embalm Jacob.

It takes forty days to embalm someone back then.⁷ The Egyptians wept for seventy days.

Joseph spoke to the household of Pharaoh. Jacob asked that Joseph and family bury him in a grave he dug for himself in the land of Canaan. Pharaoh replied that he should go to bury his father in Canaan, as he swore to Jacob, then return to Egypt. Joseph went to bury his father with all the servants of Pharaoh, the elders of his household and all the elders in the land of Egypt. How many of these where there; no one knows? Only their little ones and their livestock were left in Goshen. Who took care of these, again we do not know? A very great company went with Joseph to bury his father. They arrived at the threshing floor of Atad, beyond the River Jordan, and observed seven days of mourning for his father. Atad was probably near Hebron although described in these verses of Genesis as east of the River Jordan and associated with threshing. It was probably

---

6   EMBALMING (https://wol.jw.org/en/wol/d/r1/lp-e/1200001348) The process of treating a dead body (human or animal) with substances such as aromatic oils in order to preserve it from decay. If this art was not originated by the Egyptians, it was at least practiced by them in very early times. There are only two cases specifically called embalming in the Bible and both of these took place in Egypt. It was there that Jacob died, and after relating Joseph's expression of sorrow over his father's demise, the inspired Record states: "After that Joseph commanded his servants, the physicians, to embalm his father. So the physicians embalmed Israel, and they took fully forty days for him, for this many days they customarily take for the embalming, and the Egyptians continued to shed tears for him seventy days." (Genesis 50:2-3). Joseph died at the age of 110 years, "and they had him embalmed, and he was put in a coffin in Egypt." (Genesis 50:36). In Jacob's case the principal purpose apparently was preservation until his burial in the Promised Land. According to Herodotus, Egyptian embalming methods included placing the corpse in natron (Natron is a naturally occurring mixture of sodium carbonate decahydrate ($Na_2CO_3 \cdot 10H_2O$, a kind of soda ash) and around 17% sodium abicarbonate (also called baking soda, $NaHCO_3$) along with small quantities of sodium chloride and sodium sulfate) for *seventy* days. Yet, when Jacob was embalmed by Egyptian physicians at a much earlier time, the Bible says "they took fully *forty* days for him, for this many days they customarily take for the embalming, and the Egyptians continued to shed tears for him seventy days." (Genesis 50:3). Scholars have made various efforts to reconcile Genesis 50:3 with the words of Herodotus. For one thing, the 40 days may not have included the time of the body's immersion in natron. However, it is quite possible that Herodotus simply erred in saying the dead body was placed in natron for 70 days.

near Hebron although described in these verses of Genesis as beyond (or east of) the Jordan and associated with threshing, a process of loosening the edible part of grain or other crop from the husks to which it is attached. The inhabitant of the land, the Canaanites, saw the mourning at Atad, they named it Abel-mizraim, a site of grievous mourning for the Egyptians.

[12]Thus his sons did for him as he had charged them; [13]for his sons carried him to the land of Canaan and buried him in the cave of the field of Machpelah before Mamre, which Abraham had bought along with the field for a burial site from Ephron the Hittite. [14]After he had buried his father, Joseph returned to Egypt, he and his brothers, and all who had gone up with him to bury his father.

Jacob's sons did for him as he charged them. They carried his body to Canaan to be buried in the cave of the field of Machpelah before Mamre, where Abraham had brought along with a field for the burial site from Ephron the Hittite. He then returned to Egypt along with all who had taken the trip with him.

[15]When Joseph's brothers saw that their father was dead, they said, "What if Joseph bears a grudge against us and pays us back in full for all the wrong which we did to him!" [16]So they sent a message to Joseph, saying, "Your father charged before he died, saying, [17]'Thus you shall say to Joseph, "Please forgive, I beg you, the transgression of your brothers and their sin, for they did you wrong."' And now, please forgive the transgression of the servants of the God of your father." And Joseph wept when they spoke to him. [18]Then his brothers also came and fell down before him and said, "Behold, we are your servants." [19]But Joseph said to them, "Do not be afraid, for am I in God's place? [20]As for you, you meant evil against me, but God meant it for good in order to bring about this present result, to preserve many people alive. [21]"So therefore, do not be afraid; I will provide for you and your little ones." So he comforted them and spoke kindly to them.

We are uncertain of the time when Joseph's brothers had a feeling that Joseph, with his father dead, might have a grudge against them and pay them back for all the problems they gave to him. They sent a message to Joseph saying that before Jacob died he said to Joseph to forgive his brothers for their sin, for they did to you what was wrong. Please forgive the transgression of the servants of the God of your father. Both Joseph and all his brothers wept and they said to Joseph that they are his servants. Yet Joseph answer to them, "Do not be afraid, for am I in God's place?" Joseph was simply saying that he is not God and other people are not to be afraid of him. Then, in Genesis 50:20, Joseph made this statement to his brothers to reassure them that he was not going to seek revenge against them for what they did to him years before (read Genesis 37). Joseph was a remarkable human being. Have you ever noticed that the Bible never has anything negative to say about Joseph (two other examples might be Daniel and John)? Joseph's life mirrored Jesus' life in the sense that Joseph was a prime example of being a forgiver just like Jesus. Of course, Jesus had to shed His blood in order for us to be forgiven by God (Hebrews 9:22).

Forgiveness is to excuse a fault or an offense. To forgive another means that you have completely released and excused the person who hurt you. To forgive means to renounce whatever anger and resentment you had against another. To forgive also means to absolve a debt. Forgiveness literally means that you have removed from your mind the offense, debt and resulting resentment that you used to have against someone. Forgiveness is the supreme act of Christlike character which is why so few people, even Christians, can truly forgive.

While Joseph exemplified forgiveness, the word and act is much more emphasized in the New Testament where the word is used at least 163 times. Christians recite the Lord's Prayer all the time yet mindlessly don't pay attention to the words "forgive our debts as we forgive our debtors" (Matthew 6:12). This is the only part of the Lord's Prayer with a condition attached to a promise. We also don't remember that just a couple of verses later (Matthew 6:14-15) Jesus declared that if you don't forgive others of their debts against you, "neither will your Father forgive your debts". Think about that. You harbor resentment against someone who has wounded you without forgiving him/her, then you pray for forgiveness in your prayers, do you not know that God is not going to forgive you until you forgive first? Also, harboring resentment and bitterness and refusing to forgive another will significantly restrict/prevent peace and freedom from happening in your life.

Indeed, refusing to forgive gives Satan opportunities to take further advantage of you (II Corinthians 2:11). Refusing to forgive simply opens more doors to hate. In fact, I Peter 4:8 reads: "He who cannot forgive cannot love."

Think about these questions:

- Who do you need to forgive now? Yes, you will need to strength of the Lord to forgive someone who has really hurt you, but you know that you must forgive.
- Do you still think about an offense over and over again? If so, you have not really forgiven another.
- Is forgiveness the same as forgetting an offense?
- How many times are you to forgive another? (Read Matthew 18:21-22)
- Have you experienced the kind of result that forgiveness can produce like Joseph said in Genesis 50:20?

²²Now Joseph stayed in Egypt, he and his father's household, and Joseph lived one hundred and ten years. ²³Joseph saw the third generation of Ephraim's sons; also the sons of Machir, the son of Manasseh, were born on Joseph's knees. ²⁴Joseph said to his brothers, "I am about to die, but God will surely take care of you and bring you up from this land to the land which He promised on oath to Abraham, to Isaac and to Jacob." ²⁵Then Joseph made the sons of Israel swear, saying, "God will surely take care of you, and you shall carry my bones up from here." ²⁶So Joseph died at the age of one hundred and ten years; and he was embalmed and placed in a coffin in Egypt.

Joseph remained in Egypt, he and all his father's household, and lived one hundred and ten years, fifty-four years after Jacob died. Joseph saw the third generation of Ephraim's sons, also the sons of Machir, the son of Manasseh, born on Joseph knees. Joseph said to his brothers, "I am about to die, but God will surely take care of you and bring you up from this land to the land He promised on oath to Abraham, Isaac and Jacob". Apparently, Joseph was the first of Jacob's twelve sons to die. He made the sons of Israel swear, his brothers and others, saying that "God will take care of you and you will carry my bones up from here". Joseph died at one hundred and ten years. He was embalmed like his father, Jacob, and place in a coffin in Egypt.

Do you notice how candidly both Jacob and Joseph spoke of their death? That is not so with unbelievers. They avoid the subject with a passion. All kinds of euphemisms are employed so that death's realities need not be faced. We do not speak of the dead, but of the departed; they are not buried, but interred. People do not die; they pass away. We do not bury the dead in graveyards, but in memorial parks. Both Jacob and Joseph called their relatives to them, where they unhesitatingly spoke of their death and gave clear instructions regarding their burial. Today we do everything possible to conceal the truth from the dying. Let us look at death as Jacob and Joseph. Let us see it not as the end, but the beginning. Let us, by faith, look forward to being reunited with those we love (I Thessalonians 4:13-18) and dwelling with our Savior (John 14:1-3), forever in His presence and experiencing the things he has prepared for us. It is interested that the book of Genesis starts with God created the world and everything in it (Acts 17:24) and ends with Joseph dying and placed in a coffin in Egypt. How much we need a Savior and Lord and that person is Jesus Christ.

Milton Keynes UK
Ingram Content Group UK Ltd.
UKHW040234290124
436775UK00002BB/38